East Lothian Library

East Lothian
Library Services

Arthur Ransome's
Long-Lost Study of
Robert Louis Stevenson

Arthur Ransome's Long-Lost Study of Robert Louis Stevenson

Edited by Kirsty Nichol Findlay

THE BOYDELL PRESS

First published 2011
The Boydell Press, Woodbridge

ISBN 978 1 84383 672 8

The Boydell Press is an imprint of Boydell & Brewer Ltd
PO Box 9, Woodbridge, Suffolk IP12 3DF, UK
and of Boydell & Brewer Inc.
668 Mount Hope Ave, Rochester, NY 14620, USA
website: www.boydellandbrewer.com

A catalogue record for this book is available
from the British Library

The publisher has no responsibility for the continued existence
or accuracy of URLs for external or third-party internet websites
referred to in this book, and does not guarantee that any content
on such websites is, or will remain, accurate or appropriate.

Papers used by Boydell & Brewer Ltd are natural, recyclable
products made from wood grown in sustainable forests

Designed and typeset in Adobe Warnock Pro by
David Roberts, Pershore, Worcestershire

Printed and bound in the United States of America

Contents

List of Illustrations   vi
Acknowledgements   ix

Introduction: A Context for Arthur Ransome's
Robert Louis Stevenson: A Critical Study   1

1 Parcel Post   1
2 Ransome and Literary London, 1902–13   4
3 First Marriage and Ransome's Papers   12
4 The *Stevenson* Manuscript: Parcel and Exercise Book   19
5 Ransome and Stevenson   22
6 Writing *Stevenson*   28
7 *Stevenson* Abandoned   37
8 Ransome and the Stream of Stevenson Criticism   42
9 The Text and the Edition   45

Arthur Ransome, *Robert Louis Stevenson: A Critical Study*   49

Introductory   51
Part I   Biographical Summary   56
Part II Writings   86

Appendices

A TEXTUAL MATERIAL

A.1 Ransome's 'Stevenson exercise-book' transcribed   170
A.2 Additional material from the main manuscript   179
A.3 Published article, 'As Happy As Kings' by Arthur Ransome,
The New Witness, 5 February 1913   192

B BIOGRAPHICAL AND CONTEXTUAL MATERIAL

B.1 Ransome's first story, 'The Desert Island', 1892   198
B.2 'The Plate-Glass Window', unsigned review article, *The Eye-Witness*,
3 August 1911   200
B.3 'R. L. S.' by 'K.', *The Eye-Witness*, 28 September 1911   201
B.4 Family trees for Stevenson and Ransome   204

Index   207

Illustrations

1 Ransome's two preceding 'critical studies', his Stevenson manuscript, its wrapping paper, and the book that took its place in Martin Secker's series.
Photo: Tsendpurev Tsegmid. Reproduced with the permission of Special Collections, The Brotherton Library, University of Leeds, and by permission of The Arthur Ransome Literary Estate

2 The outside of the wrapping paper with string and sealing-wax
Reproduced with the permission of Special Collections, The Brotherton Library, University of Leeds, and by permission of The Arthur Ransome Literary Estate

3 Front cover of Ransome's earliest manuscript, 'The Desert Island', 1892
Reproduced by courtesy of The Museum of Lakeland Life and Industry, Kendal, and by permission of The Arthur Ransome Literary Estate

4 First page-opening of 'The Desert Island'
Reproduced by courtesy of The Museum of Lakeland Life and Industry, Kendal, and by permission of The Arthur Ransome Literary Estate

5 The inside of the wrapping paper showing the bootmaker's label
Reproduced with the permission of Special Collections, The Brotherton Library, University of Leeds, and by permission of The Arthur Ransome Literary Estate

6 A page of the *Stevenson* manuscript showing Ransome's hand at its most legible (fol. 131)
Reproduced with the permission of Special Collections, The Brotherton Library, University of Leeds, and by permission of The Arthur Ransome Literary Estate

7 Front cover of *The Tramp*, April 1910
Reproduced by kind permission of the Syndics of Cambridge University Library [L900.c.172]

8 The young Bohemian Ransome sketched on a piece of grocer's paper in Paris, 1908; artist unidentified
Reproduced with the permission of Special Collections, The Brotherton Library, University of Leeds.

9 'Studio Ideal' portrait of Ransome taken in Moscow between 1915 and 1917
Reproduced with the permission of Special Collections, The Brotherton Library, University of Leeds, and by permission of The Arthur Ransome Literary Estate

10 Ransome at work in Russian pine forest, 1913
Reproduced with the permission of Special Collections, The Brotherton Library, University of Leeds, and by permission of The Arthur Ransome Literary Estate

11 The daughter Ransome adored: Tabitha
Reproduced with the permission of Special Collections, The Brotherton Library, University of Leeds, and by permission of The Arthur Ransome Literary Estate

12 Arthur and Ivy Ransome with Daniel Macmillan outside the law-courts in London, a Press photograph from April 1913
Photo: Getty Images

13 Arthur and Evgenia Ransome with Taqui, Titty, Roger and Brigit Altounyan in Syria
Reproduced with the permission of Special Collections, The Brotherton Library, University of Leeds, and by permission of The Arthur Ransome Literary Estate

14 Robert Louis Stevenson and his family photographed on the verandah steps of Vailima early in 1892 by John Davis of Apia
© *National Portrait Gallery, London*

15 Robert Louis Stevenson in sleeping-bag, illustration by Walter Crane used as frontispiece to vol. I of the Pentland edition of Stevenson's *Works*, ed. Edmund Gosse (1906)
Reproduced by kind permission of the Syndics of Cambridge University Library [*Lit.6.90.753–772*]

16 R. L. Stevenson writing in bed, by Harry Furniss (pen and ink sketch)
© *National Portrait Gallery, London*

In memory of David Ian Sewart
1944–2008

Acknowledgements

Few tasks can be as enjoyable as one which yokes together writers as profoundly interesting and engaging as Arthur Ransome and Robert Louis Stevenson. For my love of both authors I am indebted to my parents, Jeanie and Stan Northcote-Bade, who told me that I spoke my first words by joining in a Stevenson poem which they were reading to me. I am enormously grateful to Arthur Ransome's literary executor Christina Hardyment and her co-executors Elizabeth Sewart and Geraint Lewis who entrusted me with Ransome's Stevenson manuscript and let me get on with it. I am above all indebted to the encouragement and assistance of Brian Findlay, whose many suggestions for improvements have all been adopted, and to Roger Savage, without whose urgings-on, constant support and careful reading this book might never have reached its publisher. I am grateful to the Red Slipper Fund of The Arthur Ransome Society for a grant towards illustrations.

In working on Ransome's manuscript over several years I am specifically indebted to the meticulous research of the bibliographer Wayne G. Hammond, whose *Arthur Ransome: A Bibliography* (2000) (and its on-line supplements) has been at my elbow throughout; to the masterly and very readable biography by the historian Hugh Brogan, *The Life of Arthur Ransome* (1984); to Ransome's own un-put-downable *Autobiography*, completed by his editor, friend and literary executor Rupert Hart-Davis (1976); and to the racy story of Ransome in Russia, *The Last Englishman* by Roland Chambers (2009). Ransome's unpublished letters, diaries, notebooks and draft manuscript and typescript papers in the archives of the Brotherton Library of the University of Leeds and at the Museum of Lakeland Life and Industry, Kendal have been a major source of new information and corroborative detail, as have letters by Ransome in private ownership. For Robert Louis Stevenson studies, the first resource for anyone these days must be the massive and impressive academic website maintained by Richard Dury and colleagues, w.w.w.robert-louis-stevenson.org. Writers on Stevenson whose work I have read or reread with enjoyment for this project include Richard Ambrosini, Oliver S. Buckton, Jenni Calder, Richard Dury, Claire Harman, Paul Maixner and Roger G. Swearingen. The standard eight-volume Yale edition of Stevenson's letters by B. A. Booth and Ernest Mehew, *The Letters of Robert Louis Stevenson* (1994–5) has been a constant point of reference.

I am indebted to many librarians, archivists, and specialist academics, historians, and others with expert knowledge for help with general and specific queries. Ann Farr, formerly of Special Collections at the Brotherton Library of the University of Leeds, Margaret Ratcliffe, librarian and archivist of The Arthur Ransome Society Library, and Ted Alexander, historian and archivist of Ransome and Walker material, have been continuously helpful and I am extremely indebted to their generosity and expertise. I am grateful to Ann and Mike Farr for having me as their guest while I was reading at the Brotherton. I am grateful to the hard-working staff of Special Collections at the Brotherton Library, including Chris Sheppard, Kasia Drozdziak, Karen Mee, and Tsendpurev Tsegmid (who took photographs used in this book) and, especially for help with things Russian, to Richard Davies. At the Museum of Lakeland Life and Industry, Abbot Hall, Kendal, I am particularly grateful to James Arnold. I am grateful to the hospitable Cambridge University Library and its generous and ever-helpful staff.

For specific information, permissions or advice I would like to thank Robert-Louis Abrahamson, Judy Andrews, James N. Bade, The Bodleian Library (Colin Harris), Nick Brewster, The British Postal Museum and Archive, Hugh Brogan, the Carlisle Library (Stephen White), Gigi Crompton, Richard Dury, Field Fisher Waterhouse LLP (Peter Titus), Penny Fielding, Brian Findlay, The Fullerton Collection, Caroline Gould, Arthur Grosset, David Groves, Wayne G. Hammond, Christina Hardyment, Jim Henderson, Hammersmith & Fulham Register Office (David Ross), Jackie Jones, Cecily Ledgard, Linklaters plc, the Lupton family (in particular the late Arthur Lupton), Andrew Nash, The National Portrait Gallery (Melissa Atkinson), The National Library of Scotland, Jerry O'Mahony, Bruce Phillips, Random House Group archive and library (Jean Rose and Jo Watt), University of Reading Library (Nathan Williams), Alan Riach, Roger Robinson, The Royal Bank of Scotland Group plc (Philip Winterbottom and archivists), Roger Savage, the late David Sewart, Elizabeth Sewart, Nicholas Spurrier, Kirstie Taylor, Taylor and Francis Group (Mindy Rozencrantz), Matthew Townend, Roger Wardale, Jonathan Wild, and the audiences at talks given by me on related material in the last few years. Every effort has been made to trace and contact holders of copyright. The editor regrets any errors or omissions – they are not attributable to anyone named here – and would be glad to receive further information.

The project has benefited from the interest and encouragement of Peter Clifford, Michael Middeke, and Catherine Larner at Boydell & Brewer, and the assistance of my copy-editor, David Roberts.

Kirsty Nichol Findlay
The Bull Pen, Hallthwaites, 2011

A Context for Arthur Ransome's
Robert Louis Stevenson: A Critical Study

1 Parcel Post

On the first day of May 1914 a stout brown-paper parcel was dispatched by post from G. H. Harris, First-Class Boot and Legging Maker, The Strand, London W.C., 'under Savoy Hotel', to A. Ransome, Esq: at Manor Farm, Hatch, Tisbury, Wiltshire. The thirty-year-old Arthur Ransome was living at Hatch with his first wife Ivy and their three-year-old daughter Tabitha. He was eagerly awaiting the arrival of the parcel. Writing to his mother, he had longingly described the 'Brands essence, A1 pair of brown walking boots, smart ones, that I have long coveted'. They would need to be tough and serviceable, since he was about to spend several summer months in Russia. It would be his second visit there; he was going to write a book about St Petersburg. Mr Harris's first-class boots would be just the thing.

Very soon after the arrival of the parcel, the stout brown paper of which it had been made was turned inside out and trimmed in order to wrap another, somewhat smaller, parcel. This time it was full of handwritten pages. It was elaborately fastened with string, and the knots sealed with sealing-wax of two colours, red and black. Ivy Ransome addressed the parcel in her firm and florid hand to 'The Manager, Parr's Bank, Regent Street, London, W.', adding 'to be delivered on demand to – *Arthur Ransome*, Esq: or *Mrs. Arthur Ransome*'. The contents were succinctly identified on the outside of the wrapping-paper, again by Ivy, as 'M.S.S.'; the date 'May 4. 1914' was written in the same hand, but in much larger characters. Arthur Ransome's own handwriting appeared nowhere on the parcel. There is no evidence that the parcel was ever delivered as addressed.

On 5 May Arthur set out from London to Paris and then St Petersburg. The parcel was never reclaimed, and the papers which it contained were never to be reunited with their author. For seventy-six years it remained unopened, unrecorded, and probably forgotten. In 1990 it *was* opened, and its contents form the greater part of this book.

Ivy had addressed the parcel to the branch of Parr's Bank where she kept an account. She seems to have used this as a 'default' address through which she could always be reached; Arthur passed it on to his mother before leaving for Russia. There is no evidence that this branch was ever used by Arthur. Whether the parcel was ever deposited there is impossible to say, since Parr's records have not survived. Arthur also banked with Parr's, chiefly (as later documents show) at the Charing Cross branch, although somewhat mysteriously he had the following year an account also at the Liverpool branch. (He is known to have visited Liverpool only once, in the company of the Russian expert and diplomat Bernard Pares.) A few bank statements from 1914 onwards are among the miscellaneous papers in the Ransome archive at the Brotherton Library in Leeds. One of these, headed simply 'Parr's Bank' (with no branch named) and 'Ransome', discloses regular monthly disbursements of £8 6s 8d to 'Mrs Ransome' during her husband's absence in wartime Russia, with associated charges on account of posting cheques. Since no other transactions are recorded on the statement, it seems likely that this account was set up for that one purpose only. He is assumed to have had another, separate account at the Charing Cross branch for normal use. (Parr's was amalgamated in 1918 into what was ultimately to become the National Westminster Bank and Arthur remained faithful to them through all these changes.) Ransome's complicated banking arrangements may indicate a desire to keep his personal financial affairs secret from his wife.

It is very unlikely that the manuscript would have been deposited at Parr's Bank, Regent Street, at Ransome's own request. Since he was already determined to seek a legal separation from his highly strung and volatile wife, it might well have seemed prudent to him to protect his work in progress from damage or destruction by removing it from his study at Hatch while he was abroad. But in that case he would assuredly have made up the parcel himself, and deposited it at his own branch of the bank until he had returned from Russia and was ready to resume work on the papers it contained. His diaries (always laconic) are silent on the subject. The page for 4 May 1914, on which he probably travelled up to London, is completely blank, and on the following day Ransome records only 'London–Paris'; and, as we have seen, it was Ivy who inscribed and dated the parcel. This suggests that she was taking the initiative. The contents were, of course, Arthur's sole property, and she was probably aware that she had no right to sequester them – hence her instruction to the bank to surrender the package to Arthur or herself. It seems likely that she went alone into Arthur's study, perhaps on the evening of his departure; that she impetuously gathered together a large quantity of papers, probably without his knowledge; and that she bundled them up in the brown paper in which his new boots had arrived. Her motive was not necessarily malicious; she may have seen this as a strategic move, a way of strengthening her bargaining position in the still unresolved dispute about the future of their marriage. She may even have hoped that the parcel might be a source of income, should Arthur not return from Russia: she had after all assisted him with his recent anthologies, *The Book of Love* and *The Book of Friendship*, and may have thought herself quite capable of sifting these papers and preparing something for publication. At all events, they were one of

Arthur's assets. She had taken control of them, and would give them back when he was in a more congenial frame of mind.

How and when the parcel of manuscript material made its journey from Parr's Bank (if indeed it ever was there) to the solicitors' office of Linklater & Paines in London where it was finally discovered and opened, is also unknown. Many of Linklaters' records were destroyed in 1941, when one of their offices suffered a direct hit in the London Blitz, but the firm is known to have had dealings with Ivy: they provided her, for example, with a character reference in 1935 and acted in 1941 as the executors of her mother Sophia's will. In 1990 they informed Tabitha Ransome that they had acted for 'The Ransome Trust', an arrangement perhaps set up at the time of Arthur's divorce from Ivy in 1923–4 by her solicitor father George Walker, so it is probable that it was Ivy who transferred the parcel from the bank (or wherever it had been kept) to the solicitors some time before her death in 1939. Linklater & Paines are not among the firms of solicitors known to have been employed by Arthur Ransome.

According to an endorsement written on the wrapper, the parcel was placed in Linklater & Paines' strong-room in London on 27 May 1947; when and by whom it had been delivered to them was not recorded. It may have been stored elsewhere in their offices before that date. It then remained undisturbed until Linklaters found it in the course of inspecting the contents of their strong-room in 1990. The words 'Arthur Ransome' and 'M.S.S.' suggested that the contents were probably of considerable importance; they therefore opened the package under conditions of some security. No covering letter was found within, and, unusually, their records contained no relevant correspondence. Having established that Ransome and his wife were both dead, Linklaters reported their discovery to the executors of Ransome's literary estate, John Bell and Sir Rupert Hart-Davis. They in turn contacted the University of Leeds, which had already received a large part of Ransome's private papers as a benefaction by his second wife Evgenia. Finally, after consulting Tabitha, now aged seventy-nine, it was decided to deposit the parcel at the Brotherton Library of the University of Leeds on indefinite loan.

On 16 September 1993 Ann Farr, a Special Collections librarian at Leeds, accordingly went to London to receive the parcel on behalf of the University. She was presented with a large pile of loose manuscript sheets, uncounted and unnumbered, contained in a large plastic shopping-bag. With great presence of mind, she asked what had become of the original packaging. Within a few days, the stout brown paper, with its string and seals and inscriptions, was retrieved and was reunited with its contents in Leeds.

2 Ransome and Literary London, 1902–13

The name of Arthur Ransome (1884–1967) is now best known for the complex and engaging series of twelve interconnected novels, the *Swallows and Amazons* series, written between 1928 and 1948. These books are profoundly innovative in narrative style, genre, and content; they are studies in the nature of childhood imagination and social realism which can be read with pleasure by readers from six to sixty – as their author had hoped that they would be. They are the crown of a long literary career that had followed many different courses and practised in many genres – so many and so different as to lead some readers to assume that there must have been several authors of the same name.

The young Arthur was indeed a very miscellaneous writer: reviewer, essayist, bellettrist, literary critic, travel writer, short-story writer, and reteller of folk-tales. He had arrived in London in 1902 from Leeds, unqualified for any profession, but anxious to get on in the literary world, to which his family had connections: both Cyril and Edith, his parents, were published authors, the poet Laurence Binyon and the playwright 'Christopher St John' were cousins, and the Macmillan family of publishers were close family friends. But he preferred to make his own way. Grant Richards, the publisher of many bright young authors, took him on as an office-boy. His enthusiasm for life and literature and his eager and entertaining conversation quickly won him many friends. Among them was Edward Thomas (to whom the young Ransome, sparking with ideas, was 'the Electrician') and older men such as John Masefield, Lascelles Abercrombie (who addressed Arthur as 'Beloved Man, and Admirable Prophet'), and Gordon Bottomley. He was ardent and heroic in friendship, once walking fifty miles to introduce Abercrombie to Martin Secker for a book on Hardy and then cycling with Abercrombie to Hardy's cottage near Dorchester, where, alas, Hardy was 'not at home'. His chief mentor however was W. G. Collingwood, once Ruskin's secretary, the 'Skald of Coniston', who adopted Arthur as a kind of honorary nephew. He rapidly grew in confidence, developing cocksure opinions about books and people; he was fluent, enthusiastic, headstrong; meticulous, hard-working; full of words, and brimming over with ideas. He came to affect a more elderly manner in his desire to seem older than his years; much-moustachioed, he was wryly proud of losing a hair or two on top. Although his impetuosity could be exasperating, his contemporaries liked him very much on the whole.

His literary life was very much bound up with his love-life. He fell in love often, mostly with young women slightly older than himself from the literary and artistic world of London. Among these enticing creatures were Stefana Stevens, novelist, Arabic scholar, archaeologist and later (as Lady Drower) the wife of a prominent diplomat; Sylvia Dryhurst, who married the essayist Robert Lynd; and Jessie Gavin, whose drawings decorated his

History of Story-Telling. She, with Eileen Gray and Kathleen Bruce (later the wife of the explorer Robert Falcon Scott), was one of 'les trois jolies anglaises' who lived in Montparnasse (the address carefully noted in Ransome's diary), young artists from the Slade School who were studying at the École Colarossi in Paris where Ransome's sister Cecily was to follow. Like countless other young writers, Ransome fell in love with Paris and used every excuse and opportunity to visit as often as possible. However, the women who were always to remain most important to him after his mother and sisters were the elder daughters of the Collingwood family, whose home in the Lake District he visited often for rest and congenial companionship. He proposed marriage first to Barbara, a sculptor, and then to the older Dora, an accomplished artist (and 'Beetle' to his 'Toad'); neither would take him seriously. It was a great disappointment to him – and, less predictably, to their parents.

Ransome's career as an author started modestly in 1904 with a number of hack-works which he later wished to forget, such as *The A.B.C. of Physical Culture*. He was prouder of his second book, *The Souls of the Streets*, a typical 'slender volume' of the time, of which the elegant but very small edition was sponsored by an ephemeral provincial publisher. (It was dismissed, accurately enough, as 'seven short essays of a rather precocious type' in the *Times Literary Supplement*'s review.) From 1906 a group of like-minded writers, including Ransome, successfully colonised a number of periodicals. *Temple Bar* that year included essays and stories by Ransome, a poem by his cousin Laurence Binyon, and, by way of adding gravitas, a tribute to his master and mentor Ruskin by W. G. Collingwood. Edward Thomas was there, writing on Richard Jefferies (another of Ransome's heroes), and John Masefield on the sea-songs which were later to be used thematically in Ransome's novels.

From the outset of his career (and for many years afterwards) Ransome's literary agents were Curtis Brown, for whom his adored Stefana Stevens was then working. He tells us that he was having tea with Cecil Chesterton one day late in 1906, when Stefana came across to their table and said 'There's a book that ought to be written, and you are the one who ought to write it, a book on Bohemia in London, an essayistical sort of book.' The next morning, Ransome took her an outline. *Bohemia in London* was published in the following September by Chapman & Hall; it was successful on both sides of the Atlantic, and a second edition was later to appear from another publisher. Stefana's novel *'– and what happened': being an account of some romantic meals* [sic] (Mills & Boon, 1916) gently satirises the young Ransome as the enthusiastic pipe-smoking Matravers:

> he is a person who writes small books in large and beautiful print in which the t's trail downwards towards the next letter [i.e. the ligatures of 'artistic' type-faces] … he contributes essays to quarterlies,

and reviews novels in a literary paper without ever having written one. He is, in print, the most fastidious and meticulous creature. In person he is bombastic, Gargantuan, thunderous, explosive, brutal, and bouncing.

It is fair to say that she and Arthur had not met for several years when this portrait was published.

Ransome was prodigiously energetic in producing books and articles over the following few years. *A History of Story-Telling: Studies in the Development of Narrative* was published by T. C. and E. C. Jack in 1909. It was a substantial and ground-breaking study, although it incorporated matter from the introductions he had written for eleven volumes of selections from 'The World's Story-Tellers'. (This series was heavily weighted towards French literature, from the *Roman de la Rose* to de Maupassant; the translations appear to be Ransome's own.) Jacks also published two substantial anthologies which he had compiled with help from Ivy, whom he married in 1909, *The Book of Friendship* (1909) and *The Book of Love* (1910). His plans for future work were now on an increasingly grand scale, as a letter from Chapman & Hall suggests:

> I do not see how we could possibly hope to cover expenses upon a volume of twelve disconnected critical essays of about 5000 words each. The prospect of twelve such books I should reckon as a prospect of a loss of at least £400, probably more … in the meantime I think your scheme is quite a Napoleonic one from an author's point of view.

No more was heard of this heroic scheme, although Ransome was still keen to publish collections of his critical essays.

The young Ransome was naturally based in Bohemian London, but he and Ivy moved into a farmhouse at Hatch, near Tisbury in Wiltshire, the year after their marriage in 1909. Here he was a near neighbour of Edward Thomas, and the two men enjoyed many long conversational walks together. Thomas was passionately attached to the English language, poetry, song, and the open air, subjects on which Ransome became increasingly fervent. He joined the cult of the Open Road. A new periodical, committed to expressing these ideals, appeared monthly during 1910 and 1911. *The Tramp* celebrated no ordinary vagabonds, but amiable, pipe-smoking lovers of the countryside dressed in Norfolk jackets and plus-fours – such as Thomas and Ransome, who were regular contributors. A typical cover of this short-lived magazine shows a well-clad gentleman-tramp pausing on a stile, appreciatively gazing out upon the landscape over which he is walking, somewhat in the proprietorial manner of a Renaissance duke. Nevertheless, the contributions of Ransome and Thomas stand out sharply from a good deal of romantic nonsense and weak nostalgia. Their clear, loving gaze had a purpose: they sought in the beloved landscape an essence which could be captured and transmitted by the writer's art; and they wanted to understand the meaning and method of that art.

Ransome was also at work in 1910 on his first 'critical study', *Edgar Allan Poe.* He corrected the proofs in bucolic, temporarily renewed bachelordom on Peel Island in Coniston Water, where he and Robin Collingwood, whose brilliant career at Oxford had recently begun, camped out and discussed philosophy and literary theory. Ursula, the youngest of the Collingwood sisters (the one to whom Ransome did not propose marriage) brought him the proofs when they arrived from the printer, swimming across to the island with a parcel fastened to her head. The book appeared that autumn.

Ransome's *Poe* was one of the first two books published by Martin Secker, a forceful young man exactly his contemporary. He had been particularly impressed by the section on Poe in Ransome's *History of Story-Telling*, and commissioned a full-length study as the first in a new series of 'Modern Monographs' on recent and contemporary writers. Ransome had originally proposed three such monographs, to be called 'critical studies', on Poe, Hazlitt, and Stevenson, writers whom he knew well, greatly admired, and revered as inspirers of his own work. He had had positive discussions about a book to be called 'Hazlitt and his circle' with Methuen in 1909, although his fatherly advisor Collingwood had been less than enthusiastic about the project. Secker doubted whether a book on Hazlitt would sell, so out of fashion had he then become. Stevenson seemed a much more promising subject, and it was agreed that Secker would publish Ransome's study of him as soon as it could be completed. In the meantime, Secker brought out *The Hoofmarks of the Faun* (1911), a compilation of previously published stories by Ransome, most dedicated to a young woman (including the Collingwood sisters and his wife Ivy). An autobiographical note was prefixed, a sign of the author's self-confidence. Ransome and Secker looked forward to a fruitful and enduring partnership.

Although Ransome believed he had originated the concept of a 'critical study', the term, at least, had been used before: George Gissing's *Charles Dickens: A Critical Study*, for example, had appeared in 1898, and Ransome could scarcely have been unaware of that. However, his interpretation of the phrase was highly individual and new, and Secker believed in it. A biographical summary would make perhaps a quarter of the book; the remainder would be a close study of the subject's techniques, methods and objectives. At twenty-six, Ransome was ready to do this. His *History of Story-Telling* and *Poe* had been widely admired; he was 'astonished by the reviews' and particularly by the admiration of the American professor G. E. Woodberry. His output of reviews, articles, and essays in *The Tramp*, *T.P.'s Weekly*, *The Bookman*, *The Fortnightly Review*, and other literary journals was prolific and influential. His reputation as a critic and a literary man was in the ascendant; but unfortunately his publisher's profits did not keep pace. In May 1911 Ransome proposed a new edition, or second volume, of his *Story-Telling* to Secker, confidently predicting a good reception. He received the following reply:

> About Story-telling, I'm afraid I can't do anything. I am very depressed and pessimistic about the outlook everywhere, and after losing £50 on Poe and £25 on the Hoofmarks, I do not think it is worthwhile adding to my list any more books for which there is apparently so little demand. What is to be done? It seems as though the only way for you to add critical volumes to your bibliography, is to serialise the articles in the reviews and magazines, and publish on a pure royalty basis ... I am sorry if this letter is so divorced from optimism, but I do not think the outlook is particularly hopeful for anyone.
>
> I am glad Wilde is going well. He shall have every chance when the time for parturition comes ...

As the last sentence of this letter shows, Secker had already changed his mind about what the next in the series of Modern Monographs should be. In his published autobiography Ransome smoothes over some aspects of the strained relationship between author and publisher at this time. Manuscript pages of his draft in the Brotherton Library collection are more revealing than the account given in his *Autobiography*:

> Secker asked me to follow the study of Poe with another. I had called my book 'Edgar Allan Poe: a critical study', and he annoyed me by using my formula for a whole series of such books [by other writers], 'Thomas Hardy a critical study', T. L. Peacock ditto' etc etc. He asked me to choose a subject. Now Poe had interested me, first because of his conscious methods of construction, instead of invention. At that moment 'native woodnotes wild' did not interest me whereas the 'P. & K.' theory [a critical theory about kinetic and potential speech, which he had published in 1911] did, and I chose to write a book on Robert Louis Stevenson. I should ...

There the fragment ends. Was he going to say, 'I should have stuck to it'?

He didn't do so. In the autumn of 1910 he had arranged to occupy Lanehead, the Collingwoods' house at Coniston, while they were away on their travels. He had planned to begin reading for his Stevenson there, among other pleasant rural themes and diversions, but his happiness was soon interrupted: his wife and their infant daughter and a Jamaican nursemaid arrived on 7 October, the very day the Collingwoods left, intent on having the baby's overdue baptism arranged as soon as possible, with the father present. Within a few days of Ivy's arrival, on 11 October, Arthur notes in his diary: 'Book on Wilde. Telegram from an excited Secker'. Secker urgently wanted a book on Wilde 'as an *esprit*', Ransome later wrote – a word which he described as being entirely without an English equivalent.

This crucial week requires careful scrutiny. It is clear that Secker's proposal was deliberated on for four days: and that the decision was not easy. On 15 October Arthur noted in his diary first 'Woe and sunshine after' – a typical sequence in his stormy relationship with his wife – and then the reply telegram sent that day: 'Secker wins Wilde book'. The characteristically terse wording of the message does not disguise a tussle of interests; the decision to accept Secker's proposal may not have been arrived at from personal inclination. Immediately on receipt of Ransome's telegram Secker posted a contract; the agreement was signed on 17 October. Reading for *Wilde* began at once.

In another fragment of draft autobiography, Ransome says ruefully,

> I ... began work on Wilde without the smallest suspicion of the trouble that book would bring me. I had finished my book on Poe, mainly concerned with his alert, self-conscious technique, and with a chapter on his influence in France, where Baudelaire's translation had made him almost a French writer. Stevenson was to have ...

Once more, the following page is tantalisingly missing, but it is clear that Ransome meant a book on Stevenson to follow. He had detected thematic and stylistic links between Poe and Stevenson, whom the French had similarly taken to their hearts, and was keen to explore them further.

In his published autobiography, Ransome says that if Secker's telegram had arrived before the Collingwoods had left Lanehead, he would have been persuaded not to write on Wilde. Collingwood had met Oscar 'as one of the undergraduate navvies under Ruskin's leadership on the Hinksey road' and had not received a favourable impression. But as it turned out, his mentor was already far away, his plans for an agreeable autumn had been wrecked, and his mental agitation can be guessed from the fact that half-pages of his diary for the days on which Ivy arrived and Secker's telegram was received have both been torn out – the only pages in any of his diaries to have been so treated. It is unlikely that the christening at Coniston church, itself postponed by bad weather, put him in a better frame of mind. His position in respect of work, marriage, and religion, were all matters of great agitation.

Still, he set to work with a will, and was for several months immersed in Wilde. Soon a new problem emerged. Despite Secker's enthusiasm for the forthcoming book, he was shocked to discover how extensively Ransome wanted to quote from Wilde's writings. There had been no such problem with *Poe*, although Ransome's quotations had been just as lavish. But the copyrights of Oscar Wilde's works were the property of the respected publisher Algernon Methuen, who despite his friendly relationship with Ransome would allow substantial quotations only in return for a substantial fee. Secker's view was that Ransome would have to make do with much less, refusing to pay more than the barest minimum. Ransome refused to change his methods: if critical study meant the close analysis of significant passages, the reader must have those passages before him. He then made matters worse by trying to conduct negotiations directly with Wilde's literary executor, Robert Ross; on 28 August 1911 he wrote:

> Dear Ross,
> I have not heard from Methuen. But, this morning there came this letter from Secker: Dear Ransome, Methuens say they will consider my application to use the extracts, on receipt of complete proofs and that it will be conditional (possibly) upon paying a fee for each extract. Yours, etc'
> Shall I let him know that I have sent you a copy of the list? ... it is horribly difficult to work when nothing is settled.
> I do hope that the making of the list and the sending it to Secker have not been undiplomatic.
> My moustache has turned gray.
> I have begun to squint and am quite unable to look my daughter in the face.

To this Ross generously and humorously replied:

> You can tell Methuen you have sent me the list. But don't write any more letters to Secker than you can help. I fear it was your interview with Secker that was undiplomatic. However your *attitude* must now be one of 'helplessness', leaving it to Methuen and Secker to fight it out. Methuen would in *any* case have cut up rough about the quotations: so that he's writing to do with the pious wish that they should eventually publish. You have only to go on with the work as if nothing happened. When Secker writes reply that 'you are really in his hands and cannot say or do anything more, but think the quotations are *essential* to your book.' If the book is held up a little it does not affect either its value or your position. You must adopt the psychology of the young lady of Sweden who went back to Weedon if you remember.

Ransome took Ross's advice despite his misquotation of Lear's limerick (the young lady, having arrived at Weedon, thought it prudent to return to Sweden). He consoled himself while these negotiations proceeded with the breeding of blue mice, a delicate matter on which he had become something of an expert. In 1912 he wrote a splendidly entertaining review of an animal book, peevishly complaining that it had got several aspects of the development of infant mice quite wrong. A room in his farmhouse at Hatch was given over to mouse breeding and selection; Ransome's successes were attested to by the prize certificates that adorned the walls. He had gone so far as to propose a book on mice to the long-suffering Methuen, who was quite charmed by the idea; but it remained unwritten.

Oscar Wilde: A Critical Study was finished in December 1911, and published early in 1912. Fifteen hundred copies were printed, as against seven hundred of *Poe*; it seems that Secker was confident of recouping his losses this time. As soon as it appeared, members of Wilde's family made objections; Ransome apologised for the matter complained of, and agreed to change his text in future editions. Then, in March 1912, Lord Alfred Douglas, vengeful and litigious in his post-Bosie days, brought an action for libel against Ransome, Ransome's publisher, the printers of the book, and The Times Book Club which had agreed to circulate it. Although Ransome never mentioned Douglas by name, he had asserted that Douglas had 'lured Wilde to his ruin and abandoned him afterwards', as Brogan puts it, and those were the grounds for Douglas's case. The printers quickly settled out of court, and Secker succeeded in buying himself out of the action in a secret agreement with Douglas, whose publisher he had recently become.

Ransome understood very well the likely financial advantages of the publicity surrounding his book. Writing to the literary agent Curtis Brown with a book proposal (never carried out) on 'the modern spirit', he had been quick to point out that 'the success of the Wilde book, which will, of course, be enormously stimulated when my case ... comes into court, should ensure a very wide notice for it both here and in America'. He was certain that he had written his *Wilde* accurately, truthfully, and without an axe to grind: Douglas' action called his integrity into question. But as his co-defendants backed away, he felt increasingly apprehensive. Secker's deal with Douglas he regarded as craven disloyalty. Matters were made worse by the delays of the law: the case was not heard until April 1913. Ransome found the suspense hard to bear, and, out of his depth, began to dread an adverse judgment.

His fears were unfounded. The jury did not take long to conclude that he had no case to answer, and that the words complained of were 'libellous, but true'. Judgment was given accordingly, and costs were awarded against Douglas. His old friend Daniel Macmillan, who was at his side during the hearing, had generously offered to pay Arthur's costs at once if necessary; happily, it did not come to that. A martyr to Arthur's cause, Macmillan had taken pains to have lunch with the Ransomes every day of the hearing, so that, as Hugh Brogan beautifully observed, 'Ivy was obliged, by mere good manners, not to go on quarrelling.' A second edition of *Wilde* rapidly appeared (published not by Secker, with whom Ransome had by now irrevocably broken off relations, but by Methuen); ten thousand copies were printed. Five further editions followed: the book was a best-seller, Ransome's first. Ironically, it was a book which, in the end, he would rather not have written.

Long before the action came to court, Ransome's patience with Secker was exhausted. In March 1912 he bought back by mutual agreement all the remaining stocks of his Secker books, as well as the rights to his still unwritten book on Stevenson, and other work which he had less formally proposed. While the court hearing was pending, copies of *Wilde* were sold by post from Ransome's home in Wiltshire. In the meantime, he had found a new publisher. He had been persuaded into the fold of a clever, charismatic, and persuasive character, a poet as well as an editor and publisher, called Charles Granville (a *nom de guerre*, as Ransome later said).

Granville had begun publishing under the name of Stephen Swift in 1911, a few doors along from Secker's office in John Street. He had had some successes already: he brought out Katherine Mansfield's first book, and in 1911 launched three influential magazines: *Rhythm* (edited by Middleton Murry), *The Eye-Witness* (edited by Cecil Chesterton and Hilaire Belloc), and *The Oxford and Cambridge Review*. The *Review* allowed Ransome his head in exploring his literary theories; to *The Eye-Witness* and its successor *The New Witness* he was such a frequent contributor that he could appear under several guises in any one issue. Best of all, Granville offered very generous terms to his authors. He had a keen and perceptive eye for talent, and recognised Ransome's capacity for hard work and consistent productivity. He encouraged him to bring together enough of his essays to make a slightly less than Napoleonic three volumes, and in the short term commissioned a translation of Remy de Gourmont's *A Night in the Luxembourg*, which was published in 1912 within a month of *Oscar Wilde*. It is easy to see why Ransome was so completely won over by this charming but unscrupulous adventurer. But Granville was too good to be true. In danger of prosecution for bigamy, he fled to the Continent with his lady, abandoning his friends and his business. Ransome's comfortable hopes of wealth and fame were no more than a pipe-dream. At first he camped out in Granville's office, determined to keep physical hold of the stock of his books; before long it became clear that very little could be saved from the wreckage. At least one volume of his collected essays appeared; Macmillans generously published it in 1913 as *Portraits and Speculations*. Ransome's other books were finally taken over from Granville by the avuncular Methuen. He was delighted to discover that Ransome was intending to write a book on Stevenson, for he was himself a great admirer, and had relished reading *Treasure Island* to the boys of the preparatory school which he had established. He would be most happy, therefore, to publish Ransome's study as soon as it was ready.

3 First Marriage and Ransome's Papers

A well-known newspaper photograph of Mr and Mrs Arthur Ransome shows them standing together on a snowy pavement outside the law-courts in London, shortly after judgment in the Wilde case had been given. In front, in topper and spats, is Arthur's gallant friend Daniel Macmillan, of the publishing family. Ivy is on tiptoe with elation, delighted to be at the centre of the picture; indeed, she seems to have enjoyed the publicity and excitement of the case from the beginning, although her determined presence in the public gallery had caused Ransome some embarrassment. Her arm is occupied by a folded cloak, and is not linked with her husband's. Arthur smiles nervously; he looks bewildered rather than happy or relieved, and considerably older than his twenty-nine years. Only his choice of a very distinctive 'squashy hat' defiantly proclaims his membership of the artistic avant-garde; he had long since broken with the trammels of respectability (and dismayed his mother) by putting the bowler hat in which he had arrived in London on the fire. The unwelcome notoriety into which the lawsuit had plunged him had plainly had a profound effect on his self-confidence. But in the body-language of husband and wife there are perhaps the signs of another, underlying, misery. Unlike the libel suit, it would not end happily.

As we have seen, Ransome had nurtured hopes of marrying one of the talented daughters of W. G. Collingwood. After his second rejection, the disconsolate young man rebounded with tremendous force into the arms of the bewitching, lively, dramatic, and volatile Ivy Constance Graves Walker from Bournemouth. Her parents were both extremely wealthy, and had little affection for each other. Unlike Ransome, she was an only child. There was an element of romance in her origins: she had a grandmother from Jamaica, a great-grandmother from Portugal, and distant connections with English nobility. When Ransome met her, she was already engaged to a rather dull cousin. Although she was keen to escape from him, her parents thought otherwise: her wedding-dress was nearly ready for its final fitting. She was older than Ransome, and understood that his family had none of the social or financial advantages of hers; but she was very ready to marry him, if only to disoblige her family. A connection with a 'Common Writer' must have seemed to them the worst of all possible disasters.

Mr Walker was a non-practising solicitor. He was evidently fond of mischief. (In his will he left a substantial annuity to his long-serving female chauffeur, a constant humiliation to his wife, who spent more and more time at Ivy's house.) Confronted with his daughter's determination to break off her engagement in favour of a struggling author, he perceived an opportunity for being intensely disagreeable to a large part of his family. Over a gentlemanly cigar, he encouraged Arthur to strike while the iron was hot, and to whisk Ivy away to Gretna Green – or, failing that, to the nearest register office. Arthur's euphoria was such that he began to write a poem in celebration of the 'respectable' Mr Walker's suggestion; but having referred to his bride as a 'corker' he could not think of any more plausible rhymes for 'Walker', and the ode remained unfinished. When the news leaked out, Ivy's paternal grandmother sent her a long, great-aunt-ish expostulation, exhorting her to do the Right Thing, not to let the family down, and above all to leave Arthur alone. Her mother sank into despair. But Ivy was delighted by the prospect. She was a charming, elegant, intriguing young lady in need of a husband; Arthur was penniless but dashing, a witty, excitingly passionate and ambitious young man. On Saturday 13 March 1909 Ransome wrote 'Got married' in his diary, in ink, adding 'Went to Paris' in pencil. The ceremony took place in a register office in Fulham – abutting bohemian Chelsea, but neither then nor now the most fashionable quarter of London.

Disenchantment, as far as Arthur was concerned, was not far away. He soon came to realise what a 'nightmarish family background of mutual hate' he had married into, and how powerless he was to detach Ivy from it. Their daughter was later (drawing presumably on her mother's account of married life) to describe Ransome as 'Wild and Bohemian', living an adventurous life in Paris with her mother on the proceeds of his first few stories. Perhaps their first few weeks of marriage were rootlessly exuberant, as they enjoyed a freedom which neither had experienced before; but Ivy's difficulties in separating reality from fantasy, her wildly romantic fabulations about herself, and her increasingly erratic behaviour, soon gave Arthur serious anxiety. He did not know how to trust her. If she was crossed, she would give way to extravagant and potentially dangerous actions, smashing things and setting them on fire. The Ransomes moved seven times in their first five months together, on one occasion being asked to leave because they had damaged the wallpaper by throwing buckets of water at each other.

This impulsive marriage was to blight Ransome's life for many years. When in 1942 his publisher Jonathan Cape urged him to write an autobiography, Ransome noted in a personal memorandum that he would be able to do so only by 'omitting the misery of 1909 to 1913, and from 1913 to 1917, so far as my affairs in England are concerned'. His gloom was lifted by the birth of his daughter Tabitha in May 1910; although he seems to have been somewhat preoccupied, since his diary entry reading 'Tabitha 10.45–50 am' was subsequently corrected by Ivy to 'Born at about 2.40 pm'. (She seems to have read his diaries without compunction, which is perhaps why Ransome confided little except factual matters to them.) As the child grew, Ransome took enormous pleasure in watching her development, encouraging her, telling her stories, and teaching her the things which he thought a child should know. He was always happy with her, and unhappy with her mother; whenever he left home he was torn between relief at being separated from his wife, and distress at being separated from his daughter. Hatch remained his family home and his base: but as time went on, he sought more and more excuses for being away. He expressed to Ivy his fear that their marriage was a failure; she coldly informed him that under no circumstances would she consider a divorce. Once the Wilde case was settled, Ransome felt that he could stay permanently with her no longer.

He had taken up the study of Russian folklore and found in it 'an undramatic way out of my personal troubles'. He would go to Russia – the first of what turned out to be many trips – to learn Russian, gather material, work on his translations, and so peacefully begin to recuperate from the stresses of recent years. He obtained a passport without saying a word to Ivy or to any of his family, informing her when he was ready to leave that his destination was Stockholm, a place far enough away from England to avoid the continuing attentions of the press, but in a country for which no passport was then required. It was not until he had reached Russian territory via Stockholm that Ivy realised that, lacking a passport, she would be unable to follow him. She did not accept the separation easily.

Upon arrival in Russia, Ransome travelled at once into Finland, to stay in a dacha belonging to a family to whom a friend in Paris had given him an introduction. There he wrote a long and distressing letter to his mother. Although probably aware that the marriage was not a happy one, she would have known only a few of the reasons why. The letter reveals so much of Ransome's tormented state of mind at the time when he was trying to continue uninterrupted work on *Stevenson* that it deserves to be quoted in full.

Datcha [*sic*] Gellibrand
Terijoki [*sic*]
Finland
Jun 30. 1913

My dearest mother,
I had just settled down to hard work here on my book on Stevenson, the Gellibrands having made everything awfully nice for me, when Ivy sent a wild and furious letter telling me to leave at once. I sent the letter to Sir George Lewis [the lawyer who acted for him in the Wilde case] with a letter from me to her refusing to change my obviously suitable arrangements. She telegraphs and writes with great violence, and I have written asking her to go and talk things out with Lewis.

I do not think I told you that 3 days before I left, in one of her terrific scenes (in this case because of a mistake I made in the name of a servant, a mistake I instantly admitted) she took up the two lighted lamps from the dinner table and broke them to pieces, narrowly escaping setting the house on fire.

I told this to Lewis before I left, and he agreed that it was more than unwise to remain in the house, as in another such scene she might without meaning it, go a little further. He is going to try to arrange a peaceable separation, at least for some months so that I can have a chance of getting some work done.

In the month before I left, I paid over to Ivy about £50, to settle our debts* so that she is all right financially. (*mostly due to her insistence on coming to London for the Case.)

Well: I did not want to worry you with all this; but, remembering what you told me about her absolutely untrue letters and telegrams on a former occasion, and her hatred of you, it seems to me that she may try to get at you in some way now: so that it is better for you to know all about it beforehand.

If she does ask you to do anything, or if she sends you violent letters, send them on to Sir George Lewis, Bart., 10 Ely Place, Holborn, E.C., with a letter saying that you are my mother, and do not want to do anything without his knowledge. He will tell you what to do or what to write in reply.

In any case, do nothing to help her to come out here in pursuit of me.

Do not hesitate to write to Lewis if anything happens in which you need advice. If only Ivy would give me a little peace I should be able to work here like anything. As it is, I live in constant terror of the post. Tabitha has been poorly, and Ivy has refused to have any nurse, even her own cousin.

Fortunately, however, Tabitha is better again. How I wish that infant were not going to be brought up in an atmosphere of lies, and dark stuffy rooms.

My dear Mother when I think of Ivy's deliberate efforts to separate me from my own family, the censorship of my letters, and all the rest, I am surprised that I am still fairly sane. Living in this calm Russian household, where there are no rows, no violent scenes, is such a relief that I feel in a different world. If only Lewis can arrange a peaceable separation, I do hope that in a calmer life you and I will be able to be the friends we used to be before that unfortunate marriage. I am so glad that we had that talk in Leeds before I left England.

One piece of very good news I have for you. Douglas has withdrawn his appeal. So the whole of that trouble is at an end. Lewis has done extraordinarily well.

Perhaps it would be a good thing if you sent this letter on to Geoffrey [his brother]. I should like him to know exactly how things stand. And in case you are at all worried it will be a satisfaction to you to know that he also knows. I told him when I was in Edinburgh how things were: but the lamp-smashing episode occurred only just before I came away, at the end of a day in which, as Ivy admitted I had given up all work and devoted myself entirely to the task of keeping her happy.

This is a beautiful place, and when my worry and anxiety allow it, I lay the foundations for Stevenson at a wooden table under tall pine trees, close to the Gulf of Finland, now and then hearing the guns from the fortress of Kronstadt far away. It is a great relief to be able to write to you without all the fear that Ivy will condemn the letter.

Your affectionate son,
Arthur.

The presence of the friendly, cheerful children of his hosts at the Gellibrand dacha was a welcome stimulus to his work on Stevenson. Ransome returned in due course to Wiltshire, drawn by his deep love for his daughter to try again, but was in low spirits there. His concentration was failing. He worked doggedly on the Stevenson, but it did not go well. A cage of comforting blue mice on his desk failed to cheer him up; he felt increasingly that he was a martyr to Ivy's jealousy and possessiveness. During this time he composed a strange philosophical allegory called *The Blue Treacle*, which he hoped his daughter might one day read and understand. Written while living at Hatch with her, it reflects his anguish at the imminent loss of her company. The story was about escape. Ransome called it 'an allegory of mental processes,' and 'merely the story of an escape from this unconscious living – a realization of a moment of experience'. The heroine, Tabitha, represents 'the poet in us, [who] reaches an imaginative height which [she] cannot explain to herself', while the blue treacle stands for 'the general stream of unrealized experience'. Ransome admitted 'I am not at all certain what all of it means myself.' It failed to find a publisher. His other projects were going badly, too. He was frantic to get away, back to Russia and safety again, as a letter from Hatch to his mother dated Saturday 14 March 1914 reveals:

> Things are very bad with me. The Caucasian Folk Tales have been rejected by the most likely of all the publishers. And I'd counted on them for getting to Russia with. All my hopes of new gorgeous books are blasted, and I'll have to take a commission for another Wilde, Poe, Stevenson type of book.
>
> Blue Treacle still homeless and likely to remain so.
>
> I've written a queer little story, short, one of the best I've done [probably 'Ankou'] which comforts me a little. But I can't help being bluer than the bluest treacle. … I am here working on Stevenson till Monday. Then just a chance of my getting a French job in Russia, and I may go to Paris 3rd class return to try for it but I don't know.

The style is uncharacteristically bleak. He did leave for ten days in Paris on the following Monday, but returned without the 'French job'. Then, at last, he was invited to write a history and guide to St Petersburg by the minor publisher Max Goschen. He jumped at the offer, and made his escape to the Continent in his good new boots on 5 May. He arrived in the city on 13 May, and, working at white-hot speed and giving time to little else, finished the seventy thousand words of the new book on 9 July. There had been a disagreeable price to pay for this remarkable achievement: most of his days had been completely taken up with a 'famished, fiendish frenzy' of fact-finding. He complained frequently about having insufficient funds, until Goschen eventually sent an advance of £50; he recorded the windfall in his diary as the 'result of my anger. Jolly good dinner.' However, political events were about to render his work obsolete. The city he had explored and described was renamed Petrograd on 31 August 1914, and before long would become a very different place. His publisher could see no commercial future for the book, withdrew from publishing it, and returned the manuscript. Ransome was to say later, 'I do not think that the book had any merit', and claimed to have destroyed the manuscript; but his recollections are not always quite reliable. Although no trace of the St Petersburg book has come to light, he was not accustomed to destroy any manuscript voluntarily. (For instance, in his autobiography he says firmly that he destroyed about a dozen stories based on proverbs which he had written at Coniston in the autumn of 1910. In fact he didn't; they survive among his papers at the Brotherton Library.) So it is at least possible that the St Petersburg manuscript survived, until a disastrous house-fire in Riga in 1923 consumed many of his personal letters, working papers and cherished possessions, and other papers relating to the years which he spent in Russia and the Baltic. Ironically, the fire happened only two months after Ivy had at last agreed to a divorce.

Such books and papers as Ransome left in England had a more complex fate. The working library (including his notebooks) which he had left behind in his study at Hatch was still, he assumed, as he had left it. As part of a difficult separation agreement, all his books remained in the farmhouse at Hatch where Ivy still lived, as her property. When she moved elsewhere in the 1920s, the books went with her; she then had a room purpose-built to receive them, always referred to as 'the Library'. Ivy seems to have treated not only the books as her own, but also (without Arthur's consent) his working papers. It was the loss of these things, rather than the one-third of his earnings which she also received, that caused Ransome the greatest pain. He had sacrificed food or fuel to buy some of the books; many were presentation copies from their authors, prized for the association. In 1929 he wrote frequently to Ivy, asking for the return of his notebooks and papers, which could not in any sense be her property. We do not know if he ever specifically asked her for his Stevenson material. Only a few notebooks were grudgingly released. It is clear that she never accepted the reality of their divorce, feeling the disgrace and social disadvantage strongly. When she died in 1939 she was, somewhat pathetically, described on her death certificate as 'wife of A. Ransome, writer'.

For Arthur, there was worse to come. He records in his autobiography the painful discovery that, after Ivy's death, Tabitha did not ask him whether he would like to have his books and papers back but had decided to sell them to a bookseller. Wounded by what he felt to be a second generation of cruelty and betrayal, he could not bring himself to accept her suggestion that he might like to make an offer for those he most wanted before the sale went through. He then suffered the additional anguish of seeing the dealer's catalogue which described them 'in painful detail, even mentioning the inscriptions in them from my friends. I bought from the bookseller some of my own manuscript notebooks, which, of course, she [Tabitha] had not had ever the right to sell.' We do not know if he had been hoping to find his Stevenson manuscript material there, or whether the 'Stevenson exercise book' (soon to be described) came to him from that source or was with him all through the intervening years.

However, the working papers of *Stevenson* which Ivy had sequestered in 1914 were not part of the collection that Tabitha sold. It is clear that they had never been restored to their former place with Arthur's other books and .papers, and so presumably did not pass to Tabitha at her mother's death. Although long estranged from her father, she appreciated his fame as a successful writer, and would almost certainly have opened the parcel if it had been available to her. Instead, she was completely surprised by the news of its discovery in 1990.

4 The *Stevenson* Manuscript: Parcel and Exercise Book

When the parcel was opened, it was found to contain an unbound holograph manuscript comprising the text and working papers of the first draft critical study of Robert Louis Stevenson. It was written on three hundred and eighty-seven sheets of small quarto (17.5 cm × 20.5 cm) paper whose watermarks indicate that it was produced between 1909 and 1916 by the Company of Riga Papermaking Factories, in what today is Latvia. Large sheets had been cut to the size he wanted.

The initial, biographical, quarter of the book is present in an almost complete fair copy, a state from which it could have been typed up and sent to the publisher. The remainder includes almost all the sections Ransome listed (both on a page within the manuscript and on a leaf of the exercise-book contemporary with that) as necessary for a complete 'critical study' of Stevenson's works, some of them still awaiting substantial revision before being ready for typing up. Inserted among the sheets of the second part are several pages of quotations from Stevenson, some in an appropriate position for incorporation into the text, others less obviously so. Other working papers in the parcel include an incomplete reading-list, a preliminary list of chapters or sections, and notes of how many pages had been written each day during July and August of 1913. Sections on Stevenson's childhood and *Weir of Hermiston*, although listed in Ransome's scheme and anticipated and foreshadowed within the existing text, are not present.

Had he been able to revise his work for publication, Ransome might well have reconsidered the order of his sections. The order in which they were numbered at Leeds (as received from the solicitors) more or less follows that of his scheme. The concluding pages of the manuscript as received deal with Stevenson and morality; Ransome's diary shows that he was writing these pages, the section planned to be last in the book, towards the end of April 1914. This seems to be the point at which continuous work ceased; and, as we have seen, Ivy dated the parcelled draft with 'May 4 1914', the last possible day on which Arthur could have been at home with it: the day before he crossed to the continent *en route* for Tsarist Russia for the second time, on 5 May.

That Ransome had projected, deferred, and in 1913 returned to work on this book had been known for a long time. His diaries (also now in the Brotherton Library) confirm that he was working steadily on the book during that year; he records the number of pages written on any one day, or (as on 11 September 1913) a running sub-total: 'Stevenson approx. 90pp. roughly'. He had a good deal of other work on hand, but it is clear that he was working fairly continuously on this book throughout 1913 and the first third of 1914. That he had come very close to completing it was quite unexpected when the parcel was opened; his autobiography tells us only that he 'worked now and then at a book on Stevenson which Methuen's were to publish (they subsequently released me from that)'. From this rather disingenuous summary, it was generally believed that the book had not gone beyond preliminary sketching. This assumption was strengthened when one of Ransome's notebooks became available after his death, an exercise-book now in the Ransome archive at the Brotherton Library. (His books, typescripts, manuscripts, and personal papers were divided between Abbot Hall in Kendal (the Museum of Lakeland Life and Industry) and the Brotherton Library of the University of Leeds by his second wife's direction.) Ransome had bought the exercise-book in Paris from 'F. Bernard, Papeterie-Imprimerie des Etudiants et de l'Odéon'. (It was in the Galerie de l'Odéon that he had seen the French translation of his *Oscar Wilde* on sale on 18 February.) While in Russia, he lettered this exercise-book on the spine in black ink 'ꜱᴛᴇᴠᴇɴꜱᴏɴ. стивенсонъ' (transliterating Stevenson's name correctly into Cyrillic script and ending with the 'hard' sign which in pre-revolutionary Russian spelling was required for a word ending in a consonant) (see appendix A.1). It contains no more than a chronology of Stevenson's life and works, headings for the sections of his own book, and extensive quotations from some of Stevenson's. On the fly-leaf is written 'Arthur Ransome. Datcha Gellibrand. Terijoki. Finland' – then part of Tsarist Russia. This address was his chief base during 1913 until his return to London in late September, and he returned to it at times in 1914 and later.

The history of this blue exercise-book is completely different from that of the parcel. Possibly it was returned to Ransome with other papers and notebooks after prolonged and bitter negotiations with Ivy in 1929 (the year in which he determined to give up the full-time journalism that had occupied him for the previous fourteen years and devote himself to a new kind of narrative, *Swallows and Amazons*). Alternatively, it may have been one of the notebooks he was obliged to buy back from the second-hand bookseller. Inserted into the 'Stevenson exercise-book' are three loose sheets of the extremely distinctive paper on which Ransome wrote his first draft of the book. One, headed 'Conclusion', contains only one paragraph, partially crossed out, that was evidently once intended for *Stevenson*. (With typical economy, Ransome used the other two sheets many years later for notes towards his autobiography.)

How and why the two sources for the book became separated is unknown. Why Ransome copied some of the quotations from Stevenson twice, on sheets within the parcel and also on pages of the exercise-book, is also somewhat puzzling. However, the exercise-book almost certainly came first. The chronology of Stevenson's life and works which it contains is evidently derived from Graham Balfour's memoir of his cousin, a new edition of which had been the subject of a review article by Ransome in 1911: 'I wrote that year on Kant, Peacock, Paracelsus and Stevenson, mostly short notes and articles hitched to new books.' (This review, signed with a pseudonym as were many of Ransome's occasional pieces, is reprinted here as appendix B.3.) It may be that the exercise-book was shelved in Ransome's study separately from the bulk of his Stevenson papers so that Ivy did not include it in the parcel; or that Ransome on that fated 4 May had already put it with the papers he meant to take to Russia. The latter is more likely.

When he made his escape from England, home, and Ivy on 5 May 1914, Ransome probably took with him (of his Stevenson work) only the exercise book and a few sheets of loose 'Stevenson' paper within it. Having already composed a fairly complete (if discontinuous) first draft, he would not have needed to take more than this. At some later point, presumably in Russia or on the way there (the ink is similar to one of the inks used in the main manuscript) he drafted a conclusion to the work on one of those blank leaves. It is unlikely that any more work on *Stevenson* was done in Russia after that; he was fully occupied in preparing the book he had gone to St Petersburg to write, and in any case would have wanted to reread and revise the whole manuscript again before attempting to write a more satisfactory conclusion. His *Stevenson*, then, was still very much 'work in progress' at the time the parcel was made. Yet he never did return to the manuscript. The reasons for this are complex, though the turmoil of his private life and the all-absorbing new direction that the outbreak of the First World War gave to his professional life, clearly have a bearing on it. Although it was a book which he had been extremely keen to write, and had been absorbed in writing, it was never completed, and (stranger still) Ransome appears never to have mentioned it again, except for the somewhat dismissive reference in his autobiography.

5 Ransome and Stevenson

1884 was the year in which Stevenson announced to his friends that he was engaged on a collection of poetry for children. 'Penny Whistles for Small Whistlers', his working title for the book, was to be published as *A Child's Garden of Verses*. 'Just about the same time it happened that I was born', says Ransome. 'It further happened that the book had just had time to percolate the provinces, and induce in provincial parents a readiness to read it aloud instead of Bunyan, when I, in the course of nature, was ready to listen to it.' He was fortunate to have parents who delighted in the company of their children, and were themselves voracious readers. His father, professor of history and literature at what was to become the University of Leeds, was the author of various academic and scholarly works; his mother was an able artist and writer, and came from an accomplished and well-travelled family. Arthur's imagination was informed from his earliest years by the books – *A Child's Garden of Verses* among them – that were read to him, and those which he very soon learnt to read for himself. There can be few other children who have received on their fourth birthday a present of their own copy of *Robinson Crusoe* 'in reward for being able to read it'.

Both Stevenson and Ransome began their education at home, and their lively imaginations found creative expression very early. At the age of eight, the boy Lewis Stevenson (always called by his given second name; the spelling became 'Louis' later) had written '"The Book of Joseph". By R.L.B.S. The author of "A History of Moses."' (The earlier story he had dictated to his mother.) 'Jacob of old married two wives; one of his wives was called Rachael [*sic*] and the other Leah. Rachael's eldest [*sic*] son was Joseph which I intend to found my story on. Well, Joseph was his father's favourite ...' Thirty-four years later, also at the age of eight, Arthur wrote his own first story, 'The Desert Island'. But for a Stevenson-inspired pirate accident he might never have written it. At home in Leeds, not merely the nursery and 'back-bedroom chairs' which the only child Stevenson had commandeered for his 'lonely Crusoes building boats' and other imaginative play, were available; the whole house, even the dining-room table, became the stage for the Ransome children's games of adventure. Huckleberry Finn, Masterman Ready, Jim of *Treasure Island*, Davie Balfour of *Kidnapped*, Ballantyne's Jack, Ralph and Peterkin of *The Coral Island*, were their inspiration. It was in consequence of Arthur's enthusiastic participation that he became a writer, as he explains:

> We were playing at ships under and on a big dining-room table which had underneath it, in the middle, a heavy iron screw pointing

downwards. It was my 'watch' below. My brother or sister was on the bridge, on top of the table, and suddenly raised a shout for "All hands on deck!" I started up, and that big screw under the middle of the table made a most horrible dent in the top of my skull, altered its shape and so, in one moment, changed my character for life. I crawled out, much shaken; and that very afternoon wrote my first book, about a desert island, in a little notebook with a blue cover. I have been writing ever since.

That little notebook still exists; the full text of Ransome's 'first book' is printed here as appendix B.1. The completeness and detail of the story, and Arthur's careful shaping of the book within such a physically small compass, are both remarkable. The notebook in which he wrote, carefully and in red ink, is no taller than an adult's thumb.

The Desert Island. By Arthur M. Ransome.

There was once a boy called Jack. His father had gone to Liverpool and had never been heard of since; everybody thought that he had been seized by a press-gang, and taken away to the South Seas. So Jack made up his mind to go and find him. When he was fourteen he went to Portsmouth and went on board a ship called the White Bird....

They rowed back to the ship the next day and took a lot of planks, guns, pistols and swords back with them.

They built a house and a stockade round it to keep it safe from wild beasts or savages if any should come. Tom shot a wild duck and a sort of pigeon which lasted for breakfast and dinner and they found some bananas and coconuts for tea. There was a little stream running through the stockade so they should never run short of water.

The pace is kept up successfully until the *dénouement:*

... Jack suddenly saw his father who was captain of the ship. Jack's father said that it was he who had written the note and built the hut, and that he had been wrecked on that very island and had been found by an English ship and been taken on board. He had afterwards got to be captain and was on his way back to England. Jack and Tom went with him and arrived safely. The End.

Here, plainly, is a homage to Arthur's favourite adventure story, *Treasure Island.* (It also owes something to *Robinson Crusoe,* and to R. M. Ballantyne's *The Coral Island,* and has the germ of thematic material familiar to readers of Ransome's *We Didn't Mean To Go To Sea.*) Both Stevenson and Ransome were powerfully influenced by Ballantyne's gripping adventure stories for boys, and both had the rare good fortune to meet him. The normally irrepressible Lewis Stevenson was so awestruck that he was speechless, despite Ballantyne's affability; and a generation later, the young Arthur Ransome was taken to tea in a garden by his grandmother 'where, silently worshipping, I shook hands with Ballantyne in the summer before he went to Italy to die.' He too was overwhelmed by his brief encounter with the aged author. But Defoe, Ballantyne and Stevenson were not young Arthur's only favourites. Before he was nine he had also read books by Catherine Sinclair, Thackeray, Lewis Carroll, Kingsley, Charlotte Mary Yonge, Mrs Ewing, Andrew Lang, the Brothers Grimm, Hans Andersen, W. G. Collingwood, and R. D. Blackmore; soon after, he began on Scott and Dickens. Some of these were perhaps the choices of his grandmother or some of his favourite aunts who, as he recalled in 1935, 'sent occasional Ballantynes. I do not think I ever had a Henty. I had "Huckleberry Finn" but not "Tom Sawyer". I had ...Stevenson's "Treasure Island" and "Kidnapped". I borrowed "The Black Arrow".' In his later autobiography he recalled: '*Treasure Island* we knew and loved, but I remember my father's shocked astonishment when I did not realise that *The Black Arrow* was in comparison a poor machine-made thing.'

Stevenson was born thirty-four years before Ransome, and circumstances of time and geography prevented them from meeting. Ransome nevertheless always felt a great affinity with the older writer, and (apart from their significant meetings with Ballantyne) there are many significant parallels between their careers and the things that influenced them. Lewis Stevenson in Edinburgh, and Arthur Ransome in Leeds were both born into comfortable, well-to-do middle-class households, where they inherited strong habits of work and were encouraged in reading, writing, story-telling, music and painting. Lewis remained an only child, whose playmates were his nurse and a number of congenial cousins; Arthur was the eldest of four children who liked playing together. Temperamentally they were both restless, impulsive romantics, and they early showed great energy and creativity. One could almost construct an alphabet of the interests that shaped them as adults: adventure, artists, boats, the Bohemian life, children and childhood, donkeys, escape, exile, friendship, France, the gypsy life, 'home' (be it Edinburgh or Vailima, Lanehead or Leeds), maps, morality, music, older women, parents, penny-whistles, poetry, politics, reading, realism, religion, restlessness, romance, the sea, stories, travel, truth, – and wives. Neither had good health: Lewis was a frail child, was thought to be consumptive, and spent many hours being nursed through fevers and nightmares. He grew up to be an extraordinarily thin young man, full of nervous energy, and often on the verge of physical collapse. Arthur was a robust child who relished outdoor pursuits, although he was never able to participate fully in sports on account of his short-sightedness. The extreme stress of his life as a young man had a powerful adverse effect on his health, and he suffered from acute digestive problems for the rest of his life. Nevertheless, both men had a tremendous capacity for hard work as writers. Both were keen to transcend the boundaries of their birth and culture, and Arthur knew from his earliest years those dreams of travel which Lewis had so enticingly expressed:

> I should like to rise and go
> Where the golden apples grow; –
> Where below another sky
> Parrot islands anchored lie,
> And, watched by cockatoos and goats,
> Lonely Crusoes building boats ...

At the age of eighteen, Stevenson loved theatricals, and was known as 'velvet jacket' to his friends because of the Bohemian clothes which he affected. He was a student in Edinburgh, briefly of engineering, and then of a slightly more congenial subject, law. Unknown to his parents, he rejected their religion, became an atheist, and joined the iconoclastic Speculative Society. He contributed a good deal to the *Edinburgh University Magazine*, and gratified his father, whom he had accompanied on lighthouse-inspecting travels, by publishing an article on 'A New Form of Intermittent Light for Lighthouses.' But the university did not detain Stevenson long. He abandoned his studies and moved to Paris, where he quickly became as intimately acquainted with the artists' colonies of Fontainebleau and Mont Lozère as he had been with the wynds of Edinburgh's Old Town and the 'advanced' student coteries of its university.

Similarly, Ransome had begun a degree course at Yorkshire College in chemistry, the subject to which his father had thought he would be best suited; but before the age of twenty he had abandoned his barren studies in favour of the profession of literature. He moved to London, rapidly finding his way into the Bohemian circles about which he was later to write affectionately; very soon, he made the first of many visits to Paris. Of this period he later said 'I lived with great content through what I have come to think was the happiest time of my life.' Perhaps in imitation of Stevenson, Arthur (who played the piano a little) now became an adept player of the penny whistle. His American artist friends Alphaeus and Peggotty Cole, with whom he lodged as a young man in Chelsea, called him 'The Piper'; his 'flageolet' made a domestic quartet with the violin, piano and cello played by his fellow-lodgers. In a discarded 'Conclusion' to the first part of his book on Stevenson (see appendix A.1.i), Ransome was to write: 'The instrument is unjustly despised, even laughed at, but it is capable of great things ... it is symbolical of [Stevenson's] career. A grown man playing the instrument of youth ... playing a penny whistle in the orchestra of English literature.'

By his late twenties, Lewis Stevenson had become Robert Louis Stevenson, the well-known author. He had published *An Inland Voyage* and *Travels with a Donkey in the Cévennes*, and contributed many articles to literary journals – on walking, rivers, Scottish songs, the Arabian Nights, and French writers such as Victor Hugo and Jules Verne. He had enthusiastically reviewed the collected works of Edgar Allan Poe, who – perhaps not entirely coincidentally – was to be the subject of Ransome's first full-length critical study. And he was about to be married. Although in miserably poor health after a cheap 'emigrant' crossing of the Atlantic and interminable railway journeys by third class across the United States, he pursued and finally won Fanny Osbourne, a divorced woman with two children. He had till now been estranged from his father, who was mortified by his confession of atheism: 'You have rendered my whole life a failure!' he grimly informed his son. But now they were reconciled, and the Stevensons offered their newly married son much-needed financial support. The company of his young stepson Lloyd was a continuing stimulus to his imagination, and he shared the planning of *Treasure Island* with him, and with his own father – boy adventurers all at heart. Then Stevenson set off on a voyage of his own, seeking relief from his ailments in the tropical waters of the Pacific. He met (and was befriended by) the 'merry monarch of Hawaii', King David Kalakaua, but settled permanently in Samoa. There he dived at once into local politics, publishing vigorously on the issues of the day, often taking the part of the underdog.

By his late twenties, Ransome also had established himself as a promising writer and a perceptive critic, with fourteen published books to his name. He wanted to write a book about Stevenson, a publisher had accepted it, and he had begun to gather material. He too had married, and now had a beloved daughter; but (as we have seen) his marriage was not a source of happiness. His visits to Russia drew him into politics, but on a much broader scale than Stevenson. Initially he found pleasure in the company of Karl Radek and other cheerfully idealistic, pipe-smoking, chess-playing revolutionaries. During the Great War he found a congenial role and a sufficient income as a press correspondent, reporting eye-witness accounts of the increasingly vigorous political unrest, and the effects of war. He was also secretly retained by the British Government as a well-placed observer of developments in Russia. During this time he sent story-letters to his daughter at home in Wiltshire, little realising how long he would be away from her: he remained in Russia for the duration of the war, and was then based in Riga until 1923. He had met a Russian woman whom he was sure he wanted to marry, and felt obliged to remain in exile until such time as Ivy would consent to a divorce.

While Ivy was very unlike her husband in temperament, Evgenia Schelepina, who was to be his second wife, was a woman of integrity, who shared Arthur's solid values of honesty and openness (except when absolutely necessary to save sanity or skin) and intelligent idealism. She had a deep appreciation of literature, and a liking for rural and aquatic pursuits. She would be with him for the rest of his life; they were married in 1924. She was then thirty to his forty, tall, well built, and blessed with robust health. She was unflappable and genial, except when she took it on herself to protect Arthur from inquisitive journalists, intrusive admirers, and aluminium cooking-pots. She was his strongest ally in all the occupations closest to his heart – sailing, fishing, and writing. In later years he came to rely utterly on her judgement of the literary value of his own work, although her critical opinions were often at odds with his, and probably with ours. But in the main she successfully deflected danger and distress, jollied him out of his mental anguish, and kept him in as good health as could be managed. It had not been easy to woo her away from her Bolshevik colleagues, and the risks which Arthur took to smuggle her out of Russia could have cost him his life; but he was convinced that she was thoroughly worth it.

There were also ten years between Stevenson and his wife, but she was the senior. Although a willing and appreciative audience for his tales and a frequent amanuensis to his flow of genius, she caused him unexpected anxiety as nervous illness and depression took hold of her. Rather like Ivy Ransome, she became a wife to be endured rather than enjoyed. John Singer Sargent painted the Stevensons in 1885, revealingly placing her in the corner of his picture, seated on a sofa and shrouded in an Indian shawl; her shadowy presence can easily be overlooked. Meanwhile, her husband paces the floor restlessly in the throes of inspiration, 'becoming' one of his own characters as narrative and dialogue well up spontaneously from within him.

As mature writers, Stevenson and Ransome both flourished when they had the support of a congenial family, domestic security, and especially the company of children. Stevenson took great pleasure in his step-family. In one of a series of photographs of his household taken in Samoa, we see him aged forty-two, two years before he died, on the palm-fringed veranda at Vailima, the tropical island home which had been built to his design. He is in the centre, arms folded, a paterfamilias. The extended family, hierarchically positioned and very much at home in their exotic setting, included his widowed mother Margaret, who came out to the South Seas in 1890; his stepdaughter Belle Strong with her son Austin in one of his mother's hats; her husband Joe Strong, in long socks and a lava-lava, with Cocky the parrot on his shoulder; his wife Fanny, and his step-son Lloyd. Despite his wife's frailty and the emerging collapse of his stepdaughter's marriage, Stevenson was looked after very well. His mother was the very efficient head of the household; all were devoted to him, not least because his writing supported them all.

Ransome, who missed his daughter acutely and scarcely saw her again after she was seven, may have looked forward to having further children with his capable new wife; but there were none. Other people's children became a kind of surrogate family, in particular the children of Dora Collingwood, a woman to whom Arthur had earlier seriously proposed marriage. In 1915 she had married Ernest Altounyan, the doctor in charge of a hospital in Aleppo. Their children provided the catalyst for the writing of his greatest novels. In 1932 he and Evgenia set out for Syria with a sailing-dinghy which they intended as a present for the Altounyan family. Photographs show them beaming with happiness, surrounded by excited children, Ransome looking, if anything, younger than he had in the 1913 photo with Ivy. While in Aleppo, he began writing *Peter Duck*, reading the family each chapter as it was written, and welcoming good ideas for the development of the plot from the children. 'Ukartha' and Aunt Genia envied the family life which they were allowed to share in Syria – a location as exotic as Stevenson's Samoa. Ransome had written the first of his great novels to please these children, and they were pleased. He was rejuvenated by their company, as Stevenson had been by Lloyd Osbourne.

6 Writing *Stevenson*

Arthur was an ebullient and even mischievous young child, but his prep-school days were miserable. He was, he says, a duffer at sport, and for that reason could make no friends there; but nobody at home or at school had yet realised that he was very short-sighted. While at Rugby, the problem was recognised. There his sense of style and love of literature was sharpened and encouraged by W. H. D. Rouse and Robert Whitelaw, under whose influence he first appeared in print in the local press. He was immersed in books, and enjoyed writing; but his father did not foresee a literary career for him. Rather, he had interpreted Arthur's interest in natural history and the physical world as a bent towards science. Presumably to fulfil his wishes, the widowed Mrs Ransome encouraged her son to study chemistry. Seeking relief in the library of Yorkshire College, he became engrossed in Mackail's *Life of William Morris*. It was a moment of epiphany. He was seduced not only by the desirability of such a life as Morris's, but by the beauty – physical as well as stylistic – of the book which had been made of it. Ransome was never to write biography of this kind, but Mackail's perceptive recreation of a writer and thinker whom he greatly admired may perhaps be seen as a remote ancestor of this book.

Writing a study of Stevenson would have been as congenial a project as Ransome could imagine, and for many reasons. And among them, he intended it to strike out in a number of new directions: to challenge received ideas, and to put into practice his recently conceived critical theories.

By 1912 Ransome had begun to make a reputation for perceptive and innovative literary analysis. He was probably best known for a theory of literary expression which was first elaborated in an article entitled 'Kinetic and Potential Speech', published in the October 1911 edition of *The Oxford and Cambridge Review*. The key terms of this theory were perhaps suggested by his earlier scientific studies; Ransome certainly believed that something of a scientific method was needed properly to investigate and evaluate the structures, materials, and effects of literature. He opens with a definition: literature in general is 'a combination of kinetic with potential speech'. Purely kinetic speech is 'prose without atmosphere … it says things.' Purely potential speech is like music. In a ballad the words may be purely kinetic, but a sea-shanty receives an extra dimension of meaning from the tune to which it is sung: a quality of potential speech. The value of potential speech in literature is that it secures profound effects entirely by means of suggestion; to illustrate his point Ransome analyses examples from Spenser, Hazlitt, Blake, Shelley, Lamb, Wordsworth and, being remarkably up to date, Mallarmé. Wordsworth, for example, when he tells us that his sonnet was composed 'on Westminster Bridge', is 'trying to ensure that we shall approach it as he did, and hear as well as the kinetic, the potential speech that he values no less'. Ransome concludes his article by claiming that his theory will provide a valuable new tool for critics, and help them to assess the changing fashions of literature.

Perhaps as a result of immersing himself in Wilde's critical writings and his doctrine of 'Art for Art's sake' in preparation for *Oscar Wilde*, Ransome began to read more widely about the development of literary theory from Sidney onwards. He was especially impressed by the essays on the subject exchanged by Henry James and Stevenson. In a long, elaborate, and highly theoretical essay published in *The English Review*, he proposed another new theory, 'Art for Life's sake'. Writing to W. H. D. Rouse, his former master at Rugby, now Head of the Perse School in Cambridge, Ransome describes his thesis as 'an identification of the act of artistic creation with *knowing* … this is the central idea of a book which I am now writing on the nature of technique.' The essays on 'kinetic and potential speech' and on Art were included in *Portraits and Speculations* (1913), which Ransome dedicated, perhaps surprisingly, to his wife. Despite their domestic difficulties, she seems at this time to have borne her husband's literary enthusiasms in much the same spirit of admiring martyrdom as Fanny Stevenson does in Sargent's portrait. It is unlikely, however, that she found this dense and extremely serious tract on Art, which would have taken two hours to read, or Arthur's equally demanding 'Friedrich Nietzsche: an Essay in Comprehension', very enjoyable or even comprehensible.

Fortunately, Ransome seems to have got his theories of literature clear in his mind and off his chest in these essays before embarking on his *Stevenson*. They are perhaps deliberately knotty, but his fresh, clear, proto-modernist eye can also be appreciated in them. He asserts, for example, that 'a work of art is a collaboration between two artists, whom I … call the speaker and the listener … the process of the speaker in the first creation of a work of art is a process of finding out.' Thus he is preparing to approach his task of writing about Stevenson in the spirit of an ideal collaborator.

He uses the open and benevolent manner of one artist-craftsman observing another, shunning the detached and sometimes esoteric terminology of purely academic assessment; and his insights sometimes seem to be far in advance of his time.

> A novel, like any other work of art, is an act of becoming conscious performed by its author. But an illusion is produced that the author has left his own life aside, and is merely chronicling the lives of others. We are faced with the difficulty of reconciling this apparent contradiction.

Ransome seems to be adumbrating the position of Lascelles Abercrombie (with whom he had often debated literary theory) in a British Academy lecture, 'A Plea for the Liberty of Interpreting' (1930), of the 'New Critics', and even of Roland Barthes and his notion of 'the death of the author'.

As a writer struggling to find his true voice as a storyteller, Ransome was very much aware of Stevenson standing to him *in loco parentis*. Writing about Stevenson almost became a way of writing autobiography, so much a part of his psyche had Stevenson's writings been from his earliest childhood. A reader now may feel grateful to Ransome's self-indulgent generosity in allowing his first draft to carry so much of his own direct personal response to text. We can, for example, reread Stevenson's *A Child's Garden of Verses* through the imagination of the child Arthur together with the adult Arthur, and so experience a double consciousness of poetry so long known and deeply loved that the experiences the words contain cannot be distinguished from those of his own 'real' life. Less than twenty years later, in 1928, Ransome the writer would himself master the skill to achieve that effect in prose. Generations of young readers have likewise read Arthur Ransome's books and savoured the experiences they contain as if they were their own; the books have lived with them to become part of their own real lives. Only the very greatest literature can achieve this.

In writing about Stevenson's poetry for children, Ransome adopts a different, more relaxed and more personal attitude and approach from the more formal and adult one in which he discusses Stevenson's essays, stories, letters and novels. He uses an engaging and authentic tone of personal reminiscence, as he approaches the moment in Stevenson's career when he himself entered the world. Writing unusually in *green* ink, he has a fine, distinctive, assured voice in sympathy with his subject.

> About this time thirty years ago, a Mr Stevenson, sorely stricken in mind and limb, severely troubled with the ridiculous details of drains and smells in a house he had taken in the hope of being well in it, was busied in composition of a kind almost entirely new to him …

But the heart of Ransome's study is his fascination with the great variety of style that can be found in Stevenson's work, a variety which he thinks is only partly related to genre. He says:

> Style is so far a man's personal rhythm, that it is as difficult to analyse
> as a personality. Its characteristics, its differences from other styles,
> are like a man's differences from other men. Yet something we can
> seize, in his choice of words, is the tone in which he uses them: and
> a vocabulary does not make so utterly flexible a vehicle of thought
> that a writer is not to be known by the repetition of particular effects
> varied only in detail, and as it were midway between perfect expres-
> sion and a private convention of his own.

That is a very knotty sentence, not very stylish, and one which Ransome would no doubt have recast had he returned to his draft. To disentangle his double negative: he says that a writer may be known by his idiosyncratic vocabulary and by a repetition of particular effects, and may finally possess 'a private convention of his own'. That is certainly true of some kinds of Stevenson's writing. It is true of all of Ransome's.

As has already been shown, Ransome was often ahead of his time as a literary critic. These words show how acutely aware he was of the impor- tance of personality and mind-set to a writer's style, and how a writer exhibits quirks of vocabulary and sentence-structure which can be iden- tified as unique to his habits of mind and thought. Literary criticism has long since passed beyond subjective enjoyment, and it is possible to apply scientific method and specific programmes to determine the author- ship of a piece of writing not so much from vocabulary (which we might have expected, and which Ransome naturally assumes is a clear mark of a man's mind) as from sentence-structures, the 'which's and 'and's, the rhythms and the 'repetition of particular effects', as Ransome puts it. And of course a sensitive reader may still intuitively feel an indefinable 'some- thing' in the turning of a sentence that marks it out as that author's, and his alone.

From earliest childhood Ransome enjoyed felicities of rhythm and words in English prose. In an autobiographical draft he remembered:

> a book [by Stella Austin] much loved and often read aloud in my
> childhood and remembered now for one continually quoted sentence:
> 'The way to Stumpie's heart is paved with strawberry jam.' 'Paved' was
> the relished word. It gives me pleasure to repeat that sentence even
> now.

The reader of Ransome's *Stevenson* will find many such pleasures in the book, from his telling placing of adverbs, to a complex intertextuality derived from direct address to the reader: 'You, I hope, who read' (although there would be no reader for almost a hundred years). And of course he discusses such matters in the work of his subject. He considers whether

Stevenson's 'familiarity' is really with his reader or with his subject, and discusses Stevenson's notions of 'charm' and his preoccupation with 'the small glamour' of authorship perceptively and with good-humoured disagreement. And he tells us clearly where and why Stevenson does not succeed (in his 'Aesopic fables', for instance). But he is fully appreciative of Stevenson's self-aware artistry and technical skills, and by careful comparison successfully places him in his context and tradition of French, American and English literature.

There is pleasure in Ransome's conversational engagement with the technical aspects of Stevenson's text, drawing analogies from enthusiasms past and present. This is the writing of a clever young critic, engaging us with mischievous but challenging convolutions of thought and imagination. Ransome betrays his personal pleasures, as when he sums up *The Wrecker* by saying, 'It is as if we are asked to solve a chess problem in the progress of the various courses of an eccentrically designed but excellent meal.' In assessing Stevenson's prose he allows an embedded memory of his own pleasure in beetle-collecting as a child: 'It included always a rhythmical, musical purpose, sound for its own sake, sonorous, reading well, an amber (if I may change to such a metaphor) very nearly if not quite as valuable in his eyes as the carefully collected coleoptera he intended to embed in it.' In defining Stevenson's accuracy of touch and tone he turns to billiards for an image: 'When he started "The Sea Cook" as an amusement only, of the most light hearted kind, he could not but write with skill and certainty, in the same way as the accomplished billiard player will frame with style even on a bagatelle board.' The metaphor suggests how important deliberation, shape and style are to the plan of a story however miniature. In reading Ransome's book we are often aware that he is on his own journey of self-discovery as an artist, as when he underlines Stevenson's observation that taking a liberty with fact is *'against the laws of the game'*.

Perhaps because the book exists only in a first draft, there is often a flavour of autobiography and an attractive immediacy of tone, as when Ransome explains that 'I am writing in a little Russian town where there are no English books ...,' or mentions 'a backhand deduction as to the childhood of my aunts', or describes himself with premature exaggeration as 'a bald-headed person', or tells an elaborate anecdote about some performing bears he once met in France, or mentions (no doubt with a thought of his own *Bohemia in London*) 'the many miraculous Londons that have been discovered in these latter years', or lets on casually that he 'cannot abide' the character of Stevenson's Davie Balfour. There are marked tonal shifts of style from third to first person, most noticeably where he is writing about *A Child's Garden of Verses* – a considerable part of which had been published almost verbatim in a periodical during Ransome's lifetime (reprinted here as appendix A.3). Although much would probably have been changed in redrafting, the immediacy of his writing adds greatly to the reader's enjoyment, as do his creative word-coinages: abracadabraical, impressional, exhilaritic, peacocking, commentatory, sur-iced … It is the voice of the young, exuberant, talkative Ransome.

One especially attractive aspect of Ransome's writing on Stevenson is the way it so easily becomes conversational that the reader has all the pleasure of a privileged participant. We become sensitive to his tone of voice: at times querulous, questioning, dogmatic, appreciative, always assured, always alert to the chameleonic nature of his subject. His judgements, almost always carefully supported by perceptive argument, are often expressed with pithy irony, as when moving in to conclusion: 'And now, let us consider not piecemeal but in a lump, the essentials of his preaching'; or in assessing Stevenson, 'the efficient man, who can build his house, cook his food, clothe himself, sail a boat, ride a horse, and read, a civilized Crusoe, the novels of Mr Henry James'; or in describing the quality of 'Tod Lapraik': 'The dialect seems to knit the words together so that there are no interstices to allow reality to slip out'; or in his personally felt response to 'Providence and the Guitar' – 'one of the most loveable stories in the world'. We can also enjoy his affectionate irony: 'Stevenson discovered a new romance: Silent upon the peak of Hyde Park Corner …' He admired Stevenson for his creative productivity, which in some ways resembled his own turbulent cauldron of book projects. 'He never complained that a man cannot do two things at once. He had seldom fewer than half a dozen on the stocks at once.'

Despite all his veneration for Stevenson, and his powerful sense of affinity with his 'romantic' temperament, Ransome is no idolater. His purpose is to place him as accurately as possible among his peers, not to make extravagant claims. 'He will not … except by a few enthusiasts of special temper, be counted among the greater writers'; and this may be because so often 'the part is greater than the whole'. He aims to discover and explore Stevenson's 'idea of art'. This especially affects his assessment of his technique:

> In art he was preoccupied with technique so largely that all he did seems now to have been by way of experiment during a prolonged adventure in the discovery of technical perfection … He was not a constructive thinker: he perceived, he felt, but was better at illustration than at argument.

He is acute in his assessment of Stevenson's oft-admired qualities of 'charm' and 'familiarity', clearly distinguishing familiarity with the reader from familiarity with the subject, and questions Stevenson's 'too sure an understanding of the moral difficulties of his subjects' (in the *Familiar Studies of Men and Books*). Why, he asks, is Stevenson's *In the South Seas* 'so curiously underestimated' in comparison with his other works? Because 'persons … conversant with Stevenson's other works, expect a different book':

The great travel books are written by Europeans, and enable other Europeans to follow the adventures of people not unlike themselves to strange surroundings. Stevenson's object was far less easy to attain. He eliminated, or almost eliminated, the common ground of race … Most of those who know of *In the South Seas,* ask themselves some such question as 'Am I the keeper of my fifteen cousins twenty times removed,' and buy *Treasure Island* instead.

Ransome's attitudes often chime with Stevenson's in relation to personal morality. He sees Stevenson's moral nature as being like that of a naïve Christian child playing at being a leader of cavalry, who in death gallantly surrendered his soul 'to a greater leader than he'. He disapproves of his whimsical false naïveté in leaving coins by the wayside on his travels with a donkey to 'pay God'. He sees in Stevenson's preaching an attitude that contains both acceptance and revolt in relation to received religion: this seems to chime with his own position. Those familiar with the novels of Ransome's maturity will know that there is no religion and no church-going in them – it is of course irrelevant to the society depicted – and may have wondered about Ransome's personal position, which is never mentioned in his *Autobiography.* The present book, alone in Ransome's work, gives us clues about his thinking – at least as it was in 1914. It is significant perhaps that the section on Stevenson's morality was written in the weeks leading up to what Ransome hoped would be a complete break with his wife. He writes with understanding and sympathy about Steven-son's 'position', which perhaps matches his own undogmatic, liberal and humanistic reduction of Christianity. He maps Stevenson's 'private intel-lectual position' and says 'I find that position extremely interesting.' As we can see also from the fervent conclusion he gives to Part I of his book, he shares with Stevenson a sense of a divine master who belongs to no partic-ular church, or, at least in the case of Stevenson's stoic minimal theism, to no particular religion either.

He looks for a tradition in which to place Stevenson, and finds (as F. R. Leavis was to do for a future generation) that Stevenson does not easily fit in. But even so he is able to identify where Stevenson belongs as a writer: he does not give us 'the filled views, for example, of Dostoevsky or Turgenev'; his characterisation pales before Balzac's:

> His is not the tradition of Richardson, Bronte, Hardy and Meredith, though just as Meredith in the beginning of his life wrote *The Shaving of Shagpat* so Stevenson, at the end of his, wrote *Weir of Hermiston* which, more than any other of his books, belongs to the other side of the gulf between the poet and the troubadours.

> A course of Balzac which, as Wilde said, 'reduces our living friends to shadows, and our acquaintances to the shadows of shades' turns Stevenson's creations into the most transparent veils, and a course of

Dostoevsky makes them altogether non-existent. But only the crudest criticism would undervalue them on that account, just as only the dullest critics measure a work by comparison with another, and only he who has no right to be a critic at all measures it by comparison with another work in an altogether different kind.

Adventure was what Stevenson cared for in life; adventure was what brought him to his twentieth reading of *Vicomte de Bragelonne*; adventure is what delighted him in his own books; and it is after a course of Dumas that the Scotch novels of Stevenson appear in their true colours, something new, something different, accomplished, graceful sacrifices on the altar of a tradition that will last as long as men are young enough to have the hearts of boys.

No man can put more virtue in his words than he practices in his life, according to Hugh Kingsmill; and this is plainly true of Stevenson and Ransome, both virtuous men whose consciences were severely tested in matters of faith, love, and artistic integrity. Ransome finds echoes and illuminations of his own torments in his subject's life and work. Later readers may be startled to find in his observations of Stevenson foreshadowings of his own struggles to come. He remarks that Stevenson's speed in composing 'The Sea Cook' 'was only made possible by the years of slow, meticulous labour that preceded it' – labour such as he himself is presently engaged in; or he mentions the need of the writer 'to re-collect himself, to refresh his personality until it could indeed translate those old adventures in to the general rhythm of his experience' – which reminds us that it was only when Ransome had returned from his Baltic exile to the Lake District with Evgenia as his wife that he was able to compose the novels of his fame. He sympathetically observes Stevenson's struggles with 'this bluidy Ebb Tide' with its narrative style 'pitched about "four notes higher" than it should have been' (an extraordinarily difficult reconciliation which few but Jane Austen have managed), prefiguring Ransome's later determined struggle and success with narrative point of view, style, and a large cast of characters in the *Swallows and Amazons* series.

Ransome was fortunate to have been writing in the innocent days of immediate personal response to books, when (apart from the primary works of his author) little but biographical information had to be taken into account by the writer of a critical study. He was able to communicate the joy of his inner conversation with Stevenson straight from the heart. It is refreshing for us to hear Ransome's clear, personal voice in his book, encouraging us and enlightening us in our own response.

What did Ransome learn from Stevenson? Much about the importance of maintaining a point of view – both negative and positive examples are carefully analysed in his book; about the difficulties of a first-person narrator; about how to leave the reader breathless at the end of a chapter;

about narrative shape. Perhaps, like Graham Greene (a cousin of Stevenson's) he learnt from him something of the 'method of describing action without adjectives and adverbs.' He learnt how to engage the whole being of the reader: 'there are delicious, perilous moments, up the mast, with Hands climbing from below, and jerking his dagger murderously through the air to pin me – or was it Jim Hawkins? – to the mast.' He learnt 'the laws of the game' of realism. He learnt how much more difficult a task it is to have a cast of six or eight, into whose minds and thoughts we can see (or partially see), than to maintain a narrative identity of one. In all this, Stevenson's struggles for perfection are mirrored by Ransome's own torments and ultimate success.

Ransome also learnt from Stevenson the power of maps to lead young readers into adventure. He learnt the power and enticement of islands, in art as in life. He learnt how to empower imagination, and to create reality through the use of deeply embedded metaphor. Most of all, he learnt about the importance of quest and romance. But he was his own man in demonstrating in his major fiction that the greatest treasure is to be found in human relationships, not in gold moidores. He certainly achieved in his mature work what he had sought for in Stevenson, 'the perfection ... which disguises from us the separateness of the planes on which he is working'. As we have seen, his was a mentality conditioned by Stevenson's imagination from childhood; indeed, he had come to know much of his work by heart. That imagination supported and coloured his narrative methods throughout his writing of the 'twelve books' of his maturity. Finally, the great slaty slabs of Stevenson's unfinished epic *Weir* may have influenced Ransome's own epically conceived and similarly unfinished 'The River Comes First'.

Clearly there are many affinities of style and imagination between Stevenson and his critic: but Ransome is never the 'sedulous ape', and the two are by nature stylistically distinct. We may intuitively appreciate that Ransome's style is marked out altogether from everyone else's by well-placed adverbs, and by the distinctive rhythms of his relative clauses, the remarkableness of which is evident in his writing from the early years of his career. In this book, we find his typical voice and turn of phrase and quality of perception more evident than in the completed studies of *Poe* and *Wilde* that had preceded it. It is a pleasure to discover that Ransome in this early book is discernibly *our* Ransome.

Lovers of Ransome's narrative voice will find much to appreciate and savour in this book. There is the pleasure of his sentences, always constructed with idiosyncratic rhythm, point, structure and flavour. There is his individual cast of mind, his love of the countryside and walking, of quiet inns, of firesides, and of pipes of tobacco enjoyed in congenial company beside them; of folk-song and poetry, of books and their writers. Above all, we hear his unmistakeable voice, both in enthusiastic but friendly disputation and in quiet companionable talk. It is a deeply personal book, and one with which he must have been pleased. And yet, only this first draft is extant. Why was it abandoned so near to completion and publication?

7 *Stevenson* Abandoned

Despite the breach with Ransome, Martin Secker had decided to continue publishing the series of 'modern monographs' that Ransome claimed to have originated. Aware that Ransome might yet complete his own book on Stevenson, Secker had no compunction in engaging another of his bright young authors to contribute the 'critical study of Stevenson' to the series. This was Frank Swinnerton, whose *George Gissing: A Critical Study* he had published in 1912, hard on the heels of Ransome's *Oscar Wilde.* The story of the literary rivalry between Swinnerton and Ransome has not been told before: its details are fascinating.

Swinnerton, Ransome's exact contemporary by birth, was to outlive him by twenty-five years. He too had started work in London as an office-boy, though in a newspaper office; and he too was determined to become a writer. For most of his long life he produced at least a book a year, although only his chronicles of the Georgian literary scene are now remembered. Like Ransome, he had energetically elbowed his way past the university-educated hopefuls in order to be accepted into the fiercely competitive literary world of London. He became associated with a coterie which included H. G. Wells and Arnold Bennett, quite different from the circles in which Ransome preferred to move. If only for this reason, his published memories of Ransome are rather sparse and not always reliable; and it is plain that they were not on friendly terms.

He may have suspected Ransome's hand in an entertainingly derisory unsigned review of his third novel *The Casement* in *The Eye-Witness*, 3 August 1911. Although the title of the article, 'The Plate-Glass Window', prepares us for wry mockery, the review begins blandly enough.

> The technique of those writers, gradually increasing in number, who usually style themselves 'creative artists' is now reasonably familiar to the majority of readers. Mr Swinnerton is a promising recruit to the band. In his third novel he proves his ability to write a novel, a stage of artistic development which many more popular writers will never attain. ... He is something of a symbolist in that he prefers suggestion to explanation.

This faint praise, with Ransome's style and preoccupations very evident, is rapidly followed by enjoyable sledge-hammer blows of damnation.

> The fact remains that he has wasted that ability in writing "The Casement". The book was not worth writing. It is a mass of platitudes

decked in the guise of subtleties. It is an attempt to make a Kemp [*sic*] window out of plate-glass. Mr Swinnerton is selling soiled goods in gilded wrappers, and the name of Swinnerton is on every packet. Mr Swinnerton calls his book 'A Diversion'. To him it may be; to us it is not. It is rather the pitiable spectacle of an artistic ability wasted by lack of courage to attack material worthy the craft. If he will throw aside his timidity and grasp at things he can only as yet apprehend he may become a novelist of distinction.

Even if Ransome was responsible for this onslaught (and it seems very likely on stylistic grounds), Swinnerton recalled him in later years as one of 'the liveliest juniors of the day', favourably mentioning his book on Wilde and his innovative theorising about kinetic and potential speech, 'the search for words and phrases that should have just so much value and meaning'. However, he did not mince his words when, as publisher's reader for Chatto & Windus, he damned Ransome's first novel *The Elixir of Life* (1915), dismissing it (not altogether unfairly) as 'pseudo-Stevensonian romance, and very juvenile.' His report perceptively sums up the more derivative aspects of the story:

> In the house is the exquisite heroine of such books, who whispers and pales and endures. And Killigrew is a man who has kept himself alive for 200 years by means of an elixir compounded of the blood of murdered humans. So he's not a very nice man.

He concludes:

> The idea is quite old, and Mr Ransome has not the imagination to work it out thoroughly. There is no illusion; but only a succession of scenes. Also, Mr Ransome writes a very clumsy, heavy style, in imitation of Stevenson, and does not at all shape like a winner.

This novel had been written by Ransome at white-hot speed – sixty thousand words in one month. He was very pleased with it; he 'had never written with so much enjoyment'; his friends said that they liked it. He had even taken the trouble to go to Moscow by sledge to buy special paper for typing up his manuscript. He told his brother Geoffrey that his 'beautiful heroine' was modelled on 'Margaret Lodge and Barbara Collingwood and Miss Gavin'. Feeling 'surprise and ecstasy' at having finished his first full-length novel, he celebrated by downing quantities of Russian Imperial Stout. Chatto & Windus acted on their reader's recommendation, and declined to take the book on, but the loyally appreciative Methuen published it within the year. Hugh Brogan's judgement is that 'it was an odd book, about which it would be too easy to be wantonly unkind.' Christina Hardyment identifies its provenance as 'by Stevenson out of Poe'. It has one redeeming feature, a vividly realised episode of a horse-race with the Devil unique in

Ransome, but it belongs indeed to the genre of sub-Stevensonian romance, and shows that Ransome still had much to learn about the craft of fiction.

Unlike Ransome, who was encumbered by *Oscar Wilde* and its consequences, Swinnerton had no other pressing claims on his energy. His *Robert Louis Stevenson: A Critical Study* was in Secker's hands even before Ransome returned from his second visit to Russia in 1914, and it was published in October that year. This must have been a severe blow to Ransome, who had hoped to finish his own *Stevenson* for Methuen that same year. Being forestalled by a rival writer can only have added to his depression.

Swinnerton's study was also, in its own way, a new approach to Stevenson. The book is physically identical to Ransome's *Wilde* and *Poe*, although it is shorter than them. There the similarity ends. If Ransome's attitude to Stevenson is that of an enthusiastic apprentice craftsman, Swinnerton's is that of a demolition man. His book is based on a relatively superficial acquaintance with Stevenson's output: preliminary reading, writing, and publication were all accomplished in less than nine months. Ransome had of course begun his reading much earlier, and had included everything then available by and about his subject. *His* book would rely on specific readings of Stevenson, and would give cogently argued reasons for admiring him as a writer and a stylist. As he had written in a different context in 1910, 'Some biographers collect their author's toothpicks or old boots; some follow his prowess on the cricket field or in the swimming-bath; a very few push things so far as to look into his books.' He was determined to be one of those few.

But Swinnerton had wanted to make a splash, and succeeded in doing so. As a publisher's reader, he had learnt to be shrewd and perceptive in assessing the work of others, and many of his criticisms are well founded. And if he took pleasure in the prospect of bursting the inflated bubble of Stevenson's reputation, he was certainly not the first who wished to dethrone the idol. (He dedicated his work to a friend who greatly admired Stevenson, 'to Douglas Gray, in malice'.) His barbs can be cruelly effective. 'It is surely better to look straighter with clear eyes than to dress life up in a bundle of tropes and go singing up the pasteboard mountain', he says of *Travels with a Donkey*. In assessing *In the South Seas*, he considers that Stevenson was 'not equal intellectually to the task', although he at least showed 'great sincerity'. Stevenson's essays show 'literary affectation'; in writing of childhood, 'only a single child provides the picture', and he tends to 'make all children delicate little Scots boys'. In *Lay Morals* he offers only 'the wagged head of sententious dogma', the 'prosaic teaching' of a lay preacher. He finds that Stevenson could never grasp a character unless it was idiosyncratic or larger than life: hence he dismisses the benign *Fleeming Jenkin* as perfunctory. Stevenson's style 'lacks vehemence' although it has 'figures and tropes in plenty'. His plays are false, lack 'real dramatic effect' and 'visual sense'. The short stories however show 'variety' and some even 'brilliance', especially 'The Bottle Imp' and 'Thrawn Janet', which he thinks perfect in form and manner. *Dr Jekyll and Mr Hyde* is merely an 'efficient piece of craftsmanship', though he concedes that the craftsmanship of 'The Treasure of Franchard' is first-class. All of Stevenson's romances fail for Swinnerton, because they 'offend our sense of form', and lack powerful inevitability. He complains of Stevenson's 'curious and unsatisfactory method, involving so much falseness, of the first person singular, with those man-traps, the things the narrator can never have known, supplied by leaves from other narratives' – a reference to *Treasure Island* – but he supposes 'the use of the "I" probably made the tale better fun for himself.' He feels that for Stevenson writing was 'an end in itself', and disparagingly notes that his 'attitude to style and the art generally' is 'essentially technical'. Finally, he observes that for most readers Stevenson 'produces a vague uncritical doting'. 'Our worship of Stevenson is founded, let us say, upon the applause of his friends, who sought in his work the fascination they found in his person.' Of the longer works he can approve only of *The Wrecker*, *The Ebb Tide*, and the unfinished *Weir of Hermiston*. He gets quickly over the subject of Stevenson's life, and ignores altogether his published letters, because his purpose is 'entirely critical' – but it is so only in an adverse sense, and it relies much more on swashbuckling assertion than on careful demonstration or argument.

Unsurprisingly, Swinnerton's book was received with outrage by the guardians of Stevenson's reputation. Later, he would congratulate himself on having set the cat among the pigeons: 'Reviewers … became as excited as the greater urgencies of a European War would allow them to be. They denounced me. They said I was horrible. They headed their reviews with such agreeable insults as "Travels with a Critic".' He admitted that his opinions were 'purposely outspoken', and modified a few especially vigorous passages in a second edition – defending himself by claiming that they had been long overdue. There is no doubt that he succeeded in initiating a sharp decline in Stevenson's reputation which continued for successive decades. Much as the renaming of St Petersburg scuppered Ransome's travel book, so Swinnerton's job of demolition seems to have put the brakes on his Stevenson project.

Meanwhile, Ransome's personal life had deflected him into quagmires of 'blue treacle'. Escape to St Petersburg had temporarily relieved his intolerable domestic pressures, but matters seemed worse than ever once he had returned. The guide-book which he had been commissioned to write would probably have been financially profitable, but the publisher had reneged. Meanwhile he had been prevented from completing and publishing his own study of Stevenson. He had stayed at Hatch for part of the summer and autumn, intent on fishing his way to recuperation after his mammoth effort with the St Petersburg book, and determined to test the water once more to see if peaceful family life might be possible. (It was not.) While still in St Petersburg he had been alarmed by Germany's sabre-rattling, and by the fierce hatred of Germans which this had provoked among ordinary Russians. Late in July 1914 he sent a telegram to his literary agents Curtis Brown 'asking to fix up job as war correspondent'. A Mr Massie replied, 'What war?' Ransome immediately returned to England, arriving on 2 August; two days later, England declared war on Germany.

Ransome would have been rejected for military service because of his poor eyesight and other health problems, but he was determined to do his best for his country. On 2 September he offered his services as a King's Messenger for the duration, writing to the Collingwoods at Coniston and to his mother about his longing for the 'glimmering glorious chance of the Messengership. That is too good to hope for, but ...' – hope he did. To his mother he admitted, 'The knowledge that I have a chance of it, real useful work, somehow sets my mind free so that I go ahead twiddling things out on my typewriter.' Although he was later to be retained by the British Government as an informant, his initial application was not successful. When he returned to Russia, he became a war correspondent for the *Daily News.*

In another letter to his mother, undated but most probably written from Lanehead in autumn 1914, he says that he was 'still struggling heavy-heartedly with Stevenson'. But what exactly he was working on is tantalisingly unspecified. He could not have had with him the parcel of manuscript which Ivy had sealed. Most likely he was writing the few remaining sections of his book, intending to add them in due course to the existing manuscript before revising the complete work. After Ransome had finally left Lanehead for Russia in December 1914, he wrote to Collingwood asking him to forward 'my notebook' which he had left behind. This can hardly have been the 'Stevenson exercise-book', which contains only one paragraph of composed text. It seems possible that this unidentified notebook contained his latest work on Stevenson. Alas, it does not survive.

Ransome had several reasons for being 'heavy-hearted' in the autumn of 1914. The war-work he hoped for had so far eluded him; his latest attempt to be reconciled with Ivy for Tabitha's sake had failed. His work on Stevenson was not far from completion, but the publication of Swinnerton's book that October spoiled the market. What was the point of going on? It might be years before any other critical study of Stevenson, however original, could be a success. His self-esteem was at a very low ebb; he needed a complete break from *everything.*

Thereafter, Ransome appears to have done no further work on his *Stevenson*. He became increasingly caught up in the currents of revolution and war in Russia; exigent daily deadlines meant that he had little time for sustained literary work, except for the feverishly composed and ill-fated *Elixir of Life.* His health deteriorated: he suffered appallingly from intestinal ulcers, and was lucky to survive an ineffective operation. (The anaesthetic failed.) He continued to include *Stevenson* in a list of work in progress entered in his diary until 1917, but it is unlikely that he had either opportunity or inclination to take it further. He tells us that Methuen finally released him from his contract. Thereafter, we can safely assume that he regarded his book as 'work abandoned'.

8 Ransome and the Stream of Stevenson Criticism

Every biographer or critic who had written about Stevenson, however superficially, found him a fascinating subject. The life he lived was unusually romantic, his personality overwhelmingly charismatic, his imagination unrivalled in creativity: these things gave him a personal charm that was powerfully sensed even by those who had never met him. But charm can have dangerous consequences, and it influenced the reception of his books both positively and negatively. Even before the end of his life, admiration of his story-telling and of his own life-story had reached the point of adulation. Between 1894 and 1924 there were eight collected editions of his works, a number achieved by no other contemporary author. Admirers who had the means had gone on pilgrimage to Samoa to meet the great man and listen to his table-talk. After his death his friends and his public felt genuinely profound and prolonged grief, feelings that were sharpened and prolonged by the posthumous publication of the master's unfinished works – not to mention a flood of hyperbolic tributes. 'High on the Patmos of the Southern Seas our Northern dreamer sleeps ... He is gone, our Virgil of prose', laments Richard Le Gallienne in his elegy; and 'He is gone, our Prince of storytellers', sighed *The Illustrated London News*. In the first years after his death appeared his *Songs of Travel*, other unpublished poems, autobiographical work such as *The Amateur Emigrant, Vailima Letters* – and *In The South Seas*, part essay, part autobiography, in a category of its own and considered by Ransome as an unrecognised masterpiece. More novels and stories followed: *St Ives*, and then his last work, so good that it had 'frightened' him, the unfinished *Weir of Hermiston*. The story of Stevenson's death in the middle of writing a sentence of this story gave an especially agreeable *frisson* to many of his readers, provoking awed speculation about its significance. Stevenson's widow, stepson, and extended family, who had been financially dependent on him in life, were amply provided for after his death through stimulating the flow of Stevensoniana. They were however perhaps surprised to discover that he was rapidly becoming a kind of secular saint, and his life a source of moral inspiration.

Many of Stevenson's contemporary writers admitted to falling under the spell of his charm, although for more discriminating reasons. For Oscar Wilde, whose style and ideas on art had so engaged the young Ransome, Stevenson was 'that delightful master of delicate and fanciful prose'.

G. K. Chesterton, in *Twelve Types* (which had been the young Ransome's constant pocket-companion and inspiration in early days in London) admired Stevenson for qualities most others had ignored: his principles of art and ethics, 'things that Stevenson nearly killed himself to express' – a theme expanded by Ransome in his book. He was admired by writers as disparate as Henry James, Rudyard Kipling, and John Masefield – (whose tribute 'A Ballad of John Silver' speaks for generations of boys: 'a big black Jolly Roger flapping grimly at the fore, We sailed the Spanish water in the happy days of yore'). By 1910 several of Stevenson's books were established as classics, and even studied at school. His gripping narratives of adventure were universal favourites.

In the year Ransome may first have published on Stevenson, 1911 (see appendix B.3), interest in the man and writer had received fresh stimulus from several sources. There was the publication of the first four volumes of the twenty-five volume Swanston edition of his works; the newly enlarged edition of Stevenson's letters in the 'four red volumes' edited by Sidney Colvin; and the augmented sixth edition of the 'standard' biography of Stevenson by Balfour, which had prompted Ransome's review essay. But in embarking on a critical response to Stevenson *as a writer* when he returned to this subject late in 1912, Ransome was venturing into much more hazardous territory than might be supposed. In 1887 Stevenson wrote 'My biographer, if I ever have one', perhaps unaware that various friends, not least his young cousin Graham, were already storing up their materials. He could scarcely have guessed what a deluge of memorial writing would be let loose after his death. Ransome's aim was to give a fair and just account of the man and his work, to elucidate his personal moral code and his 'principles of art', and to achieve 'gradually clearing perspectives' of the artist. He was no doubt aware of the many toes that might be trodden on in the process, not least those of Fanny Stevenson, Lloyd Osbourne, and the adulatory Graham Balfour. 'All biography would be autobiography if it could', Balfour had said in the preface to his biography. Ransome might well have taken those words as his motto when beginning his study of Stevenson.

Most of the Stevensoniana which Ransome had read concentrated on Stevenson's personality, and it included a good deal of sentimental nonsense. Neil Munro, a fellow Scot, in a contribution to *The Bookman*'s special collection of essays on Stevenson (1913), finds 'only in his language sometimes he minces; his nature steps breast-high like a stag, regardless of the weather ... his style, in fine, is an incarnation of his thought and character'. An anonymous poet in 1905 had characterised him as 'an elfin wight', a 'genius bringing delight and joy'; one Alice Browne (1893) confessed that 'it is difficult to regard his critical work studiously, save with a wandering eye, drawn momentarily away from the canvas to the artist himself'.

This cult of Stevenson the man had already begun to create ripples of dissent, expressed notably as early as 1901 in an outburst by his once great friend and collaborator W. E. Henley (an inspirer of the character of Long John Silver), who seems to have resented his flight to the South Seas as a kind of desertion. His attack on the 'overstrained stylist' struck many orthodox admirers of Stevenson as disloyal and near-blasphemous, and provoked a flurry of fervent counterblasts. Many who had learned to love and admire Stevenson the writer were embarrassed by this pamphlet war; but they were in the minority. Later, and not least in the wake of Swinnerton's book, some of these admirers were to revise their opinions. G. K. Chesterton remained fascinated by Stevenson, and wrote on him again in 1913, this time somewhat perversely interpreting him as an inadvertent apologist for imperialism, and finally in 1927, returning to the subject he had hinted at in 1902:

> I mean to attempt the conjectural description of certain states of mind, with the books that were the 'external expression' of them. If for the artist his art is a fizzle, his life is often far more of a fizzle: it is even far more of a fiction. It is the one of his works in which he tells least of the truth. Stevenson's was more real than most, because more romantic than most. But I prefer the romances, which were still more real. I mean that I think the wanderings of Balfour more Stevensonian than the wanderings of Stevenson: that the duel of Jekyll and Hyde is more illuminating than the quarrel of Stevenson and Henley: and that the true private life is to be sought not in Samoa but in Treasure Island; for where the treasure is, there is the heart also. In short, I propose to review his books with illustrations from his life; rather than to write his life with illustrations from his books. And I do it deliberately, not because his life was not as interesting as any book; but because the habit of talking too much about his life has already actually led to thinking far too little of his literature. His ideas are being underrated, precisely because they are not being studied separately and seriously as ideas. His art is being underrated, precisely because he is not accorded even the fair advantages of Art for Art's Sake.

We can only speculate on the effect of Ransome's *Stevenson* on so acute a reader as Chesterton, had it been possible for him to read it.

Stevenson's best-loved books never fell out of print, and collected editions continued to sell. Nevertheless, critical enthusiasm for his writing cooled. Stevenson gradually fell out of the academic canon of English literature: partly because of the great variety of genres in which he wrote; partly because of the perceived superficiality of his 'boys' books' when contrasted with, say, the depths of Conrad's novels; partly through suspicion of his 'charm'; and partly through sheer change of taste, under the influence of academic critics such as F. R. Leavis, who dismissed him in a footnote to the 'great tradition'. But now the tide has well and truly turned. In the last twenty years Stevenson studies are pursued increasingly in universities, and the interested reader risks being engulfed by an avalanche of articles and books on every aspect of his life and work. In the last decade alone, academic industry has brought forth more than four hundred books and articles with every imaginable theory and approach applied: aesthetical, anthropological, biographical, cross-cultural, colonial, comedic, commercial, comparative, conceptual, cultural, dramaturgical, epic, folkloric, gender, generic, geographical, historical, narratological, national, pathological, pedagogic, pictorial, political, populist, psychological, receptionist, representational, rhetorical, Scottish, semiotic, sexual, sociological, structural, stylistic, symbolical, textual, transformational. Stevenson continues to excite the imagination in a world in which he finds ever more readers. The narrative power of *Treasure Island* and *Dr Jekyll and Mr Hyde* also seems to grip an ever-growing mass audience, albeit in every kind of abridged, pictorial, film, and television versions.

Jorge Luis Borges once described Stevenson as 'a form of happiness'. Ransome would have agreed. And the transformative influence of Stevenson's imagination seems to remain as strong as ever amongst writers of many cultures. Jeanette Winterson's wry nod towards him in *Lighthousekeeping*, with a heroine called Silver, is perhaps the most recent and unexpected of many tributes to a great master of English fiction.

9 The Text and the Edition

Ransome's study of Robert Louis Stevenson, commissioned in 1910 and written mostly in 1913 and 1914, now meets its readers for the first time. 'None but an idiot or an enemy would wish to possess any book written by me before 1914', wrote an elderly and irascible Ransome to someone who had enquired about his early work. This book shows that we need not agree with him.

In 1994 Ransome's literary executors had the manuscript photocopied in order to help them decide what could or should be done with it. They, and publishers they showed it to, felt that the material was excellent, and still merited publication. But there were serious problems to overcome. Ransome's handwriting, clear enough when he is writing relaxedly once the reader has got used to it, quickly deteriorates into a scrawl when he is ill or tired (which he often was), or writing at speed (which he often did). Some sections seemed to defy decipherment altogether. The range of Ransome's references was also an obstacle. He was extremely widely read in English and European medieval and renaissance literature, French and Russian literature (the Russian he met in French translation, only beginning his study of the language in 1913), as well as in more recent British and American literature and literary theory. Some of the authors and stories that he and his intended readership would have been familiar with have vanished from the ken of the modern reading public. Proper names posed their own difficulties: many of them were not English, and because of their density and range it was often not immediately clear whether Ransome was referring to a fictional character or a real-life person.

The order of pages when the executors read the manuscript was also puzzling. They were evidently not all in a coherent sequence, and were not numbered consecutively. Some sections of continuous fluent text clearly related to one topic, such as a specific book by Stevenson: pages headed (for example) 'Fleeming Jenkin', were numbered consecutively 1–5. However, the pagination for each separate topic was the start of a separate sequence, and there are very many topics, some (for example a page headed 'Style') amounting to only a page or less. It was also hard to establish what the intended sequence of sections might be. The status of a few sheets was problematic: some bore quotations which Ransome had copied out for future use, many of which he had drawn into completed sections of the text; others had quotations which had not been used. Had Ransome discarded them, or had he intended to include them somewhere? He always preferred to be lavish in his use of quotation.

From the outset of his career, Ransome does not seem to have worked steadily through any piece of work, in the sense of starting at the beginning and going on until he had come to the end of it. His preferred method of composition, having read round his subject and made his notes, was to map out a working structure of chapters and narrative order, and then to begin composing any section which happened to be clear in his mind. The present manuscript includes one leaf which sketches a possible chapter-structure (see appendix A.1.iv); but even that scheme is hedged about with arrows and question-marks, and may be far from what would have been Ransome's final construction. There is a similar page in the 'Stevenson exercise-book', with a different outline order of chapters for the projected book. Which came first, and which should take precedence?

Neither can we tell in what order the various sections of the manuscript were composed, although there are occasional clues from physical evidence such as a change of ink, from internal linguistic evidence, and from Ransome's correspondence, notebooks and diaries. As we have seen, a few sections are missing, and nothing has been found to show that they were ever written. Nor is every section of the same quality. Some are written in the fluent authoritative manner that would have satisfied Ransome in print without further revision: indeed, as we have seen, a few pages did appear as an article in 1914 (see appendix A.3). At other times we have what seems little more than Ransome's Stevenson commonplace book, quotation following quotation with little or no linking thread of argument.

It was not at all certain to those who first looked through the contents of the parcel in 1994 that it contained anything like a complete book, or indeed that all the sheets related to the one piece of work. Many pages consisted of fragmentary one-line jottings, whose relevance to Stevenson was not obvious, or simply a heading such as 'Schwob'. The parcel's contents were, after all, clearly identified on the wrapper as 'M.S.S.', not as 'Stevenson MS'. As a result of all this, the literary executors could not decide how best to proceed. Sir Rupert Hart-Davis had, with great dedication, pieced together (from a rather chaotic assemblage of typescript and manuscript) Ransome's autobiography, and written a conclusion to it. But that had been twenty years earlier, and both he and his fellow-executor John Bell were now aged and lacking the energy required for the task of editing. Their successors, Christina Hardyment and David Sewart, were also determined to bring Ransome's long-lost book to public attention. David, with his wife Elizabeth, offered to produce a complete transcript. This labour was undertaken in intervals from their daily work and occupied ten years. There were understandable lacunae in their transcription, and not all their guesses at the hopelessly indecipherable seemed correct to other readers, but the text presented here would have taken much longer to prepare without their work. They are to be thanked most sincerely for providing an extremely valuable starting-point for this edition, which is based on a careful scrutiny of the manuscript afresh.

The present book contains not only the first publication of a major Ransome manuscript, but includes in its appendices all Ransome's other extant work on Stevenson. Here can be found the Stevenson-inspired story which he wrote as a child, available to the general public for the first time; a first reprinting of his published articles on Stevenson contemporary with the manuscript; and a transcription of all his working-notes from the separate 'Stevenson exercise-book'. Thus, in conjunction with the main text, we present here the fullest evidence known of Ransome's methods of composition. If only for this reason, all his own footnotes, source-citations, and memoranda have been retained; as an essential part of the text as we have it.

Ransome copied out many passages of Stevenson for commentary or quotation; those few that have found no place in the main text of this edition can be found in appendix A.2.iv. Some longer passages copied out in full by Ransome, such as Stevenson's character-study of 'Spring-Heeled Jack', which may have been intended for selective quotation in the next draft, have been retained uncut in the main text, as found. Ransome clearly felt that only by a liberal use of quotations could the effect of the writer's style be fully demonstrated; as we have seen, it was a policy which caused him great trouble in relation to his *Oscar Wilde*, but which had the support of Robert Ross. It has not been possible to ascertain which of the many editions or reprints of Stevenson's works were used by Ransome; references to these are therefore generally by title only (and chapter, where relevant). (Between Stevensonians and lovers of Ransome the editor has tried to be as even-handed as possible, but in this matter has chosen to favour Ransome: the letters can in any case readily be found in the current standard edition by B. L. Booth and Ernest Mehew.) Most of Ransome's quotations from Stevenson's letters are from 'the four red volumes', *The Letters of Robert Louis Stevenson* ed. Sidney Colvin, 4 vols. (London, 1911), abbreviated to '*Letters*', with volume and page number following, and from *Vailima Letters, being correspondence addressed by Robert Louis Stevenson to Sidney Colvin, November 1890–October 1894* (London, 1895), '*Vailima Letters*'. Letters not in these works are identified by date. Ransome's own footnotes are given within double quotation marks, e.g. "*Across the Plains*, p. 143". All Ransome's own footnotes are reproduced verbatim. Where Ransome does not identify the source of a letter quoted, reference is given to books he is known to have used.

As for other matters of editorial detail: punctuation has been modernised – for instance, full-stops after book-titles in Ransome's notes become commas, as in the example above; full-stops after the titles 'Mr' and 'Mrs' are omitted; the colon with dash [:–] becomes a colon; italics instead of quotation-marks are used to identify book-titles. But Ransome's Edwardian habits of nomenclature, which are so much part of the flavour of his text, have been retained. People living at the time of writing are referred to him by title, 'Sir J. M. Barrie', 'Mr W. B. Yeats', 'Mrs Stevenson', whereas those have died are not: 'W. E. Henley', or 'Henley' – although there are exceptions, such as (the deceased) 'Dr Baildon'. His sectional running headings (which were effectively his aides-memoires) are generally omitted, although some have been editorially incorporated in order to ease continuity. Thus 'Stevenson. Criticism. Victor Hugo. He distinguishes ...' becomes 'Writing on Victor Hugo, he distinguishes ...' Such expansions are few, and all are identified in footnotes. The few misspellings in the manuscript have been silently amended, for example 'Ferguson' to 'Fergusson', 'Ori a Ori' to 'Ori-a-Ori', and 'Dostoieffsky' is given the more modern form 'Dostoevsky'. Occasional inconsistencies with verb-agreement have been corrected. Numerals within the text such as 'at 33' are spelt out in full, and dates such as '89' expanded to '1889'. Ransome's handwriting has very occasionally nonplussed the editor and her advisors. She has done her best to decide on contextual grounds whether the intended word is (for example) 'fever' or 'power' – on the grounds that an informed guess is potentially of more value than an admission of defeat. Hardly any editorial linking passages have seemed necessary, and these are printed in italics.

Arthur Ransome
Robert Louis Stevenson: A Critical Study

Introductory

The book, as I see it now, should be really two books. The one should be the plain tale of an adventurous romantic's progress through life in the nineteenth century; and the other should be a kind of log-book, kept by the clerk of a workshop, retaining perhaps a little of the abridgement and hurried character of notes made in the whistle and hum of the machinery, its pages smudged a little with iron filings, and here and there a shaving to keep the place. It should, I think, retain the sharp clean smell of new sawdust. And yet, different in character as the two books should be, it ought not to be possible for the reader of the tale to forget that its hero was, in fact, prospecting for metal and timber that was afterwards to go into the workshop, and the reader of the mechanic's record should be reminded that he who wrestled so merrily with the problems of machinery, was also the man who sailed and rode and played at being a consul[1] away in the South Seas, and, in earlier manhood, had walked on Princes Street, exultant in his youth, and from the Calton Hill[2] had swelled at the vision of the town beneath him, and in wild northern seas[3] had done his day's work with the rest.

Stevenson, perhaps more markedly than any other Scottish writer born in the nineteenth century, stands a little apart from English literature. Even such writers as Sir J. M. Barrie,[4] for all their rather aggressive

---

[1] Stevenson described the politics of Samoa as 'a distracted archipelago of children, sat upon by a clique of fools,' because of the conflicting interests of America, Germany and Britain. Ransome correctly implies that Stevenson had much diplomatic influence there. It was his home from 1890 until his death in 1894. In 1892 he forwarded to the 'Three Powers' through the consul in Apia proposals for amendments to the Treaty of Berlin, and chaired the public meeting that adopted them.

[2] At the north end of Princes Street, Edinburgh.

[3] Stevenson accompanied his father on lighthouse-engineering sea-voyages in the North of Scotland, and to the Isle of Mull, where he explored the islet Erraid on which he later caused his hero David Balfour to be marooned in *Kidnapped*.

[4] James M. Barrie (1860–1937), Scottish playwright and novelist, author of *Peter Pan*, *Quality Street*, *The Admirable Crichton*, *A Window in Thrums*, and many other well-received novels and plays.

dialect, have their eyes on English books and their ears attuned more particularly to English prose. Stevenson was a contemporary of Wilde's;[1] but it would be hard to imagine two intellectual backgrounds more essentially different. And the background of Irish legend adopted by Mr W. B. Yeats,[2] adopted only in its periods of vivid dream and action, is quite other in character than the continuous tradition not only of history but also of literature in which Stevenson, as a Scotsman, grew up. His short-winded Latinity and his still shorter-breathed knowledge of Greek[3] confined him closely to his own language, and in that language for him Burns and Scott and Drummond of Hawthornden[4] were not Scottish islands in a sea of English literature, but the peaks of a main land whose lower hills and valleys were no less familiar to him. He knew Fergusson[5] as well as Burns, and his knowledge of Scottish ballads was not bounded by 'Chevy Chase' or that stirring invitation to assault the walls of Carlisle,[6] which the descendants of the assaulted sing with sturdy relish and cosmopolitan toleration. The figure on which

[1] Oscar Wilde (1854–1900), Irish playwright, novelist and poet. Ransome's work on Stevenson was interrupted by the demand of his publisher Martin Secker for a critical study of Wilde (1912).

[2] William Butler Yeats (1865–1939), Irish poet, dramatist, and statesman, a leader of the late-nineteenth-century Irish nationalist revival of Irish legend and myth.

[3] Ransome's lack of prowess in the classics, endearingly demonstrated in mistakes in Latin in *Missee Lee* (1941), is only one aspect of the affinity he feels with Stevenson as man and writer. He re-works a famous phrase in Ben Jonson's elegy on Shakespeare: 'For though thou had'st small Latin and less Greek ...'

[4] Ransome here summons up heroes of the Scottish literary establishment: Robert Burns (1759–96), poet and icon of Scottishness; Sir Walter Scott (1771–1832), immensely popular Scottish historical novelist and poet, whose towering memorial dominated Princes Street in Stevenson's Edinburgh as it does today; William Drummond of Hawthornden (1585–1649), 'the Scottish Petrarch', poet, essayist, laird and lawyer.

[5] Robert Fergusson (1750–74), the 'ill-fated genius! Heaven-taught Fergusson', much admired by Burns. 'The Ballad of Chevy Chase' is a traditional ballad about the Earl Percy of Northumberland's ill-fated hunting in the Earl Douglas of Scotland's forest.

[6] Writing in *New Witness*, 7 May 1914 under the pseudonym 'Svidatel' ('witness' in Russian), Ransome remarked: 'I do not forget that not two hundred years ago there were young men's heads on the Scottish Gate at Carlisle. Yet, whatever the side on which our ancestors fought, we cannot now regard their enemies as vermin only, and with this in mind, I find it hard to believe that the opponents of revolutionaries in Russia are a set of devils.' Perhaps he had in mind here 'The Ballad of Kinmount Willie', which relates a border action

his imagination brooded in boyhood was not Robin Hood in Lincoln green under the oaks of Sherwood, but Hackston of Rathillet[1] sitting on horseback muffled in his cloak watching the assassination of his spiritual and private enemies, and refusing, for conscience' sake, to strike a blow.

The period of Stevenson's activity in writing lies, roughly, between 1870 and 1890. Its background is not altogether easy to construct. His delight in vigour and gallantry inclined him to look beyond the Pre-Raphaelites[2] in search of adopted ancestry, preferring to follow on a moonlit road the exploits of an incredibly courageous musketeer than in a green-house to listen to the talk of an intenser but less spectacular personality. But if Dumas,[3] Hugo,[4] and as much as their works the traditional romantic attitude, influenced his view of life, his demands from art, Flaubert[5] – and that later, more scrupulous, generation – dictated his punctilious tech-nique. His heart was born in 1830; his critical faculty in the time of the Parnassians,[6] and under the tutelage of that inexorable master who paced

of 1596, and was revived after the Jacobites' imprisonment in Carlisle Castle; it contains the lines:

> O were there war between the lands,
> As well I wot that there is none,
> I would slight Carlisle castell high,
> Tho it were builded of marble stone.
>   I would set that castell in a low,
> And sloken it with English Blood;
> There's nevir a man in Cumberland
> Should ken where Carlisle castell stood.

The allusion is also reminiscent of Lord Macaulay's 'The Armada', 'Till Skiddaw saw the fire that burned on Gaunt's embattled pile, And the red glare on Skiddaw roused the burghers of Carlisle', quoted in his *Swallowdale* (1931).

[1] Ransome here contrasts the legendary Robin Hood of traditional English ballad, with the historical David Hackston (d. 1680), a leader of the Scottish Covenanters wrongly executed for murder.

[2] A 'brotherhood' of artists and poets, a movement founded in 1848 with the aim of restoring painting to a primitive truthfulness They were much admired by the painter and influential critic John Ruskin.

[3] Alexandre Dumas, père (1802–70), French novelist, author of *The Three Musketeers* and many other popular novels of adventure.

[4] Victor Hugo (1802–85), French poet and novelist, stalwart of the French Romantic movement, author of *Les Miserables* and *The Hunchback of Notre Dame* etc.

[5] Gustave Flaubert (1821–80), born in Rouen, author of *Madame Bovary* and many other novels; a more conscious stylist than Dumas.

[6] Derived from Mount Parnassus, the home of the Muses in Greek mythology, this refers to a French literary movement in the mid-nineteenth century.

roaring like a lion in his room at Rouen in a ferocious rather then graceful search for accuracy of expression.

To these influences, felt, it is politic to notice, not only directly, from books, but also in the air at Fontainebleau,[1] where the students' camp in a village inn was in its way a Royal Exchange[2] of half-assimilated ideas, he brought a mind already furnished in a manner not at all like that of most English writers of his age. He brought a mind to which its own nationality was not a question of indifference, as it is to most,[3] a mind exultantly Scottish, romantically in love with its country, as Byron[4] was with the East, as Johnson[5] with London, as Hazlitt[6] with England, and full of Scottish history and literature, which had for him something of the special vividness and sanctity of family traditions.

It is worth remembering that, as Stevenson quoted from an imaginary Encyclopaedia, the English are 'a dull people, incapable of comprehending the Scottish tongue. Their history is so intimately connected with that of Scotland, that we must refer our readers to that heading. Their literature is principally the work of venal Scots.'[7]

The group was influenced by the French romantic writer Théophile Gautier (1811–72), who is also associated with Rouen, and his doctrine of 'art for art's sake'; it included the symbolist poets Mallarmé and Verlaine.

[1] After Stevenson left university in 1875 he made extended visits to France, staying in several artists' colonies there including that of Fontainebleau, where he met his future wife, Fanny Osbourne, in 1876.

[2] The Royal Exchange, in Threadneedle Street, London, had been more than a financial institution; a frequent rendezvous for Samuel Pepys and his coffeehouse friends, it is often mentioned in his *Diary*.

[3] As it seemed then to Ransome, the Yorkshire-born Englishman. The vicissitudes of his later life changed his mind, and his major novels evoke a fierce pride of place.

[4] George Gordon, Lord Byron (1728–1824), English Romantic poet, author of *Don Juan*, autobiographical narrative poem of his adventures in the East etc.

[5] Samuel Johnson (1709–84), essayist, poet, lexicographer, and subject of the famous biography by his friend James Boswell.

[6] William Hazlitt (1778–1830), English critic and essayist much admired by Ransome and Stevenson. His *Table Talk* was Ransome's constant companion at this time, and he had unsuccessfully proposed a study of him for the series that was to have included this present book.

[7] This paragraph is editorially constructed from "Scotch paragraph. Scotland. From an imaginary Encyclopaedia. Letter to Jason, July 24, 1879. *Letters*, I, 236." (Double quotation marks are used in these footnotes to indicate a verbatim quotation of Ransome's own notes.)

These elements at least, the scrutiny of technical processes[1] which followed the over-productive facility of the great Romantics,[2] the Romantic attitude which no close attention to technique was to divert into a realism, charm, and an engaging reliance on charm, not only in life but in literature also, a deeply engraved Scottish background, and, due perhaps partly to that background, to discussions in the Edinburgh students' Speculative Society,[3] to studies prosecuted with his friend Ferrier,[4] a definite though narrowly circumscribed knowledge of certain philosophers: these elements are important to any critical examination of the phenomenon which, in Stevenson's works, we are about to discuss. It will be our business as we proceed to search more narrowly into them, to place them in gradually clearing perspectives, and not to forget that, important as they are, they are no more than perspectives, in and out of which flits, far more difficult to seize, or even to perceive, the personality they partly formed, which left with their collaboration so vivid, so individual an imprint.[5]

[1] He is thinking of (and being influenced by) the stylistic scrupulosity of Henry James; these were high matters of debate to Stevenson in the 1880s. His essay 'A Gossip On Romance' was first published in *Longman's Magazine*, 1882, and James's reply 'The Art of Fiction' was published there in 1884. The literary debate was extended by Ransome, whose own explorations in narrative stylistics include an essay of 1911, 'Kinetic and Potential Speech' (see Introduction).

[2] Ransome is alluding to the French Romantic movement and its novelists, rather than the earlier English romanticism and its poets.

[3] The Speculative Society of Edinburgh, founded in 1764, is a prestigious literary and debating society. In Stevenson's day the most famous former member was Sir Walter Scott.

[4] Walter Ferrier was Stevenson's best friend in Edinburgh student days; with him he read Friedrich Schiller's *Briefe über die ästhetische Erziehung des Menschen* (*Letters upon the Aesthetic Education of Man*) (1794); Stevenson mourned his death in 1883.

[5] This sentence applies equally to Ransome and the literary heritage that formed him. He too steeped himself in French romanticism and had been a literary pilgrim in France; by this time he had published *A History of Story-Telling: Studies in the Development of Narrative* (Jack, 1909), which includes chapters on 'The Romanticism of 1839', 'Sir Walter Scott', 'Poe and the new technique', 'Gautier and the East', 'Balzac and Romantic analysis'. Working notes for this section are in appendix A.2.v.

PART I

Biographical Summary[1]

Any consideration of the life and work of Stevenson must be a study of the reaction continually in progress between a delight in physical doing and making and being and an irresistible and more or less contradictory desire to write, to knit words together and to be absorbed wholly in an intellectual business. Stevenson felt that delight and this desire to be more or less opposed to each other; but, speaking with strict accuracy, the desire was no more than a result and at the same time a stimulus of the delight. Art with him as with all other artists was for life's sake; with him more obviously than with some others because of the comparative simplicity of the life of which he sought by means of art to make himself more intensely conscious. He '*felt* action' he wrote in a letter: his art was a means of feeling it more clearly. It was precisely because he was an artist that he could write, 'I am one of the few people in the world who do not forget their own lives.'[2]

This must not be forgotten when we read his laments for an active life. These laments are mere greedy desire for yet more of what he already possessed. He lived like a candle flame and towards the end of his life climbed higher and higher in hopes to catch and consume a little more of that life which he had valued with steady wisdom from the first. There was no form of activity which he would not have liked to share for a moment at least. He felt in a different way something of the eighteenth century reverence for the natural man; not for the gentle creature whose love in the pages of Chateaubriand[3] is conducted under palm trees and blessed by a hermit; but for the efficient man, who can build his house, cook his food, clothe himself, sail a boat, ride a horse, and read, a civilised Crusoe,[4] the

---

[1] Much of this section was written between 16 and 20 April 1914, as Ransome's diary shows. Stevenson's 'contradictory desires' were his also.

[2] To Henry James, 28 May 1888, quoted by Graham Balfour as epigraph to chapter III, 'Infancy and Childhood' of his *Life of Robert Louis Stevenson* [1901] (1911) (henceforth 'Balfour').

[3] François-René, Vicomte de Chateaubriand (1769–1848), writer and diplomat, credited with being the founder of French Romanticism; the 'gentle creature' is perhaps Amélie in his novella *René* (1802).

[4] Narrator and hero of *The Life and Strange Surprising Adventures of Robinson Crusoe of York, Mariner* (1719) by the journalist and writer Daniel Defoe (*c.* 1630–1731); cast on his desert island, he had no such wonderfully civilised

novels of Mr Henry James.[1]

I think it will be easier to realise how oddly his life came, without his knowledge, perhaps, to conform to his ideal, if I print one of his laments over the specialisation of modern man, before an account of the varied, vigorous activity from the enjoyment of which not even his uncertain health was able to prevent him. Jim Pinkerton in *The Wrecker* remarked, 'Why in snakes should anybody want to be a sculptor, if you come to that? I would love to sculp myself. But what I can't see is why you should want to do nothing else. It seems to argue a poverty of nature.'[2]

'That problem,' wrote Stevenson to Mr W. H. Low in January of the year of his death,

> why the artist can *do nothing else*? is one that continually exercises myself. He cannot: granted. But Scott could. And Montaigne. And Julius Caesar. And many more. And why can't RLS? Does it not amaze you? It does me. I think of the Renaissance fellows, and their all-round human sufficiency, and compare it with the ineffable small-ness of the field in which we labour and in which we do so little. I think *David Balfour* a nice little book, and very artistic, and just the thing to occupy the leisure of a busy man; but for the top flower of a man's life it seems to me inadequate. Small is the word; it is a small age, and I am of it. I could have wished to be otherwise busy in this world. I ought to have been able to build lighthouses and write *David Balfour*s too. *Hinc illae lacrymae*.[3] I take my own case as most handy, but it is as illustrative of my quarrel with the age. We take all these pains, and we don't do as well as Michael Angelo or Leonardo, or even Fielding, who was an active magistrate, or Richardson, who was a busy bookseller. *J'ai honte pour nous*; my ears burn.[4]

It is curious to think that this was written when Stevenson could look back upon the vivid, adventurous career which it is now my business to record.

---

pastime as reading Henry James available to him. This is Ransome's first known reference to Crusoe, so important to the imaginative life of his 'Swallows'.

[1] Henry James (1843–1916), major American novelist and critic, author of *The Golden Bowl*, *Portrait of a Lady*, *The Turn of the Screw* etc.; a Franco-phile with tremendous knowledge of French literature, much admired by Stevenson and respected by Ransome.

[2] *The Wrecker* by Robert Louis Stevenson and Lloyd Osbourne (1892), chapter 4.

[3] 'Hence these tears', used first by the classical Latin poet Terence and later by Horace.

[4] *"Letters*, IV, 243, Jan[uary] 15, 1894. Quote Crichtonic letter".

From the beginning[1] Stevenson's life was affected by his health, his parents abandoning one house because its three outside walls let in the cold, and choosing another because its protected position was likely to benefit their continually ailing child. They, perhaps fortunately, had no other children, and from his earliest babyhood Stevenson's most constant companions were his father and mother and Alison Cunningham, his nurse, the Cummy of his familiar letters, to whom he dedicated *A Child's Garden of Verses*, for whom he always felt the most lively affection. 'My ill health,' he wrote, 'principally chronicles itself by the terrible long nights that I lay awake, troubled continually by a hacking, exhausting cough, and praying for sleep or morning, from the bottom of my shaken little body.' He remembered his father inventing conversations with guards, innkeepers, and coachmen and the other great characters of childhood to quiet the terror in which he woke from snatches of feverish sleep, and, when sleep would not come, his nurse lifting him to the window to see lights over the way, where, perhaps, another nurse and another little boy were watching for the morning.

In the lives of few writers has regular education been of so little importance as in Stevenson's. He moved from day-school to day-school, Edinburgh Academy among others, attended fitfully, was often prevented by illness, and perhaps as much by his father's attitude, from ever trying to get any serious benefit from his many masters. For his father, the engineer, the processes of whose mind was learned in observation of wind and current and shifting foreshore, despised the copy-book learning of the pedagogue. 'Tutor,' says Stevenson, 'was ever a byword with him; 'positively tutorial,' he would say of people or manners he despised; and with sure consistency, he bravely encouraged me to neglect my lessons, and never so much as asked me my place in school.' He took him early abroad, and early to England; when Stevenson was twelve he went on his first tour of inspection of lighthouses, with his father, and, a less exciting adventure, was taken to London to see the Second International Exhibition.

Robert Louis Stevenson was born on November 13th 1850 at 8 Howard Place, Edinburgh. He was christened Robert Lewis Balfour but his father later altered the spelling of Lewis and Stevenson himself omitted and prescribed the omission of Balfour. His father was a civil engineer who, like others of his family, was especially interested in the work of lighthouse building, and has secured for himself an immortality in stone towers and shifting lights no less respectable than his son's in frailer but perhaps more persistent material. He was thirty-two at the time of Stevenson's birth and his wife (Stevenson's mother) was a daughter of the Manse, of the Manse

---

[1] "*Letters*, II, Childhood." Other notes: "Health and friends. Mrs Sitwell, Colvin, Fleeming Jenkin, R. A. M. S."

which Stevenson described, with perhaps half a memory of Lamb's[1] essay on a similar subject, in *Memories and Portraits*.

Mrs E. B. Simpson relates how: 'His father severely criticised the tawdry make of a toy sword given to his small Louis in Crimean times, when war-fever was rampant in every nursery. 'I tell you,' replied the proud owner, examining his gew-gaw weapon anew, 'the sword is of gold and the sheath of silver, and the boy who has it is very well off and quite contented.'[2] The best summary description of his childhood is Stevenson's own. 'My childhood was in reality a very mixed experience, full of fever, nightmare, insomnia, painful days and interminable nights; and I can speak with less authority of gardens than of that other 'land of counterpane.'[3] His youth was more robust. When his friend Walter Turner died he wrote, 'to think that he was young with me, sharing that weather-beaten, Fergussonian youth.'[4]

Stevenson's career at the University was shaped by his father's hopes, though it woefully cheated them before the end. He abandoned Greek as an impossible task, and soon left Latin aside in exchange for studies more likely to be useful to an engineer. Even these he did not too diligently pursue, and boasted afterwards that few had 'more certificates of attendance for less education.' In vacation time also he was supposed to be training for his father's profession, and did indeed have lively adventures among the light-house builders in the north. At Wick he went down to the sea-bottom in a diving suit, and at Anstruther heard himself referred to as the man in charge. These portions of his education he always remembered grate-fully. That kind of engineering, he wrote, 'takes a man into the open air; it keeps him hanging about harbour-sides, which is the richest form of idling; it carries him to wild islands; it gives him a taste of the genial dangers of the sea; it supplies him with dexterities to exercise; it makes demands upon his ingenuity; it will go far to cure him of any taste (if he ever had one) for the miserable life of cities.'[5] Boats, the sea, dexterities, and a distaste for cities were the best corrections for the exercise of writing in which alone he was diligent. He may, in the momentary enthusiasm of these things, have looked complacently, even eagerly, on the future his father had planned for him, but when they sat together above an estuary, the elder Stevenson discerning the hidden forces of the waters, the younger wearing him out

---

[1] Charles Lamb, 1775–1834, author of *Essays of Elia* (1823)

[2] "'Robert Louis Stevenson's Hills of Home' in *Chambers' Journal*," (1901) by Evelyn Blantyre Simpson, and in her *Robert Louis Stevenson* (1906).

[3] *"Letters*, II, 238, to William Arbor, March 1885."

[4] *"Letters*, II, 133." The reference is to the Scottish poet Robert Fergusson. This section is headed "Edinburgh Days. Memory & the Casco;" this paragraph is editorially reconstructed.

[5] From the chapter 'Random Memories' in *Across the Plains* (1892).

with indifference to his virtuoso skill in this kind of theorising, it was clear enough that sooner or later some well laid plans would go agley.[1]

The embryo R. L. S., that was to burst the smooth shell on which his father wrote so legibly, is to be discerned in quite different employment. There is, for example, an exultant memory of long lamp-lit evenings, toes to the fire, reading *The Vicomte de Bragelonne*[2] in Swanston Cottage. And the unspecialised side of all these events and places of this time recur in his later writings to show how vividly Stevenson had realised them when he was supposed to be merely pressing past them to succeed to the glorious tradition of the light-house builders. Swanston Cottage, in the hamlet under the Pentlands, taken by his father in 1868, became the house where St Ives suffered after his escape from Edinburgh Castle.[3] David Balfour was cast ashore, by an odd coincidence, on the island where the youthful engineer had spent three weeks in 1870.

His friendship with Fleeming Jenkin,[4] the professor of engineering, had no basis of common interest in mechanics, but rather of a common interest in morality, in argument, and in life. And his father might have found a danger signal to his hopes in the character of his son's delight in the Edinburgh students' Speculative Society. Stevenson's place in that body, which 'has counted among its members Scott, Brougham, Jeffrey, Homer, Benjamin Constant, Robert Emmett, and many a legal and local celebrity besides', was not that of a student of engineering. He was there by virtue of another self, who wrote in penny exercise books, and dreamed of books. From its library he was called by 'three very distinguished students' to take his share in editing and writing a College Magazine. Here he was no truant, but remained at his editorial post after his three distinguished colleagues had fallen away with faint hearts.

His father, from excellent motives, allowed him no more than twelve pounds a year for his personal expenses – a sovereign, payable monthly. Stevenson got the most out of his monthly pound in a manner that would not have pleased his parent. He was a student, idle, at the University; he

---

[1] Ransome here recalls Robert Burns, 'To a Mouse':

> The best laid schemes o' mice an' men
> Gang aft agley,
> An' lea'e us nought but grief an' pain
> For promis'd joy.

[2] The third part of *The Three Musketeers* (1847–50) by Alexandre Dumas *père*, usually known in English as *The Man in the Iron Mask*.

[3] The hero of Stevenson's unfinished novel *St Ives: Being the Adventures of a French Prisoner in England*, published posthumously in 1897 with final chapters added by 'Q' (Sir Arthur Quiller-Couch).

[4] Fleeming Jenkin (1833–85), Professor of Engineering at Edinburgh University: also actor and dramatist; subject of Stevenson's *Memoir of Fleeming Jenkin* (1887).

boated, without conspicuous skill in his friends' canoes on the Firth; but in his evenings, like Deacon Brodie (who always had a friendly glow in his imagination), he lived another life, was known as 'Velvet Coat' among the disreputable, had his seat in the chimney corner of a tavern, and was a puzzle to his strange but largely tolerant associates. Perhaps he had a model in his mind, not to imitate, but for reference and encouragement, and, perhaps, that model was Robert Fergusson. Years afterwards, in a starlit night in the South Seas, he lay under a blanket on the deck of the yacht *Casco*, and had a vision of Drummond Street:

> It came on me like a flash of lightning: I simply returned thither, and into the past. And when I remember all I hoped and feared as I pickled about Rutherford's in the rain and the east wind; how I feared I should make a mere shipwreck, and yet timidly hoped not; how I feared I should never have a friend, far less a wife, and yet passionately hoped I might; how I hoped (if I did not take to drink) I should possibly write one little book, etc. etc. And then now – what a change! I feel somehow as if I should like the incident set upon a brass plate at the corner of that dreary thoroughfare for all students to read, poor devils, when their hearts are down.[1]

In another way also, he was moving on lines divergent from that so clearly illuminated path to his father's ideal. When 'Velvet Coat' fled from Calvinism he ran to a distance, and, like many another young man, made faces at it and called himself an atheist. Stevenson once in youth was himself tempted to raise the Devil. He had read old books on magic, and, alone in his room, inscribed the mystic figures on the floor, zodiac and pentagram, and abracadabraical lettering. 'And I got into the very happiest fright you can just imagine.'[2] This was play, but he had long argued with his father, too well to make their conversations pleasant. He joined the 'L. J. R.,'[3] which seems to have been a rather high-spirited specimen of that kind of club satirised by Goldsmith, from whose mock-rules I quote:

> V. All them who brings a new argument against religion, and who being a philosopher and a man of learning, as the rest of us is, shall be admitted to the freedom of the Society, upon paying sixpence only, to be spent in punch.[4]

---

[1] "*Letters*, III, 65. To Baxter. 7a.m. Sept[ember] 6, 1888. At sea."

[2] "*English Illustrated Magazine*, May 1899", an article by J. and M. C. Balfour, 'Robert Louis Stevenson by Two of his Cousins'.

[3] 'Liberty, Justice, Reverence.' A student club of six members founded by Stevenson with his cousin and close friend R. A. M. Stevenson (1847–1900), later to become Professor of Fine Arts at the University of Liverpool.

[4] From a satirical essay by Oliver Goldsmith (1730–1774), 'On the Clubs of London.'

The L. J. R. probably used better grammar, but it was the sight of its 'rules and constitution' which caused the most serious of the differences between Stevenson, father, and Stevenson, son.

In 1871, his father was encouraged by seeing a paper of his son's on 'A New Form of Intermittent Light for Light-houses' awarded a medal by the Royal Scottish Society of Arts, but, in that same year Stevenson told him that he did not wish to be an engineer, and that he wanted to write instead. The old man stoically agreed, on condition that his son was to have some visible profession, and Stevenson forthwith proposed to be an advocate. His father must have felt him wasted, for two years after this decision the Royal Society accepted another scientific paper by Stevenson on 'The Thermal Influence of Forests'.

Stevenson was now free to study the art of writing, so long as that did not hinder his progress in the law. He wrote continually, talked continually, but passed in 1872 his preliminary examination for the Scottish Bar, and spent some time, sitting as squarely as he could on a three legged stool, learning conveyancing in the office of an Edinburgh solicitor.

Stevenson was now twenty two, delicate in health, shaking, reed-like, in the tempestuous Edinburgh writers, avoiding ordinary society, Velvet Coat among associates who could not understand but liked him, writing continually, and beginning to choose his friends for life. Much may be learnt of a man by a survey of the friendships of his first youth. And we get a vivid stereoscopic picture of Stevenson if we set by the side of the friends of Velvet Coat the four who, though he had known some of them before, began from this time to be determining influences on his development. Robert Alan Mowbray Stevenson, exalted by a gust of malice into a rival of R. L. S., when both were dead, was his cousin, a fine, peacocking talker, a brilliant, suggestive, achieving man, more in stimulating others than in any private output, a man keenly interested in the processes of art, and able to supplement Stevenson's deductions with analogies from painting, a witty, an argumentative companion. Fleeming Jenkin was a moralist capable of reproving Stevenson with a perspicuity that made reply impossible – and at the same time, a large, cheerful, boyish man, full of whimsies that were a pleasure to himself as well as to those who loved him, a lover of private theatricals, but happiest at 'playing himself among his friends.'[1] The other two were Sir Sidney and Lady Colvin, then Mr Sidney Colvin and Mrs Sitwell.[2] All the more intimate confessions of Stevenson's early letters are

[1] "See later Stevenson's account in his *Memoir of Fleeming Jenkin*."

[2] Sir Sidney Colvin (1845–1927), Slade Professor of Fine Art, literary critic and art historian, friend and frequent correspondent of Stevenson, editor of the Edinburgh edition of Stevenson (1894–7) and of Stevenson's *Letters* (1899, 1911); Mrs Frances Sitwell (1839–1924), 'Fanny', beloved friend and early mentor of Stevenson and his sympathetic correspondent from 1873; she married Colvin in 1903.

addressed to Mrs Sitwell, and it is easy to learn from these letters how large a part she played in helping him to know his own road, and in giving him, as it were, a private castle in life to which he felt he could retire, when his own keep and battlements were in danger of falling by storm.

Stevenson met Mrs Sitwell at a country parsonage in England where Mr Colvin was also staying. Mr Colvin was older than Stevenson, and had already earned the reputation as a critic which his admirable study of Keats[1] was afterwards to confirm. He became Stevenson's most consistent correspondent; he introduced him to the Savile Club, where Stevenson was 'Velvet Coat' to a far more circumspicuous audience than in Edinburgh; he helped the publication of his first essays, and, in the end, edited the posthumous publication of Stevenson's letters. If he was not in perfect sympathy with Stevenson's later activities, if the South Seas were a little too far from the British Museum, we must not forget that they were not too far for friendship, and that at this earlier, more critical stage of Stevenson's career Mr Colvin was just such an ally as the young Scottish law-student would have asked of the gods if he had not had him.

Stevenson had other friends or was soon to have them, notably Mr Charles Baxter and W. E. Henley;[2] but I think that the four I have chosen for particular mention were those who had most influence on his future. Mr Baxter and he had been schoolboys together, and their friendship lasted through life and was one of Stevenson's best loved possessions; perhaps he was not strange enough to Stevenson to be a determining factor in his life. Henley indeed influenced him, sometimes, as I think, for bad, in worrying him with plays at a time when he wished to write other things; he was a vivid stimulant, but something of the nature of a squall which fills the sail, bends the mast, furrows the sea with silver and black, and passes leaving blue calm and the boat upright and steady in the water. He saw Stevenson very clearly, once, in a sonnet,[3] and obscurely when he gave him the

---

[1] The study of Keats had been published in 1887.

[2] Charles Baxter (1848–1919), friend and correspondent from Edinburgh days, became his solicitor. William Ernest Henley (1849–1903), poet and playwright, first met Stevenson in 1875 at the time of his amputation in Edinburgh. The two collaborated in three plays including *Deacon Brodie: or, The Double Life* (performed 1884). Henley is a plausible inspiration for Stevenson's Long John Silver; his 'doubleness' is separately attested by his post-mortem attack on Stevenson (see Introduction).

[3] His sonnet 'Apparition' characterises Stevenson as having 'brilliant and romantic grace, / The brown eyes radiant with vivacity' and as being 'a spirit intense and rare ... valiant in velvet':

> Most vain, most generous, sternly critical,
> Buffoon and poet, lover and sensualist:
> A deal of Ariel, just a streak of Puck,
> Much Antony, of Hamlet not at all,
> And something of the Shorter-Catechist.

nickname of 'Fastidious Brisk;'[1] he had no sympathy with the later developments that were really to be foretold by his beginnings, and he wrote him a malicious epitaph,[2] full of truth and yet so distorted by feeling as to make even its truth both false and unwelcome.

In the later months of 1873, after the beginning of his friendship with Mr Colvin, he had thought of becoming a barrister instead of an advocate, and, with that purpose of entering one of the English Inns of Court. He went to London to see if this was possible, fell ill, was examined and found to be in danger of phthisis,[3] and on doctor's orders was sent to winter at Mentone.

No previous winter had been so valuable to him. The essay on 'Ordered South', written in the succeeding spring, set the keynote (in prose not in subject for he did not care to publish his ill health) for several years of subsequent work. He had not yet been disillusioned in the pursuit of health, as he afterwards was, at Davos. He learnt for the first time what Nietzsche calls 'the sweetness and spirituality almost inseparable from extreme poverty of blood and muscle,'[4] and with the peculiar lightness of delicate health found the pleasures that go with it: idleness, sunshine, and friendships like the flowers of the birds-eye[5] that are said to blossom only for a day. These friendships of convalescence are like those on ship board, filling life to the brim for a moment, and afterwards painlessly evaporating. Some Russian ladies who found him quite delightful, and a Russian baby girl, 'a little polyglot button', kept him fully amused in the intervals when his more permanent friends could not be with him.

He tasted, too, though in the diluted form that is all that ill health allows, the sensation of independent manhood. The money was his father's but his was its disposition, and the feeling was altogether different from that of the schoolboy spending his pocket money which he had known before. On his return his father made him a regular allowance of seven pounds a month, and, though Stevenson had scruples sometimes as to his right to

---

[1] A character in Ben Jonson's *Everyman Out Of His Humour* (1599): 'a neat, spruce, affecting courtier.'

[2] Probably a metaphorical reference to Henley's famously resentful article 'R. L. S.' in the *Pall Mall Gazette* xxv, December 1901, 'this Seraph in Chocolate, this barley-sugar effigy of a real man,' etc.

[3] Tuberculosis of the lungs. "Graham Balfour, p. 82." All Ransome's page-references to *The Life of Robert Louis Stevenson* by Graham Balfour (London, 1901) are to the enlarged sixth edition of 1911 (henceforth 'Balfour') which he had apparently reviewed, and later used to make a chronology for this book (see the appendices for his chronology and review).

[4] Friedrich Wilhelm Nietzsche (1844–1900), German philosopher on whom Ransome had written in his *Portraits and Speculations* (1912). Here he paraphrases an idea from Nietzsche's *Beyond Good and Evil*.

[5] A speedwell, *veronica chamaedrys*.

this unearned wealth, yet at twenty three he began, really for the first time, to feel 'grown up'.

On his return from Mentone he visited Paris where R. A. M. Stevenson was studying art, and there began the friendship with Will H. Low, which that romantic artist has delightfully chronicled.[1] His health was so far improved that he was fit for boating expeditions with Sir Walter Simpson, the Edinburgh friend with whom he afterwards made an inland voyage. His father and he no longer had such violent discussions on their religious differences, and, with pleasant interludes, he moved steadily towards the Scottish Bar. In July 1875 he passed the First Examination, was duly called, and took the taste out of his mouth with a visit to Fontainebleau.

He had been[2] at Fontainebleau before, in the April of that year when he found it 'very be – , no, not beautiful exactly, just now, but very bright and living. There are one or two song-birds and a cuckoo, all the fruit-trees are in flower, and the beeches make sunshine in a shady place.'[3] Now that he had earned the right to walk in wig and gown in the big, hollow, dimly lighted hall of the Advocates in Edinburgh, he fled to the forest again and found much more there than he had expected. Thenceforward for some time he was often at Barbizon, and in the end the forest seemed to usurp dominion over all his other memories of France and to mark a definite stage in his life and also in his work. He became one of an informal colony of young painters whose headquarters was an inn, and their occupations a modest kind of revelry, conversation, hopes for the future, and the making of studies from nature. He busied himself with old French poetry, and though he loved, physically, 'to smell the wet forest in the morning,'[4] the trees and glades became for him an epitome of French history, an illustration of the French poets. Old wars and phantom hunting parties passed through the green shadows with hours of chase or battle; he lay against a tree and hummed with Charles d'Orléans:

> Allez-vous-en, allez, allez,
> Soussi, Soing et Merencolie,
> Me cuidez-vous, toute ma vie,
> Gouverner, comme fait avez? ...[5]

---

[1] *"Chronicles of Friendships*, W. H. Low etc": *A Chronicle of Friendships, 1873–1900* by Will Hicok Low (1908).

[2] For an earlier version of this paragraph see appendix A.2.iii.

[3] To Mrs Sitwell, *"Letters*, I, 182."

[4] To his mother, from Barbizon, August 1875.

[5] Charles, Duc d'Orléans (1391–1465), Rondeau 55: 'Be off with you, Grief, Care and Melancholy! Would you influence me all my life the way you have in the past!'

and recaptured not only the moral but also the artistic mood in which such songs were lived and written, by himself experimenting in the old French measures. 'I have had some good times,' he wrote, sending Mrs Sitwell two not very notable specimens, 'walking along the glaring roads, or down the poplar alley of the great canal, fitting my own humour to this old verse.'[1]

He ascribed to the influence of this place, and of his companions' employment, the love of style, of form, which was his before he went there. It may well have been encouraged by the circumstance of being one of a number of young men all busy learning the rudiments of an art; 'stupidly, all else being forgotten, as if they were an object in themselves.' In an essay written afterwards he said:

> there is something, or there seems to be something, in the very air of France that communicates the love of style. Precision, clarity, the cleanly and crafty employment of material, a grace in the handling, apart from any value in the thought, seem to be acquired by the mere residence; or if not acquired, become at least the more appreciated. The air of Paris is alive with this technical inspiration. And to leave that airy city and awake next day upon the borders of the forest is but to change externals. The same spirit of dexterity and finish breathes from the long alleys and the lofty groves, from the wildernesses that are still pretty in their confusion, and the great plain that contrives to be decorative in its emptiness.[2]

I quote this passage here, because, in spite of its special application, it seems to me indirectly to set the key and indicate the motive of the light, bodiless, exhilaritic[3] true Stevenson, a writer among painters, whose exploits he could admire but not emulate, found at Fontainebleau.

We must imagine Stevenson at this time as a young man whose interest in words made it impossible for him even to take his private letters as other than literary exercise and made him play in conversation with the technique he was laboriously acquiring. I think of him talking precisely, with a relish for clear imagery, a care for concision that gave delicacy to his jokes, and, with Edinburgh in the background, a whole-hearted acqui-escence in the scorn of the bourgeois which was the one article of creed unanimously held by his companions. Long afterwards, one at least of them remembered his peculiar humor, and told a story of him, so slight as, perhaps, to seem disproportionately emphasised in this, which should be the briefest of biographies, and yet seeming, for all its slightness, to carry

---

[1] "To Mrs Sitwell, August, 1875." He had enclosed two verse translations.

[2] Stevenson, *Across The Plains*, chapter 3, 'Fontainebleau'. A separate noting of this quotation is headed by Ransome "Technical Importance of France".

[3] One of Ransome's coinages, suggesting a mix of jubilant and romantic breathlessness.

with it the private atmosphere of the man. Low, Stevenson and R. A. M. S.[1] had taken part in a christening feast, and so well drunken that, long after midnight, they has lain full length in the middle of a road in the forest, holding high converse, and only very late indeed found their way to bed. R. A. M. S., waving a candle, told Low to see Stevenson safe to bed, and so seriously did he do it, so carefully did he tuck in the counterpane, that Stevenson 'smiling broadly from his pillow, murmured: 'How good you are, you remind me of my mother.'

It was perhaps a tribute to his delicacy in conversation, as it certainly illustrates their attitude towards him, that his familiar companions placed him to sit next at table to the first women students to find their way to the inn at Barbizon. These were a mother and daughter, both painters, who had come to Paris, and then to Fontainebleau from America. With the mother Stevenson was presently in love.

The years following his meeting with Mrs Osbourne were feverish with activity, and restless with his most uncertain hope. He wrote now here now there, stories, essays, *The New Arabian Nights*[2] at one end of the scale and *Lay Morals*[3] at the other. In July 1879, he learnt that a divorce was possible between Mrs Osbourne and her husband. She was also very ill. On August 7 he sailed as a second class passenger in the *Devonia*, bound for New York. His parents knew nothing of his enterprise; he was facing a new continent and the probability of having for the first time to live entirely on his own earnings, the possibility of being able to share those earnings with another. As he set foot on the gangway of the *Devonia*, he must have felt all that a schoolboy feels who runs away to sea, and more, because he was going in eager hope of being trusted for the first time not only with his own life but with a larger responsibility. His friends were all against him. He stepped on board out of one existence into another utterly different and infinitely more dangerous.

He wrote 'The Story of a Lie' on the voyage: and even on the uncomfortable journey on the emigrant train from one side of America to the other, he was making notes for a book. In that tale, characteristic as much of it is, and in that book, I seem, perhaps with the bias of extraneous evidence, to detect for the first time in Stevenson's writings, a faint covering tint, a shadow, a suspicion, of the attitude of the professional tradesman of letters. This Stevenson could not be; but the knowledge that he was perilously near that tradesman's position must have intruded itself often in his mind and gave that thin, but I do honestly believe noticeable, flavour to the work he professed so zealously even in the very throes of his adventure.

[1] Stevenson's cousin Robert.

[2] (1882).

[3] *Lay Morals and other papers* was published posthumously (1911).

It is possible to look on that adventure with the eyes of health incarnadined and to say that the worst of it was discomfort. For me, for you, I hope, who read, it would be nothing more serious. But, if we would realise what it was for Stevenson, we must remember that it very nearly shook the life out of his frail body. A second class cabin and coarse food on the sea-voyage did him no harm; but it was followed by a shilling's worth of sleep in a dockside lodging house in New York, and then by many days of slow, jolting, train journey, a plank for a bed, in a stuffy railway carriage, or on its windy roof, from one side of that continent to the other. His health weakened from day to day, and he reached the Pacific Coast so ill that he thought he had but a heroic chance, and went up into the mountains to die, or to recover, camping by himself. He was rescued by two old goat-ranchers and nursed back to some sort of vitality.

> Two nights I lay out under a tree in a sort of stupor, doing nothing but fetch water for myself and horse, light a fire and make coffee, and all night awake hearing the goat-bells ringing and the tree-frogs singing when each new noise was enough to set me mad. Then the bear-hunter came round, pronounced me 'real sick,' and ordered me up to the ranche. It was an odd, miserable piece of my life; and according to all rule, it should have been my death; but after a while my spirit got up again in a divine frenzy, and has since kicked and spurred my vile body forward with great emphasis and success.[1]

He went down to Monterey, which had not yet turned, as it was on the point of turning, into an American sea-side resort. There, lodging with a doctor, and comforting himself at a little French restaurant, he wrote 'The Pavilion on the Links', and *The Amateur Emigrant*,[2] and grew frightened, because he worked too slowly. 'I hope soon to have a greater burthen to support, and must make money a great deal quicker than I used.'[3] And again: 'I am so haunted by anxieties that one or other is sure to come up in all that I write.'[4] He fell ill with pleurisy but recovered with 'that peculiar and delicious sense of being born again in an expurgated edition which belongs to convalescence.'[5] In December he moved to San Francisco, where he lived on three or four shillings a day, including rent. There he wrote or prepared essays[6] on Thoreau, Yoshida-Torojiro, finished *The Amateur*

---

[1] "*Letters*, I, 249."

[2] *The Amateur Emigrant from the Clyde to Sandy Hook* was published posthumously in 1895.

[3] "*Letters*, I, 251."

[4] "*Letters*, I, 257."

[5] "*Letters*, I, 259."

[6] In *Familiar Studies of Men and Books* (1882). 'Henry David Thoreau: his character and opinions' is chapter 4, 'Yoshida-Torojiro' is chapter 5. Thoreau

Emigrant, calculated continually and apprehensively his possible earnings, and again fell ill, this time with a malaria. But on January 23rd the Osbourne divorce had made it possible for him to announce his engagement to be married, and three days later, he had to reduce his daily expenditure on food to one shilling and ten pence and a half penny. In March he was very ill again.

> I have been very very sick; on the verge of a galloping consumption, cold sweats, prostrating attacks of cough, sickening fits in which I lost the power of speech, fever, and all the ugliest circumstances of the disease; and I have cause to bless God, my wife that is to be, and one Dr Bamford (a name the Muse repels), that I have come out of all this, and got my feet once more upon a little hill-top, with a fair prospect of life and some new desire of living.[1]

Two months later, a convalescent ghost, safe in his father's telegraphic promise of £250 annually, he married, as it were among the very reeds of the Styx, and went up into the mountains with his wife.

With the episode described in *The Silverado Squatters*,[2] the little book the scene of which 'is on a high mountain', where Stevenson and his wife spent their honeymoon, his life settled again into something like calm after the gusty interlude of his American journey. He was married, happy, confident, safe so far as he need look in immediate financial concerns, at peace with his parents, and anxious only to justify himself by good work.

In marrying Mrs Osbourne, he leapt suddenly from bachelorhood to the parentage of a growing and lively boy. He had fallen in love years before with the polyglot button Russian baby at Mentone, but had had no other intimacies with children until he became the step-father of Samuel Lloyd Osbourne, to whom he taught Latin and Euclid, to whom also he owed the impulse that set him writing *Treasure Island*.[3] To understand Stevenson's married life we must remember that it never passed through the stages of a man and a woman being together, or the later stage of babies, but began as a man and his wife with a son of twelve and a marriageable daughter,

(1817–62) was an influential American philosopher; Yoshida-Torojiro (b. *c.* 1830) was a hero of the American invasion of Japan (1852–4) under Commodore Matthew C. Perry; Stevenson was demonstrating his range. Ransome too wrote on Japanese culture, for instance on Japanese poetry in 1906 and 1910.

[1] "*Letters*, I, 286." This section is headed "Scotland and Davos. Drawings. War Game."

[2] This book (1883) is Stevenson's account of his honeymoon journey.

[3] (1883); originally titled 'The Sea Cook', it had been earlier serialised in *Young Folks* magazine as '*Treasure Island; or, The Mutiny of the Hispaniola* by Capt. Geo. North' (1881–2).

and that for long before he died Stevenson had tasted all the sensations of grand-parentage.

In August 1880, Stevenson, his wife, and his stepson were met at Liverpool by his parents and Mr Colvin. After a short stay in Scotland, Stevenson was ordered to winter at Davos and lived in a hotel there with his wife and Lloyd Osbourne, from November to the following April, when he returned by way of Paris. He wrote to his parents, 'If we are to come to Scotland, I *will* have fir-trees, and I want a burn, the firs for my physical, the water for my moral health,'[1] and they took a cottage at Pitlochry. While there he determined to apply for the Chair of History and Constitutional Law in the University of Edinburgh, which Professor Mackay[2] was resigning. He got excellent, though for the most part un-academic testimonials, but his literary reputation was not wide enough, and the memory of his truancies while a student was too fresh, to give him any real chance of election.

At Pitlochry he began a series of short tales, some of which were to be written by Mrs Stevenson, and 'Thrawn Janet' and 'The Merry Men' proved that the weakness perceptible in the work he had done just before his marriage was not more than the temporary effect of unusual and harassing conditions, more harassing, that is, than the ill health to which he had been long accustomed. The whole family moved in August to Braemar, where *Treasure Island* was accidentally begun, and exultantly continued as far as its nineteenth chapter. In October he went again to Davos, under the immediate compulsion of his throat and lungs, which had been seriously affected by the Scots autumn. Here for the first time, after their rickety hut in the Californian mountains, Stevenson and his wife had a house of their own. It was not always extremely happy. 'Fanny and I have both been in bed, tended by the hired sick nurse; Lloyd has a broken finger; Wogg (the dog) has had an abscess in his ear; our servant is a devil.'[3] But, in spite of these occasional woes, Stevenson enjoyed himself in unexpected ways. Lloyd Osbourne had had a printing press at Silverado, and now at Davos the business was taken more seriously and engaged the attention of the whole household. Wood-engraving drove suddenly between Stevenson and the sun, and he and his wife did some lively woodcuts to illustrate little books (written by himself) printed by his stepson. A few of these are very good in the ancient manner, and it is impossible not to delight in their crudities when the white slash of a slipt tool is thus excused:

> A blemish in the cut appears;
> Alas! it cost both blood and tears.

---

[1] "*Letters*, May 1, 1881."

[2] Aeneas Mackay, 1839–1911, Professor of Constitutional History, and generous benefactor to the University of Edinburgh Library.

[3] To Gosse, 9 November, 1881, *Letters*, II, 57 ('the dog' is Ransome's interpolation, and Colvin has slightly abbreviated the original).

> The glancing graver swerved aside,
> Fast flowed the artist's vital tide!
> And now the apologetic bard
> Demands indulgence for his pard![1]

Some of these woodcuts have been reproduced in *The Studio*; particularly I remember a very noble elephant nosing his trunk for the abstraction of a hat, and a fine study of Nelson on a pier-head looking out to sea at a ship and a floating champagne bottle. There were reproduced at the same time three or four quite pleasant pencil drawings, done in a sketch book at Monastier, at the time of his journey with Modestine.[2] He was then fresh from Fontainebleau. He had met Mrs Osbourne and her daughter, both art students, and perhaps these drawings by one who had never been able to draw as a youth was something in the nature of an offering on the altar of his love's gods: like Browning –

> Does he paint? he fain would write a poem, –
> Does he write? he fain would paint a picture,
> Put to proof art alien to the artist's,
> Once and only once, and for One only,
> So to be the man and leave the artist,
> Gain the man's joy, miss the artist's sorrow.[3]

The woodcuts were a different matter altogether, a more rollicking pleasure, though serious enough as was all Stevenson's play, serious like a child's, like the war-game which, shared with engraving all the time when he was not finishing *Treasure Island*, working at *Otto*,[4] or writing verses for *A Child's Garden*.[5] They played the war-game at Davos with toy soldiers in 'an attic, reached by a crazy ladder, and unlit save for a single frosted window, so low at the eaves and so dark that we could seldom stand upright, nor see without a candle.'[6] The country was mapped on the floor.

[1] *"Studio*, Winter number, 1896–97." *The Studio: An Illustrated Magazine of Fine and Applied Art* (1893–?) The verse is 'The Graver the Pen: or, scenes from nature, with appropriate verses', v, 'The Foolhardy Geographer'.

[2] His donkey, from *Travels with a Donkey in the Cévennes* (1879).

[3] "Quote Browning 'paint a picture'. *Studio*, Winter number, 1896–97." The lines are inserted from 'One Word More. To E. B. B., London, September, 1855'; the capitalisation of 'One' is Ransome's.

[4] *Prince Otto: A Romance* (1885).

[5] *A Child's Garden of Verses*. A trial version was first published as *Penny Whistles* (1883).

[6] "'Stevenson at Play,' with an introduction by S. Lloyd Osbourne. (Article in some Am. magazine ?Century." The article, drawn from Stevenson's notebooks, was in fact published posthumously in *Scribner's Magazine*, December 1898.

There were elaborate rules, and even war correspondence in an imaginary paper, the editor of which was so rude to Mr Osbourne that the indignant general had him summarily hanged.

In April 1882, they were again in England, in Edinburgh in May, and at the end of June tried to live in the manse of Stobo in Peeblesshire. Stevenson was ill, went to London, and was ordered elsewhere. He went to Kingussie, stayed a month in bad weather, and was presently on the way to the south of France with R. A. M. Stevenson. His wife was ill, but had recovered sufficiently to meet him at Marseilles in October when his cousin had left. They found a house, but Stevenson's health grew worse, and he went to Nice. In March 1883, they settled again in the Chalet la Solitude, Hyères, where, with 'a garden like a fairy story and a view like a classical landscape', they were very happy for nine months, in which Stevenson continued the *Child's Garden of Verses*, enjoyed his first popular success with the book publication of *Treasure Island*, worked on *Otto* and was ill again and again. In May 1884 he nearly died from a haemorrhage, and unable to speak, tried to comfort his wife by scribbling on a bit of paper 'Don't be frightened; if this is death it is an easy one.'[1] After a very painful convalescence, he returned to England in July 1884. It is hard with dates and so few details to give a just picture of these years, in which Stevenson seems to have been like a child with all the fervour of happiness chased from room to room, in every one of which he could have played so merrily, by a Bogie Man of coughs and blood and fears. Much of his most delightful work was written in the intervals of escape from this pursuing monster.

Soon after reaching England Stevenson went to Bournemouth, where for some months he lived in furnished houses. Then, as the place seemed to suit him, though it was far from turning him into a healthy man, his father bought a house there and made a present of it to his daughter-in-law. At this house, called Skerryvore, after the lighthouse, with the exception of a few short holidays which usually ended in illness, Stevenson lived until August 1887. The three years at Bournemouth were the least exciting in his life, though as he said, he never knew what it was to be bored, his own lively spirit, even in illness, being always a sufficient entertainment. He lay abed and wrote with great industry. The works published during his stay there included *The Strange Case of Dr Jekyll and Mr Hyde*,[2] *Kidnapped*,[3] *More New Arabian Nights*,[4] *Prince Otto* and *A Child's Garden of Verses*. He made several new friends, and was visited by many old, so that the period seems now to have been almost a designed prologue to the then unforeseen

[1] "Balfour, 149."

[2] (1885).

[3] (1886); first published in *Young Folks Paper* from May to the end of July that same year.

[4] (1885); with stories by Fanny Stevenson also.

departure to America and the South Seas. Sargent[1] painted his portrait, and, on a visit to Mr Colvin,[2] he met Burne-Jones,[3] Browning and Lowell,[4] on which he remarked that his path was paved with celebrities.

He had already written one play, *Deacon Brodie*, in collaboration with Henley,[5] and when he first came to Bournemouth Henley visited him and they wrote two more, and, a few months later, another, but, though his collaborator was most helpful, Stevenson felt that 'It was bad enough to have to live by an art – but to think to live by an art combined with commercial speculation – that way madness lay,' and refused to be turned from the more immediately promising labour of *Kidnapped*.

He added another to his many games[6] by becoming interested in music. He began by picking out tunes with one finger, then with two, and as thorough in this as with his battles of lead soldiers when Sir Edward Hamley's *Operations of War*[7] was at his elbow, he flung himself at the theory of music, and was presently announcing compositions. He wrote with one of them to his cousin a letter that well illustrates his rather tremulous solemnity in the matter:

> Dear Bob, – Herewith another shy; more melancholy than before, but I think not so abjectly idiotic. The musical terms seem to be as good as in Beethoven, and that, after all, is the great affair. Bar the dam bareness of the bass, it looks like a piece of real music from a distance. I am proud to say it was not made one hand at a time; the bass was of synchronous birth with the treble; they are of the same age, sir, and may God have mercy on their souls! – Yours, *The Maestro*.[8]

In his executant capacity he went so far as accompanying Lloyd Osbourne's penny whistle with the piano, and this was, I believe, his first step towards that congenial instrument[9] which was the delight of later years.

---

[1] John Singer Sargent (1856–1925), American portraitist.

[2] Sir Sidney Colvin was knighted in 1911.

[3] Sir Edward Burne-Jones (1833–98), painter and member of the Pre-Raphaelite Brotherhood.

[4] James Russell Lowell (1819–91), American Romantic poet and diplomat in London from 1880.

[5] W. E. Henley.

[6] 'Games' is a word oddly used by Ransome. As late as 1960 in an unpublished letter he advised his sister Joyce to 'consider Stevenson's games, such as "Providence and a Guitar", "The Sire de Maletroit's Door", etc.'

[7] Sir Edward B. Hamley, *The Operations of War Explained and Illustrated* (1878).

[8] "*Letters*, II, 291." Ransome double-underlines the words 'The Maestro'.

[9] In a discarded alternative 'Conclusion' to the first part of his book (see appendix A.2.iii) Ransome wrote: 'The instrument is unjustly despised, even

The two events of his stay in Bournemouth were the death of his father and of Fleeming Jenkin.[1] Jenkin had been his friend since his student days in Edinburgh, and, in collaboration with his widow, Stevenson prepared the memoir that was affixed to his works, and, as he learnt more and more of the man he had loved and admired, finding him shine still brighter. The elder Stevenson had long been failing. No longer the downright disputant, fire in cloud,[2] the eager man of science, he had become a child, playing at parentage, talking to his son like a mother to a baby, the more pathetic for the memory of his sterner prime. Stevenson was summoned to Edinburgh in May 1887, and saw his father die. The advice of physicians on his health, and melancholy after his father's death, determined him to undertake a second journey to America. On August 20th 1887 he sailed from London, not knowing that he was never to return.

On his first voyage[3] to America he had sailed without the approval of his family or friends, and arrived in a country where was scarcely one who knew his name. On the second he sailed with his wife, his mother, Lloyd Osbourne and a Swiss maid, and was received by Mr Low, one of his best friends, and a host of journalists. The voyage was almost as uncomfortable as in the emigrant ship, but to Stevenson at least, who loved the sea, infinitely delightful. They sailed from London in *The Ludgate Hill*, and afterwards Stevenson wrote:

> I was so happy on board that ship, I could not have believed it possible. We had the beastliest weather, and many discomforts; but the mere fact of its being a tramp-ship gave us many comforts; we could cut about with the men and officers, stay in the wheel-house, discuss all manner of things, and really be a little at sea. And truly there is nothing else. I had literally forgotten what happiness was, and the full mind – full of external and physical things, not full of cares and labours and rot about a fellow's behaviour. My heart literally sang; I truly care for nothing so much as for that ...[4]

laughed at, but it is capable of great things ... it is symbolical of his career. A grown man playing the instrument of youth... playing a penny whistle in the orchestra of English literature.'

[1] "Death of Fleeming Jenkins and his father. Pub[lished]: *Jekyll. Kidnapped. More New Arab. Prince Otto. C[hild's] G[arden of] V[erses].* Friends. Plays with Henley. Music."

[2] See Exodus 40:38: 'For the cloud of the Lord was upon the tabernacle by day, and fire was on it by night, in the sight of all the house of Israel, throughout all their journeys;' for Ransome, a rare but commonplace Biblical allusion.

[3] Ransome's headers for this section are: "Saranac. Penny Whistling. Wild Men of the Woods. Buffalo robes. Fame. *Ludgate Hill.*"

[4] "To R. A. M. S. Saranac Lake Adirondacks. Oct[ober], 1887. [*Letters,*] III, 9."

It was perhaps the pleasure of that voyage which decided Stevenson's destiny, his cruising in the South Seas and so his eventual settlement in Samoa.

On reaching New York he knew, for the first time, the sensations of the travelling prize-fighter or Cabinet Minister. *Jekyll and Hyde*[1] had completed the work of *Treasure Island* and made him a public character, and in America fame is more obvious, more vociferous than in England. He was at the same time pleased and sardonic. 'One thing is,' he wrote, 'they do not stick for money to the Famed One; I was offered £2000 a year for a weekly article; and I accepted (and now enjoy) £720 a year for a monthly one.'[2] And 'I begin to shirk any more taffy; I think I begin to like it too well. But let us trust the Gods; they have a rod in pickle;[3] reverently I doff my trousers, and with screwed eyes await the *amari aliquid*[4] of the great God Busby.'[5] The excitement of fame brought no release from the chains of ill health. Stevenson had caught cold on the Newfoundland Banks, and almost immediately after his arrival was in bed and too ill to be moved. The younger Mrs Stevenson went with her son to find a fit lodging for the writer, and soon afterwards Stevenson and his mother followed them to a small house outside Saranac in the Adirondack mountains, on the Canadian border, where Stevenson worked at his monthly essays and planned *The Master of Ballantrae*.[6] They had the worst of Canadian winters but though his wife and mother suffered his own health steadily improved.

The country was wild, and Stevenson loved to walk in it in fitting costume. W. H. Low was to paint his portrait, but Stevenson wrote to him, smiling, saying that he 'won't have you till I have a buffalo robe and leggings, lest you should want to paint me as a plain man, which I am not, but a rank Saranacker and wild man of the woods.'[7]

Such a robe he did get, and walked in it, in the cold of the wilderness, enjoying himself in this setting, and thinking of the last resurrection of the Master of Ballantrae. Indoors in the evenings his mother read Mr Henry James' *Roderick Hudson*[8] aloud in the evenings, and Stevenson worked with difficulty and amazement at the *Aeneid*.[9] His lighter amusements

---

[1] *The Strange Case of Dr Jekyll and Mr Hyde* (1886).

[2] "To Sir Walter Simpson. Saranac Lake, Oct 1887. *Letters*, III, 11."

[3] i.e. harbour revenge.

[4] 'Something bitter': evidently a caning.

[5] "Gosse, Saranac, Oct[ober] 8 1887. *Letters*, II, 13." Dr Busby was a famous flogging headmaster of Westminster School.

[6] *The Master of Ballantrae: A Winter's Tale* (1889).

[7] "W. H. Low. Saranac Lake, Oct[ober] 1887. *Letters*, III, 14."

[8] (1876).

[9] Virgil's epic poem on the adventures of Aeneas. Stevenson was working at a translation by way of encouraging his stepson's Latin.

were Patience and the penny whistle, the full possibilities of which instrument he was beginning to discover. 'I am a great performer before the Lord on the penny whistle,'[1] he wrote to Mr Colvin, and to Miss Boodle of Bournemouth:

> We now perform duets on two D tin whistles; it is no joke to make the bass; I think I must really send you one, which I wish you would correct ... I may be said to live for these instrumental labours now, but I have always some childishness on hand.[2]

Outside his own family he had few friends at Saranac, but he had always a power of getting an intense pleasure from accidental acquaintances. Mr Low gives an amusing example. After Stevenson returned to New York from Saranac, a newspaper artist called, while Mr Low was with him, and asked to be allowed an hour in which to finish a drawing of him he had begun from a photograph. He took off his watch and gave it to Stevenson and said that it would be seen he was a man of his word. 'Let us begin now, and stop on the minute that the hour has elapsed.' Mr Low continues: 'I left them, but on coming later in the day I found Stevenson delighted with the experience. He had been everywhere – has seen everything, and talked extremely well about it all. Do you know what I did? *I turned his watch back an hour,* I was so afraid to lose him.'[3] The act is an allegory of Stevenson's manner with almost all he met. He was a most inviting listener.

His health had so far improved, the memory of *The Ludgate Hill* was so happy, that he spent much time at Saranac planning voyages, and considering the possibility of chartering a yacht. In April his wife went to California and was charged to hear if possible of any available boats in San Francisco Harbour. Stevenson and Lloyd Osbourne went, after a fortnight in New York to Manasquan, New Jersey, where they sharpened their ardour for the sea by sailing a cat-boat. Mrs Stevenson found the yacht *Casco*, and though there were difficulties of mistrust, yet as soon as the owner met Stevenson, these were whisked away, and on the 28th June 1888, he sailed from San Francisco for the South Seas.

Stevenson did not set out[4] on his cruising as a mere light-hearted holiday-maker. It was an adventure, but it was also a serious bid for health. He wrote to his friend Mr Baxter, who managed his affairs for him in Edinburgh:

---

[1] *"Letters*, III, 54."

[2] "Penny Whistling. Miss Boodle, Saranac, April 1888. [*Letters,*] III, 56."

[3] "W. H. Low, p. 404."

[4] This section, "Cruising in the South Seas. Near Death. The Sea", was mostly written on 9 January 1914, according to Ransome's diaries.

I have found a yacht, and we are going the full pitch for seven months. If I cannot get my health back (more or less), 'tis madness; but, of course, there is the hope, and I will play big... If this business fails to set me up, well £2000 is gone, and I know I can't get better.[1]

And as he had said in New York: 'Fame is nothing to a yacht.'[2]

The yacht *Casco* was a fore and aft schooner, ninety-nine feet over all, 'like most yachts, over-rigged and over-sparred, and like many American yachts on a very dangerous sail plan.' They had an admirable sailing master in Captain Otis, but a not so satisfactory crew, and their fill of the perils of the sea. 'We have been thrice within an ace of being ashore: we were lost (!) for about twelve hours in the Low Archipelago, but by God's blessing had quiet weather all the time; and once, in a squall, we came so near gaun heels ower hurdies, that I really dinnae ken why we didnae a'thegither.'[3]

In spite of this sombre background, the yacht glittered in the more hopeful sunshine of excitement. 'From festering in a sick-room all winter' (thus he ungratefully forgot his walks in buffalo-robes) 'to the deck of one's own ship, is indeed a change.'[4]

> One stirring day was that in which we sighted Hawaii. It blew fair, but very strong; we carried jib, foresail, and mainsail, all single-reefed, and she carried her lee rail under water and flew. The swell, the heaviest I have ever been out in – I tried in vain to estimate the height, *at least* fifteen feet – came tearing after us about a point and a half off the wind. We had the best hand – old Louis – at the wheel; and, really, he did nobly, and had noble luck, for it never caught us once. At times it seemed we must have it; Louis would look over his shoulder with the queerest look and dive down his neck into his shoulders; and then it missed us somehow, and only sprays came over our quarter,

[1] *"Letters*, III, 56."

[2] Ransome's approximation. The letter to R. A. M. Stevenson of October 1887 reads:

> I know a little about fame now; it's no good compared to a yacht; and anyway there is more fame in a yacht, more genuine fame; to cross the Atlantic and come to anchor in Newport (say) with the Union Jack, and go ashore for your letters and hang about the pier, among the holiday yachtsmen – that's fame, that's glory, and nobody can take it away; they can't say your book is bad; you HAVE crossed the Atlantic.

> Again to his cousin Bob that same month Stevenson had written: 'Wealth is only useful for two things: a yacht and a string quartette.' Elsewhere Ransome notes: "Fame is nothing to a yacht; *experto crede*. They do not stick for money to the Famed One ...' To Sir Walter Simpson, Saranac Lake, Oct[ober], 1897."

[3] *"Letters*, III, 68." 'Hurdies': buttocks.

[4] *"Letters*, III, 57."

turning the little outside lane of deck into a mill race as deep as to the cockpit coamings. I never remember anything more delightful and exciting.[1]

It is interesting to compare this swift description with the account of the storm on page 173 of *The Wrecker*, where the demands of story necessitate a change of mood:

What I liked still less, Johnson himself was at the wheel, which he span busily, often with a visible effort; and as the seas ranged up behind us, black and imminent, he kept casting behind him eyes of animal swiftness, and drawing in his neck between his shoulders, like a man dodging a blow.[2]

Nor did Stevenson's health show any immediate sign of the improvement that afterwards justified his stay in the tropics. Once again he had an opportunity of showing his perfect calm in the face of[3] imminent disaster.

In Tahiti his life was despaired of. He had been taken ashore, and lodged in a hotel. He sent for Captain Otis, who records:

He told me in his ordinary tone, and without a flicker of excitement, that he had sent for me, fearing that he might take a turn for the worse; if he did, he said, the doctor had told him he probably would not live till morning. Then he added with a smile, 'You see, the doctor does not give me much time; so I have divided what there is left into three equal portions, one for each, only reserving the last for Mrs Stevenson.' He then proceeded to inform me, as calmly as though he had a century to spend, how I was to dispose of the yacht and settle the business, if disaster fell – which happily it did not. After that he bade me adieu as quietly as if no danger threatened his life and hopes.[4]

In Tautira[5] they learnt that the mainmast was rotten and they were detained for two months in the house of a sub-chief, Ori-a-Ori, who became a most devoted friend, and when he left wrote him a letter which Stevenson said

---

[1] *"Letters, III, 100."* Ransome quotes rather more than the extract he had elsewhere copied for use, where he observed "changes of mood" and noted the recipient: "R. A. M. S., Honolulu, Feb[ruary] 1889." The following sentence is editorially completed.

[2] *The Wrecker* (1892) by R. L. Stevenson and Lloyd Osbourne, chapter 12, 'The North Creina'. This paragraph is inserted from a separate sheet; it appears to belong here.

[3] The sentence breaks off here and is editorially completed.

[4] *Recollections of Robert Louis Stevenson in the Pacific*, by Arthur Johnstone (1905), 39.

[5] A village on the south-east coast of Tahiti-iti.

he would rather have received than written *Redgauntlet*[1] or the sixth book of the *Aeneid*.[2]

Discussion of Stevenson's *In The South Seas*[3] will bring with it discussion of the islands, and I propose here to say nothing of the impression they made on him, but to keep strictly to an abridged account of his actual cruisings. They visited now the Marquesas, the Low Archipelago in the Society Islands. It was here that Stevenson was so ill, here that he was detained by delay in repairing the mast. From the Society Islands they sailed south to Honolulu (a map is really necessary to anyone who would have a clear idea of what they did.) At Honolulu they 'got the yacht paid off in triumph,'[4] and settled for six months some three miles out of the town. That was in February. Stevenson here finished *The Master of Ballantrae*, but already, in March, they were planning a further cruise, and in June, after Stevenson had visited Molokai, the island set apart for the lepers, they were again at sea, on board *The Equator*, a trading schooner bound for the Gilbert Islands, and to Samoa, where Stevenson was so pleased with the climate that he bought the estate on the mountain behind Apia, 'three streams, two waterfalls, a great cliff, an ancient native fort, a view of the sea and lowlands or (to be more precise) several views of them in various directions,'[5] which was to be his last home. He stayed some weeks in Apia, and then sailed for Sydney, where he wrote the 'Letter to Dr Hyde,'[6] and was ill with fever and haemorrhage. In April 1890, he set sail in another trading steamer, the *Janet Nicoll*. He wrote hard on board, even in a gale, 'spearing his inkpot like a flying fish,'[7] stayed a week in New Caledonia, while his wife and stepson went on, and then joined them in Sydney in August. In October he left Sydney for Samoa, and a settled habitation, after nearly two and a half years of intermittent cruising. 'It is a singular thing,' he wrote during this time of sea-going, 'that as I was packing up old papers ere I left Skerryvore',

[1] A Jacobite novel (1824) by Sir Walter Scott.

[2] Book VI describes Aeneas's journey to the underworld.

[3] *In The South Seas* (1896) was first published in the *New York Sun*, 1891. It was Ransome's favourite of Stevenson's travel books. He is right to say a map would be necessary. Stevenson's pencil sketch from 1881 was the basis for the map published as frontispiece to the book in the Tusitala edition (1924).

[4] To Charles Baxter, 8 February 1889, *Letters*, III, 95.

[5] "*Letters*, III, 149."

[6] *Father Damien: An Open Letter to the Reverend Dr Hyde of Honolulu* (1890), a characteristic championing of an underdog. This was Stevenson's first influential intervention in Pacific politics. Fr Damien was a missionary priest.

[7] In his letter to Colvin, Stevenson says he worked 'four to six hours per diem, spearing the ink-bottle like a flying-fish …' *Letters*, III, 163. This is Ransome's approximation.

I came on the prophecies of a drunken Highland sibyl, when I was seventeen. She said I was to be very happy, to visit America, and *to be much upon the sea.* It seems as if it were coming true with a vengeance. Also, do you remember my strong, old, rooted belief that I shall die by drowning? I don't want that to come true, though it is an easy death; but it occurs to me oddly, with these long chances in front. I cannot say why I like the sea; no man is more cynically and constantly alive to its perils; I regard it as the highest form of gambling; and yet I love the sea as much as I hate gambling. Fine, clean emotions; a world all and always beautiful; air better than wine; interest unflagging; there is upon the whole no better life.[1]

A delightful picture of Stevenson's arrival in Samoa[2] has been preserved by the Rev. W. E. Clarke. He writes:

Making my way along the beach – the sandy track with its long, straggling line of stores and drink saloons – I met a little group of three European strangers – two men and a woman. The latter wore a print gown, large gold crescent earrings, a Gilbert-island hat of plaited straw, encircled with a wreath of small shells, a scarlet silk scarf round her neck, and a brilliant plaid shawl across her shoulders; her bare feet were encased in white canvas shoes, and across her back was slung a guitar.

The younger of her two companions (Mr Osbourne) was dressed in a striped pyjama suit – the undress costume of most European traders in those seas – a slouch straw hat of native make, dark blue sun-spectacles, and over his shoulder a banjo. The other man (Stevenson) was dressed in a shabby suit of white flannels that had seen many better days, a white drill yachting cap with a prominent peak, a cigarette in his mouth, and a photographic camera in his hand. Both the men were bare footed ... my first thought was that, probably, they were wandering players en route for New Zealand, compelled by their poverty to take the cheap conveyance of a trading vessel.[3]

As soon as Stevenson had bought the Vailima estate, the building of a house had been begun, and was carried on during his absence. When he returned it was hurried towards completion, and in April 1891 it was ready for its owners. 'The house,' says Mr Balfour, who stayed there, 'was built of wood throughout, painted a dark green outside, with a red roof of

---

[1] "Colvin. Honolulu, April 2, 1899. [*Letters,*] III, 111."

[2] This is preceded by working notes: "*Vailima.* Open air life. Politics. Work. The idiot boy. War. First appearance."

[3] "Personal Recollections of Robert Louis Stevenson, by the Rev. W. E. Clarke. Article in *The Chronicle of the London Missionary Society*, April, 1908."

corrugated iron, on which the heavy rain sounded like thunder as it fell and ran off to be stored for household purposes in the large iron tanks.'[1] It had three living rooms downstairs, five bedrooms above, with a verandah on each floor, part of the upper one boarded in to make Stevenson's bedroom and writing room. In May 1891, Stevenson and his wife and stepson were joined by his mother, and by his step daughter Mrs Strong and her son. He was thus the head of a clan which soon included the servants on the estate who, as it were, adopted themselves into his family. In a very short time he had thus passed from the position of the visiting tourist to that of the established resident on the little island, and his obvious intention to live and die where he was accounted for much of the influence with the natives which he was soon to possess.

These last years of his life were very different from any that had preceded them. For the first time since he had been taken for the man in charge at Wick, he was living with vivid gusto the life of a man of action. He dug, cut trees, weeded (a heroic battle against the swift growth of tropical plants), made roads, drove cattle, rode, and was able to do all this without the immediate retribution of the sick-bed. 'Remember', he says exultantly,

> remember the pallid brute that lived in Skerryvore like a weevil in a biscuit, and receive the intelligence that I was rather the better for my journey. Twenty miles ride, sixteen fences taken, ten of the miles in a drenching rain, seven of them fasting and in the morning chill, and six stricken hours' political discussions by an interpreter; to say nothing of sleeping in a native house, at which many of our excellent literati would look askance of itself.[2]

He got all that he could out of this release from ill health.

In youth the delicate experimenter in the breaking and harnessing of words, the virtuoso in riding prose rhythms, driven perhaps a little further than was quite natural into virtuosity by contrast with his firm-standing, keen-eyed practical father whose eye followed the course of a current better than a fugue of skilfully disguised alliteration, Stevenson reverted as he grew older to the paternal type and became perhaps a little more practical than was natural, in reaction from superfluous virtuosity. House-builder, road-maker, diplomatist, virtuous politician, planning with deeds instead of with words, he gave himself a taste of the life which as a boy he had chosen, rightly on the score of health at least, to reject.

Nor did this bright, external activity at all prevent, though it often broke into, his ordinary work. Here is his account of a day.

[1] The more substantial Australasian colonial houses of the period were very similar in structure.

[2] "To Colvin, May 9, 1892. *Letters*, IV, 45."

I am now an old, but healthy skeleton, and degenerate much towards the machine. By six at work: stopped at half-past ten to give a history lesson to a step-grandson; eleven, lunch; after lunch we have a musical performance till two; then to work again; bath, 4.40, dinner, five; cards in the evening till eight; and then to bed – only I have no bed, only a chest with a mat and blankets – and read myself to sleep. This is the routine, but often sadly interrupted. Then you may see me sitting on the floor of my verandah haranguing and being harangued by squatting chiefs on a question of a road; or more privately holding an inquiry into some dispute among our familiars, myself on my bed, the boys on the floor – for when it comes to the judicial I play dignity – or else going down to Apia on some more or less unsatisfactory errand.

Even when chronicling all their jostling business, he compares himself ruefully with Scott, unsuppressed by his immense work, and says, 'But the lean hot spirits, such as mine, become hypnotised with their bit occupations – if I may use Scotch to you – it is so far more scornful than any English idiom. He suffered from writer's cramp, and used to work by lamplight in the early mornings and at eight o'clock began dictation from his notes.

Much of his thought was occupied with island politics. This is not the place to discuss them. Most of his views have since been adopted, and it says much for his tact that Mr Johnstone records the fact that though in his writing on the South Seas he was seldom if ever polite to the representatives of civilisation, he left few enemies though many critics among the whites and on the other hand a host of friends. Mr Johnstone quotes the opinion of Captain Otis, the sailing master of the *Casco*:

> Well, gentlemen, it seems this way to me: Stevenson was first and last a man of convictions – in fact he always acted promptly and vigorously when he reached a conclusion that satisfied his own mind – but his mental make-up was such that he always took the side of the under-dog in any fight that arose, without waiting to inquire whether the under-dog had the right of it, or was in the wrong. That was the man, gentlemen; and I know from personal experience that he did not understand what fear was, when he defended what he thought was right.

'*He defended what he thought was right.*'[1] That old seaman's view should content us here.

The natives expressed their opinion on Stevenson in many ways. One native king remained on friendly terms with him. The chieftain of the other built a road for him in gratitude for his kindness to them when in prison.

---

[1] For a slightly different presentation of this, see appendix A.2.iii.

And, when there was war in the islands, he could work in peace. Mrs Strong writes in March 1894:

> Our woods are full of scouting parties, and we are occasionally inter-
> rupted by the beating of drums as a war-party crosses our lawn. But
> nothing stops the cheerful flow of 'Anne'. I put in the words, between
> sentences, 'Louis, have we a pistol or gun in the house that will
> shoot?' to which he cheerfully answers, 'No, but we have friends on
> both sides,' and on we go with the dictation.[1]

It was a strange translation from Davos, or Bournemouth, and must have been entirely delightful to one who had always thought in terms of romance, who had pictured himself not on a sick bed but turning to wars or his band of irregular cavalry, or listening to the highwayman's taps on windows of the inn at Burford Bridge. Few invalids can ever have had so clear, so fresh a taste of the better kind of barbarism.

On January 3rd of the year in which he died, Stevenson wrote to his life-long friend Dr Baildon:[2]

> Yes, if I could die just now, or say in half a year, I should have had
> a splendid time of it on the whole. But it gets a little stale, and my
> work will begin to senesce; and parties to shy bricks at me; and
> now it begins to look as if I should survive to see myself impotent
> and forgotten. It's a pity suicide is not thought the ticket in the best
> circles.
>
> But your letter goes on to congratulate me on having done the one
> thing I am a little sorry for; a little – not much – for my father himself
> lived to think that I had been wiser than he. But the cream of the
> jest is that I have lived to change my mind; and think that he was
> wiser than I. Had I been an engineer, and literature my amusement,
> it would have been better perhaps. I pulled it off, of course, I won the
> wager, and it is pleasant while it lasts; but how long will it last? I don't
> know, say the Bells of Old Bow.
>
> All of which goes to show that nobody is quite sane in judging
> himself. Truly, had I given way and gone in for engineering, I should
> be dead by now. Well, the Gods know best.[3]

---

[1] "*Memories of Vailima*, p. 55." By Isobel Field and Lloyd Osbourne (1902).

[2] Dr Henry Bellyse Baildon (1849–1907), a friend from the University of Edinburgh, who was author of *Robert Louis Stevenson: A Life Study in Criticism*
(1901) a work strongly criticised by G. K. Chesterton in *Twelve Types of Biography* (see Introduction).

[3] "To H. B. Baildon, Jan[uary] 30, 1894. *Letters*, IV, 246." An earlier version of
this paragraph is in appendix A.2.iii.

It is to be presumed that the gods did know best. Less than a year later, Stevenson died as good a death as a man can ask, in the midst of the best work of his life, in full vigour, without pain. Nor is it extravagant to find in *Weir of Hermiston*[1] a work in words nearly resembling the work of his father in stones against the beating of the seas. Here, at last, Stevenson was building on a promontory in dangerous waters, with a solidity and strength to which he had never attained. In happy consciousness of this, knowing that his latest work was not as he had feared 'senescent', he died. His letters seem, after the event, to prove that he had felt a coming end, but those who were with him had not perceived it. Their fear was, for the moment, elsewhere. "Do I look strange?" he asked abruptly, and died, almost at once.[2]

There is no need here to Describe His Funeral, that romantic journey to the mountain top, the tomb on the summit. That has been done by his stepson, in the letter printed in Mr Balfour's *Life* which everybody who cares for Stevenson has read.

We need only look back over those forty-four years, more than half of them occupied continually in writing, and realise how adventurous a life this writer led. The outward facts are full of incident, lighthouses, walking, boating, the emigration, the South Seas; but if we would realise how romantic the life was to him who lived it, we must remember his attitude towards himself, his dramatic vision, and the two personifications he chose for his own epitaph.[3] The hunter from the hill, the sailor from the seas; these were the men who died in Stevenson. The child cut off in a Red

---

[1] Stevenson's last novel, often considered his most powerful, incomplete at his death, and published posthumously in 1896.

[2] A different, apparently discarded version of this paragraph may be found in appendix A.2.iii.

[3] Stevenson's 'Requiem', the final sentence of which (with the interpolation of 'the' before 'sea') is carved on his gravestone at Mt Vaea in Samoa:

> Under the wide and starry sky
> Dig my grave and let me lie:
> Glad did I live and gladly die,
> And I laid me down with a will.
>
> This be the verse you grave for me:
> *Here he lies where he longed to be;*
> *Home is the sailor, home from sea,*
> *And the hunter home from the hill.*

Ransome constructs a fine peroration; his affirmation of hope may be no more than the sort of thing which his masters at Rugby School and contemporary readers might approve. Neither Stevenson nor Ransome had formal Christian beliefs. This passionate, image-upon-image laying-to-rest of man and writer is unique in Ransome.

Indian game, surrenders even in the solemnity of death his little scalp with heroism. And in the writer of so many books, dying in the hall at Vailima, a leader of irregular cavalry, mortally wounded at last, gallantly surrendered his soul to a greater leader than he.

PART II
Writings

Throughout the chronicle of illness, adventures, and all kinds of play, have been scattered the names of books, and with them implicit reference to quite another life, ceaselessly carried on in the midst of most various activities, the life of a writer, an obstinate determined struggle with intangible difficulties, most of them not to be perceived even by those who were most often with him. It is the business of the rest of this book to consider that other intricate life, and to follow its progress, to observe a series of adventures on a plane quite different from that on which its hero played the penny whistle, loved, learnt the ways of boats, and weeded in a Samoan plantation.

Although Stevenson wrote essays even at the end of his life, and Scottish stories at the beginning, yet it is not only convenient but essentially just to discuss each one of the many facets of his art in an order almost chronological, following generally the times when each of these facets was so brightly illuminated as to leave the rest at least in partial shadow. My plan[1] is, to begin with an analysis of Stevenson's attitude towards the techniques of literature, and to follow it with chapters on his essays, criticism, short stories, boy's books and *Prince Otto*, poems, fables, the Scotch novels, the South Seas, collaborations, and unfinished work, ending with a summary of his character and achievements.

I have sketched other plans,[2] but rejected them one after another, this because it permitted insufficient detail, that because it insisted on too

---

[1] Ransome's check-list for this section reads "Stevenson. Techniques of Literature. *Technical Questions. Characters in Novel;* how far dictated by the book: how far contributed as elements of the game: Schiller's play theory fits perfectly Stevenson's method. He Stevenson separates the imagining of the book from the writing of it. Find a psychological statement of that too Noyes. Is the first art at all: or is it merely a plan, which gains in enjoy thereon from an assumed perfection in the as yet unattempted execution of the work of art? His general ideas on *art*. Schiller. His own development in knowledge. *Points.* Realism: the laws of the game. Realism qua danger. Observation & euphony. Styles. The offset of every word into technique. Omission & suppression."

[2] An example of another plan can be found within the 'Stevenson exercise-book', transcribed and reproduced in appendix A.1.iii. Ransome always began with careful preliminary note-taking and detailed planning. Then he wrote up sections in whatever order seemed congenial.

much, this other because it seemed to me to concentrate the light unfairly, that because it hid the proportions which I believed more just. Let me hope that it will not seem tedious to follow as pedestrians[1] the road he galloped and to stop at the inns, one after another, to consider the adventures of the day.

Perhaps the reason why Stevenson remained a charming, a skilful writer, and in life a delightful but not a commanding personality lay in his attitude towards life and towards art. In life he looked for romance, and made of his own a romantic adventure: in art he was preoccupied with technique so largely that all he did seems now to have been by way of experiment during a prolonged adventure in the discovery of technical perfection. He will not be remembered as a great man of action: he will not, except by a few enthusiasts of special temper, be counted among the greater writers: but, even by men who are impatient of all his finished achievements, he will be counted as one of the greatest exponents of the objects and the methods of literature. And in the history of writing there are few more romantic tales than this of the man who knew himself when all his efforts failed, and died at last, suddenly, in the full glow of a work which would perhaps have been perfect, and certainly had not gone far enough to show a sign of eventual failure.

I have been led, almost against my will, to chronicle poem and story, fable, novel and essay, with a mind that looked forward to a discussion of what in Stevenson's mind was more important than any of his actual achievements, the gradual development of his idea of art, the lineaments of the dryad who fled him through the brushwood and undergrowth of realising dreams, seemed ever and again to be within his reach, and came near enough at last to let him die with something of the exultation of capture.

His pleasure then, as in life, was to be on the way. He talked of writing an 'Art of Literature', but he never sketched its contents, and could scarcely have done so, for his ideas were always those of the craftsman, not the systematic falsehood of the philosopher. There is falsehood even in the ideas of the craftsman, but of a different kind. Stevenson, as craftsman, knew how, but he did not always know why, and in stating ultimate aims he was nearly always so far in error as almost to disguise the truth of his original observation.

It is not possible to describe enthusiasm, and to say that a man was enthusiastic is a cold speech that may either be a complement or a reproof. I cannot do better, if I wish to show Stevenson's attitude towards these technical matters than illustrate it by quotation. And if it were not to be

---

[1] An apt series of metaphors for Stevenson's art. (Concurrently with this book, Ransome was planning another, on roads and walking, but only one or two separate essays were written.)

illustrated his pursuit of technical knowledge, and of technical proportion, would lose its most imprinting quality. In October 1883, he wrote to Mr W. H. Low:

> Yet I now draw near to the Middle Ages; nearly three years ago, that fatal Thirty struck; and yet the great work is not yet done – not yet even conceived ...
>
> Eight years ago, if I could have slung ink as I can now, I should have thought myself well on the road after Shakespeare; and now – I find I have only got a pair of walking-shoes and not yet begun to travel. And art is still away there on the mountain summit. But I need not continue; for, of course, this is your story just as much as it is mine; and, strange to think, it was Shakespeare's too, and Beethoven's, and Phidias's. It is a blessed thing that, in this forest of art, we can pursue our wood-lice and sparrows, *and not catch them*, with almost the same fervour of exhilaration as that with which Sophocles hunted and brought down the Mastodon.[1]

And a month or two earlier he wrote to Henley in a more lyrical spirit, a letter which though long I must enrich my book by quoting in full:

> I beg to inform you that I, Robert Louis Stevenson, author of *Brashiana*[2] and other works, am merely beginning to commence to prepare to make a first start at trying to understand my profession. O the height and depth of novelty and worth in any art! and O that I am privileged to swim and shoulder through such oceans! Could one get out of sight of land – all in the blue? Alas not, being anchored here in flesh, and the bonds of logic being still about us.
>
> But what a great space and a great air there is in these small shallows where alone we venture! and how new each sight, squall, calm, or sunrise! An art is a fine fortune, a palace in a park, a band of music, health, and physical beauty; all but love – to any worthy practiser. I sleep upon my art for a pillow; I waken in my art; I am unready for death, because I hate to leave it. I love my wife, I do not know how much, nor can, nor shall, unless I lost her; but while I can conceive

---

[1] "Hyères. Oct[ober] 23, 1883. *Letters*, II, 151. To W. H. Low." A telling metaphor for the supreme classical dramatist's heroic art, after reference to three artists supreme in their own fields. Stevenson and Ransome would agree about the power of the relatively recently discovered Mastodon to create awe: it had done so in Jules Verne's *Journey to the Centre of the Earth* (1864), a book that later fed the imaginations of Ransome's characters Dorothea and Titty. 'The Mastodon' becomes a character in his *Secret Water* (1939).

[2] A "series of burlesque sonnets he had written at Davos" in 1881 commemorating Peter Brash, who had kept a tavern in Edinburgh when Stevenson was a student.

my being widowed, I refuse the offering of life without my art. I *am* not but in my art; it is me; I am the body of it merely.

And yet I produce nothing, am the author of *Brashiana* and other works: tiddy-iddity – as if the works one wrote were anything but prentice's experiments. Dear reader, I deceive you with husks, the real works and all the pleasure are still mine and incommunicable. After this break in my work, beginning to return to it, as from light sleep, I wax exclamatory, as you see.

> Sursum Corda:
> Heave ahead:
> Here's luck.
> Art and Blue Heaven,
> April and God's Larks.
> Green reeds and the sky-scattering river.
> A stately music.
> Enter God!

> RLS

Ay, but you know, until a man can write that 'Enter God,' he has made no art! None! Come, let us take counsel together and make some![1]

Stevenson always heightens the pitch of voice and thought when he is writing to Henley.

The realism of which Stevenson warned his friends to beware, the realism of which he was heartily frightened himself, and into which he had once or twice fallen in error, needs a more precise definition than ever he gave it. His remarks on the subject are for the most part negative, with the exception of perhaps a few examples of thing itself. For example: he thought he had trodden in realism by mistake when he wrote the last sentence in 'The Treasure of Franchard':[2] '"Tiens," said Casimir. I thought it was what Casimir would have said and I put it down.' I suppose what he means here is, that it was more harmonious with Casimir than with the whole story. By defining his error as realism, he meant that that sentence

---

[1] "Stevenson. His art: Aetat. 33. To W. E. Henley, Hyères, 1883, June." [*Letters*, II, 124.] This sequence of quotations may imply that Ransome concurs with the traditional notion that every true artist aspires to be possessed by god-like creative power. The mention of God, and a quotation from the Eucharistic Preface 'Lift up your hearts' (*sursum corda*) occurs in a letter to a man considered by some to be 'devilish' and the prototype for the morally ambiguous Long John Silver; it is fascinating that Ransome enjoyed this 'heightened pitch' of thought and chose to quote this in full to enrich his book.

[2] An eight-chapter novella, in *The Merry Men and of Other Tales and Fables* (1887).

was true to ordinary life[1] instead of to 'The Treasure of Franchard'. And so we may use this tentative interpretation as a rushlight[2] in our explanation of what realism in general meant to Stevenson and why he distrusted it.

Writing to Trevor Haddon (who had just got a Slade scholarship) he says:

1. Keep an intelligent eye upon all the others. It is only by doing so that you will come to see what Art is: Art is the end common to them all, it is none of the points by which they differ.

2. In this age beware of realism.

3. In your own art, bow your head over technique. Think of technique when you rise and when you go to bed. Forget purposes in the meanwhile; get to love technical processes; to glory in technical successes; get to see the world entirely through technical spectacles, to see it entirely in terms of what you can do. Then when you have anything to say, the language will be apt and copious. ...

4. Beware of realism; it is the devil; 'tis one of the means of art, and now they make it the end! And such is the farce of the age in which a man lives, that we all, even those of us who most detest it, sin by realism.[3]

There is but one art – to omit! O if I knew how to omit, I would ask no other knowledge. A man who knew how to omit would make an *Iliad* of a daily paper.[4]

And again:

It is not by looking at the sea that you get 'The multitudinous seas incarnadine,' nor by looking at Mont Blanc that you find 'And visited all night by troops of stars.' A kind of ardour of the blood is the mother of all this; and according as this ardour is swayed by knowledge and seconded by craft, the art expression flows clear, and

---

[1] Ransome here prefers the word 'ordinary' to 'real' which he deleted. 'Real life' is a key concept for the novels of his greatness, and includes the life of the imagination – a distinction which Ransome is already making clear.

[2] A primitive form of candle made from steeping the pith of a rush in tallow. In Edwardian England this would already have been an archaic and seldom-met form of cottage-lighting; a deliberately romantic image of flickering weakness. Just such an amount of light does Ransome unassumingly imagine he will cast on the subject.

[3] "*Letters*, II, 125. July 5, 1885."

[4] "*Letters*, II, 147." The *Iliad* is Homer's verse epic. Ironically, Ransome himself has not yet thoroughly 'learnt to omit', as his occasionally winding and florid sentences in this work demonstrate. He was soon forced to learn this art by becoming a newspaper correspondent in Russia. His skill with telegrams is most famously demonstrated in *Swallows and Amazons* (1930), 'Better drowned than duffers if not duffers won't drown'.

significance and charm, like a moon rising, are born above the barren juggle of mere symbols.[1]

Yet again he praises concision.

> If there is anywhere a thing said in two sentences that could have been as clearly and as engagingly and as forcibly said in one, then it's amateur work. Then you will bring me up with old Dumas. Nay, the object of a story is to be long, to fill up hours; the story-teller's art of writing is to water out by continual invention, historical and technical, and yet not seem to water; seem on the other hand to practise that same wit of conspicuous and declaratory condensation which is the proper art of writing. That is one thing in which my stories fail: I am always cutting the flesh off their bones.[2]
>
> 'Or opulent rotunda strike the sky,' said the shopman to himself, in the tone of one considering a verse. 'I suppose it would be too much to say 'orotunda,' and yet how noble it were! Or opulent orotunda strike the sky.' But that is the bitterness of arts; you see a good effect, and some nonsense about sense continually intervenes.'[3]

The shopman was Mr Somerset, newly employed by Prince Florizel in his cigar divan, and his sentiments are Stevenson's own. He had a delightful consciousness of the effect of words as words, or rather of syllables as syllables, regardless of their meanings, and his most difficult battle, although he won it, was in subduing to the needs of sense elaborate and tantalising designs of consecutive sounds. 'Style' meant different things for him at different periods of his life, as we shall presently see, but whatever was its meaning it included always a rhythmical, musical purpose, sound for its own sake, sonorous, reading well, an amber (if I may change to such a metaphor) an amber very nearly if not quite as valuable in his eyes as the carefully collected coleoptera[4] he intended to embed in it.

[1] *"Letters*, II, 147. 1883, to R. A. M. S."* (Stevenson here quotes Shakespeare's *Macbeth* and 'Hymn before Sunrise, in the Vale of Chamouni' by S. T. Coleridge.) "Stevenson. Technique. of Storytelling. [the quotation follows] 'I would rise from the dead to preach.' Refer to remarks on techniques of story-telling in letter to Archer, [*Letters*,] III, 42."

[2] *"Letters*, III, 42. Archer. Saranac, Feb[ruary] 1888."

[3] *More New Arabian Nights: The Dynamiter* (1885) by Robert Louis Stevenson and Fanny Vandergrift Stevenson, 'Epilogue of the Cigar Divan'. The composition of this page can be precisely dated from Ransome's diary to 7 January 1914.

[4] 'Coleoptera' is an order of sheath-winged insects, mostly beetles. As a boy Ransome had been a keen beetle-hunter, and in later life named his own sailing dinghy 'Coch-y-bondhu' after a Welsh beetle, also the name of a trout-fly, and named its fictional counterpart in *The Picts and The Martyrs* (1943) after an ancient Egyptian beetle, 'Scarab'.

And so in Stevenson's books (except perhaps *Treasure Island*, and for a more honourable reason *Weir of Hermiston*) we are conscious of the style as well as of the book. We are conscious of it as a separate, a separately admirable thing. It produces an illusion of being a veil not obscuring the significant object behind it, but itself of great price and not to be duplicated. This illusion, sometimes pleasant, sometimes a little exasperating, I ascribe to the touch of Somerset in Somerset's inventor.

It is not a question merely of marked personality. It was too wilful an illusion for that. It is a question of Stevenson's attitude of mind towards his work, which allowed him in his own view of what he was doing, to separate matter and manner, as few other writers have ever been able so to separate them. Remembering the significant phrase in the paragraph where he describes the novelist's task: 'for so long a time you must keep at command the same quality of style' – we can find a score of other sentences indicative of this preoccupation. He speaks for instance of 'the constipated mosaic manner' he needed for *Weir of Hermiston*, and had adopted successfully in *The Ebb Tide*.[1] Then there were *The New Arabian Nights* and *Otto*, 'pitched pretty high and stilted.'[2] Then the pathetic little episode of Mr Somerset, and again flat, direct statements as in a letter to Henry James in 1893:

> Your jubilation over *Catriona* did me good, and still more the subtlety and truth of your remark on the starving of the visual sense in that book. 'Tis true, and unless I make a greater effort – and am, as a step to that, convinced of its necessity – it will be more true I fear in the future. I *hear* people talking, and I *feel* them acting, and that seems to me to be fiction. My two aims may be described as –
> 1st. War to the adjective.
> 2nd. Death to the optic nerve.
> Admitted we live in the age of the optic nerve in literature. For how many centuries did literature get along without it? However, I'll consider your letter.[3]

And again:

> We begin to see now what an intricate affair is any perfect passage; how many faculties, whether of taste or pure reason, must be held upon the stretch to make it; and why, when it is made, it should afford us so complete a pleasure. From the arrangement of according letters, which is altogether arabesque and sensual, up to the architecture of the elegant and pregnant sentence, which is a vigorous act of the pure

---

[1] *The Ebb Tide: A Trio and Quartette* (1894), by Robert Louis Stevenson in collaboration with Lloyd Osbourne (1894).

[2] See below, p. 121.

[3] "[*Letters*,] IV, 231." The quotation is editorially inserted.

intellect, there is scarce a faculty in man but has been exercised. We need not wonder, then, if perfect sentences are rare, and perfect pages rarer.[1]

In 1878[2] Stevenson had finished *An Inland Voyage*[3] and written *Travels with a Donkey*.[4] In the next year he had his first experience of real travel, voyaging done without too firm a consciousness of the Savile Club at home, without an immediate translation of experience into telling and humorous anecdote. The travelling he did in pursuit of his private romance was touched by realism, whereas the little journeys he had undertaken for fun were at least gilded by the sunset of the Romantic movement – a very different thing. In the two little sentimental journeys,[5] Stevenson pervaded his material: in the journey dictated by a real sentiment he was a dragon fly tossed by a wind of irresistible experiences, blown far from his accustomed reeds, and taking notes while in immediate danger of not finding his way back. In some such way I represent the change in character between *An Inland Voyage* and, for example, *The Amateur Emigrant from the Clyde to Sandy Hook*.[6]

Let me review the circumstances.[7]

'Every book is, in an intimate sense, a circular letter to the friends of him who writes it. They alone take his meaning; they find private messages, assurances of love, and expressions of gratitude, dropped for them in every corner. The public is but a generous patron who defrays the postage.'[8] The first of these sentences from the dedication of *Travels with a Donkey in the Cévennes* is strictly true; except in a few rare cases, and of the books of

---

[1] "Technique of literature. [*Essays in the*] *Art of writing*, 43:".

[2] "*Essays*, II."

[3] Stevenson's lively account of a canoeing holiday in France (1878), in which he paddled the Arethusa, and his friend the Cigarette.

[4] *Travels with a Donkey in the Cévennes* (1879).

[5] The 'sentimental journey' genre of travel writing became very popular in the eighteenth century, imitating Laurence Sterne's *A Sentimental Journey through France and Italy by Mr Yorick* (1768). Stevenson's *Inland Voyage* and *Travels* were very consciously part of this tradition.

[6] *The Amateur Emigrant from the Clyde to Sandy Hook* (1895).

[7] Here he intended to consider Stevenson on "Thoreau. Turajini. Pavilion. The story of a lie – ? in the ship. Planning Prince Otto," but his next running-heading is "Essays". Ransome put a colon after 'circumstances', but did not complete his review.

[8] The dedication takes the form of a letter to Sidney Colvin. The letter continues: 'Yet though the letter is directed to all, we have an old and kindly custom of addressing it on the outside to one. Of what shall a man be proud, if he is not proud of his friends? And so, my dear Sidney Colvin, it is with pride that I sign myself affectionately yours, R. L. S.'

great and isolated men. The third is an ingenious, charming corollary to the second. And the second is not by any means generally true, though it is so of much of Stevenson's own work, and partly explains its peculiar intimate quality. He was thinking of *Otto* when he wrote to Mr Gosse that it was a deadly fault 'to forget that art is a diversion and a decoration, that no triumph or effort is of value, nor anything worth reaching except charm';[1] but the opinion had long been his, and the expression of it is in the manner of writing, dangerously infectious, easily recognisable, that he early developed for himself.

Style is so far a man's personal rhythm, that it is as difficult to analyse as a personality. Its characteristics, its differences from other styles, are like a man's differences from other men. Yet something we can seize, in his choice of words, is the tone in which he uses them: and a vocabulary does not make so utterly flexible a vehicle of thought that a writer is not to be known by the repetition of particular effects varied only in detail, and as it were midway between perfect expression and a private convention of his own. He thinks in these effects, but they are approximations stamped with a trademark; he moulds a bust with them, but they do not precisely follow the curves and hollows that they represent. Dr Johnson always spoke in thunder but sometimes his thunder was a loud and roaring imitation of some smaller noise. Bottom[2] will roar you like the lion, or as gently as a sucking-dove, but the roar is always Bottom's and lion or sucking-dove must be attributed by courtesy to his wild wood-notes.[3] In so far, every artist is another Bottom, another Johnson where little fishes talk like whales,[4] or, commoner case, when whales converse like little fishes. The wise know the gamut of their own voices and are careful not to stretch them to points where courtesy breaks down and the illusion passes.

This is very unsatisfactory, but it is illustrated with particular clarity by Stevenson's early books.

---

[1] "*Letters*, II, 177." 'Mr Gosse': later Sir Edmund Gosse (1849–1928), literary critic, art critic, and author of the autobiographical *Father and Son* (1907) and *The Life of Philip Henry Gosse* (1890), a work that held resonance both for Stevenson and Ransome.

[2] The rustic actor in Shakespeare's *A Midsummer Night's Dream*, II. i., 'Let me play the lion too. I will roar ... but I will aggravate my voice so I will roar you as gently as any sucking-dove; I will roar you as 'twere any nightingale.'

[3] An allusion to John Milton, 'L'Allegro', '... or sweetest Shakespeare, fancy's child, Warble his native wood-notes wild'.

[4] The playwright and poet Oliver Goldsmith is recorded by Boswell as having said to Dr Johnson, 'If you were to make little fishes talk, they would talk like whales.'

Charm is the power of impressing on the minds of your hearers a loveable picture of yourself, and, in describing your experiences to make them share a pleasurable participation. It is, however, achieved in many indirect ways. It is to participate pleasurably in prodding a donkey with a pinpointed stick over unknown boulders in the pitch dark. But the reader is not called upon so to do; he is only asked to sympathize with a philosophic mood of reminiscence in which such adventures, most obnoxious at the time, are playthings with just that quality of safe danger that a pair of scissors in a cork or a closed box of matches has for an imaginative child. It is never merely delightful to walk in wet clothes: but few things are more pleasant than the warm caress of approval and fearful admiration that the dry man sitting besides a fire gives to that uncomfortable memory of himself.

Here I think we are near the scent of at least one kind of literary charm. It depends not on the description of circumstances pleasurable in themselves, but on tenderness exhibited by the writer for his subject, on the infectious quality of a mood in which a man looks affectionately upon the past. Examples are not difficult to find. The title of one of Daudet's books betrays this purpose: *Le Petit Chose*,[1] the little thing, applied to an early edition of the long-haired married man then writing of himself. And in *Lettres de mon Moulin*,[2] there are many specimens of mutual caresses bestowed upon the past. I am without the book;[3] but I remember particularly the chapter in which Daudet remembers himself sitting in the cottage of two old people, and pretending for their sakes to like some cherry brandy from which some essential ingredient was missing. Nor need it always be self-reminiscence: at the end of that same story[4] of Daudet's the old woman begs the old man, who sees his visitor some hundred yards upon his way, not to be out too late, and he makes a whimsical reply 'quite like a grown up man'[5] instead of a weak, white-haired, baby. Stevenson does all that Daudet does and more. He trusts his reader not to laugh at his weaknesses: he describes himself lovingly beneath the stars: he overflows with

[1] Alphonse Daudet, *Le Petit Chose* (1868); the 'little thing' of the title refers to paternal weakness.

[2] Daudet, *Lettres de mon moulin* (1869), 'letters from my windmill,' a collection of short stories.

[3] This section may have been written in Russia.

[4] The story is the twelfth, 'Les Vieux' (the old folk). Ransome's recollection of the story is not accurate in detail.

[5] 'Quite like a grown-up man' is not an exact quotation, but Ransome's paraphrase of Daudet is true to the final emotion: the old man's 'petit air malin', his rascally youthful bravado in suggesting he might be out late, walking arm-in-arm 'like a man' with the narrator, and his wife's final rueful 'My poor husband! At least he's still walking', as she gazes after him.

affection for the stout lay brother who carried him home in both his arms: he greatly dares and describes himself hitting his unresisting donkey over the head, no pleasant picture in real life, and yet softened by a pity less for the donkey than at his defection from himself: he even throws the mood of gentle personal reminiscence over the echoes of the fierce and bloody fighting of the Camisards[1] where men were burnt, and hundreds of villages made desert places, two hundred years ago.

And within this governing mood of tender memory, subservient to it, dictated by it, are a continuous series of small fancies, only to be stolen from serious thought in such light-hearted moments as it is a pleasure to share. Of them are his recognition in the donkey he was belabouring of 'a faint resemblance to a lady of my acquaintance who formerly loaded me with kindness; and this increased the horror of my cruelty': the flight of the inland voyagers from competition with the champion canoeist, 'this infernal paddler':[2] the unsuccessful stove 'voyaged like a gentleman in the locker of the *Cigarette*.'[3]

And then there are point blank discharges of charm at the head of the reader. These I do not like so well. You can see the charmer loading his cannon, training it to hit you between the eyes, firing, and expectantly looking to see the destruction he has wrought. I will give two examples. The first is the payment for lodging under the stars by leaving money by the side of the road: not only wilful but thoroughly false, since, if he were paying God for his hospitality he would never have done, and Stevenson adjudged a certain amount and no more. The second is the last paragraph of the book: on the sale of the Modestine, the donkey:

> Father Adam wept when he sold her to me; after I had sold her in my turn, I was tempted to follow his example; and being alone with a stage-driver and four or five agreeable young men, I did not hesitate to yield to my emotion.

Now that is pure *feu d'artifice*,[4] with materials borrowed from Sterne,[5] betrayed by the phrase 'agreeable young men'. We have time to watch

---

[1] Militants in the Cévennes and Southern France who resisted the persecution of Protestantism by Louis XIV (1638–1715).

[2] Stevenson and his friend had fled from 'the champion canoeist of Europe'.

[3] In *An Inland Voyage,* a stove called an Etna failed to cook an egg.

[4] Fireworks. In a later note, Ransome approved Stevenson's ability to "smile at his own mannerisms [he crossed out the word 'artifice'] of style. When Mrs Strong said to him 'At least you have no mannerisms,' he took the book out of my hand and read 'It was a wonderful clear night of stars.' 'Oh,' he said, 'how many many times I have written "a wonderful clear night of stars."' *Memories of Vailima*, p. 10."

[5] Laurence Sterne (1713–68).

its preparation, and, since it is the last paragraph of the book, time to be amazed at its effect.

Most of my examples have been taken from *Travels with a Donkey*, but they could be paralleled without difficulty from *An Inland Voyage*, the earlier book. I am not sure which is the pleasanter of the two. Both have their defects that follow on the too resolute, the too industrious pursuit of charm; but both are actually charming, idle little books full of a sort of philosophy that is sometimes very welcome; both are tributes to the romance of life, written by a young man in love, and in love also with himself, with the world, and with a wisdom which has not yet been paid for in sad experience, but as it were bought on credit and not the worse for that. The gentle, cheerful insistence on death, on the pleasures of chance meetings, of handkerchiefs waved by persons one has known for two minutes or not at all and will never see again; the combination of romance and sanity makes these books among the friendliest that Stevenson wrote. 'The most beautiful adventures are not those we go to seek,'[1] and the purposeful cannonades of charm fade into silence and are forgotten as we read the half-serious half-smiling theorising which Stevenson had not to seek but found in the legacy from his Scottish ancestry which he softened and sweetened before he passed it on.

Edinburgh, originally a series of short essays published in *The Portfolio*[2] and called *Picturesque Notes* is, like the other ten little earlier books, an exercise in style. The manner was everything: Edinburgh itself was less important in Stevenson's mind than the even mellifluous harmony of sentences for which it was the ostensible excuse. ''Tis a kind of book nobody would ever care to read; but none of the young men could have done it better than I have, which is always a consolation.'[3] For all that, in spite of the many little hints that it is a tour de force, and an admirable piece of juggling, it is a delightful miniature, and does indeed convey between its smooth Italianate sentences much of the Gothic air of that pinnacled grey northern town, with the crags above it, the blue hills at the end of each long street, and the continual memory of old events, all of which have a kind of dry robustness, quite different from the histories of other towns.

'Day by day,' says Stevenson, 'when we are put down in some unsightly neighbourhood ... we perfect ourselves in the art of seeing nature

---

[1] *An Inland Voyage*, chapter 23.

[2] "Edinburgh 1878". *Edinburgh: Picturesque Notes* (1879) was first published in the artistic periodical *The Portfolio.* The book was used by Ransome's mother, sisters and brother as a handbook to Edinburgh when they settled there while his brother Geoffrey began to learn the printing business. Arthur gave his mother's address on his daughter's birth certificate (May 1910), and he, Ivy and their baby spent six weeks there after the birth.

[3] "Letters, I, 227."

favourably.'[1] 'As for Wick itself, it is one of the meanest of man's towns, and situate certainly on the baldest of God's bays.' Here Stevenson uses a deliberate but lively cleverness or smartness, 'man's towns', 'God's bays', and the 'certainly' is put in carefully to lessen the prepared impromptu effect of that antithesis, to colour the memory of the baldness and meanness of the place.[2] Most of his essays are a kind of practice in this art. 'I regard them,' he says, 'as contributions towards a friendlier and more thoughtful way of looking about one,'[3] and indeed one of their qualities, and one which accounts for much of the fervour with which their lovers love them, is a benignance so confidently attributed to this world that, for those who have just risen from *Essays of Travel* for example, this would seem entirely smiling and benign. Here may be a touch of Hazlitt, as when the countryman bewildered in a town remarks 'there seems to be a deal of meeting hereabouts.'[4] Here may a hint of the firm jawed manner of Borrow:[5] 'While she was telling all this in the most matter-of-fact way, I had been noticing the approach of a tall man, with a high white hat and darkish clothes. He came up the hill at a rapid pace, and joined our little group with a sort of half-salutation.'[6] So do strangers appear in *Wild Wales*. But Borrow, or Hazlitt, or their ghosts manipulated by Stevenson, or Stevenson himself, are all sweetened, become tolerant, kindly, smiling men who bring the world into tune with their own cheerful hearts.

The persons they meet are kindlier than those we meet in sullener works. The coarse language of the lacewomen of Monastier[7] becomes a social grace. The officious hatmaker of Cockermouth turns into a benevolent maker of memories for other people.

---

[1] *Essays of Travel* (1905), the quotation slightly rearranged from chapter 14, 'On the enjoyment of unpleasant places': 'For when we are put down in some unsightly neighbourhood, and especially if we have come to be more or less dependent on what we see, we must set ourselves to hunt out beautiful things with all the ardour and patience of a botanist after a rye plant. Day by day we perfect ourselves in the art of seeing nature more favourably.'

[2] This sentence is editorially put together from a working page headed "*Prose examples of Stevenson's style*;" but the example quoted (from chapter 6 of *Across the Plains*) is the only one listed.

[3] "To Colvin. Summer, 1874. *Letters*, I, 149."

[4] "Roads. 1873" Stevenson's actual words were 'a great deal of meeting ...' (*Essays of Travel*, chapter 13.)

[5] George Henry Borrow (1803–81), novelist, travel writer, linguist, author of *Wild Wales, Lavengro, The Romany Rye, The Bible in Spain*; subject of a biography (1912) by Ransome's friend the poet and essayist Edward Thomas.

[6] *Essays of Travel*, chapter 2, 'Cockermouth and Keswick'.

[7] The place from which Stevenson set out on his travels with a donkey.

He began by saying that he had little things in his past life that it gave him especial pleasure to recall; and that the faculty of receiving such sharp impressions had now died out in himself, but must at my age be still quite lively and active. Then he told me that he had a little raft afloat on the river above the dam which he was going to lend me, in order that I might be able to look back, in after years, upon having done so, and get great pleasure from the recollection.[1]

It is not reality and yet – perhaps it is reality after all.

One of the best of the essays of travel is called 'An Autumn Effect.'[2] It is rich with sketches of persons, of scenery, and of philosophical digression, all gleaned upon a three day walking tour. It amused me to take the map and learn that the total distance covered did not exceed twenty-four miles of which the last six were conquered in a dog cart. This is not Hazlitt's 'thirty, forty miles along the Great North Road,'[3] but something much nearer the gentlemanly dalliance of Sterne with his calèche.[4]

In this essay ('An Autumn Effect') it is amusing to see that Stevenson anticipates Wilde by more than ten years in saying that nature imitates art.[5] It is worthwhile to give the quotation:

The whole scene had an indefinable look of being painted, the colour was so abstract and correct, and there was something so sketchy and merely impressional about these distant single trees on the horizon that one was forced to think of it all as of a clever French landscape. For it is rather in nature that we see resemblance to art, than in art to nature; and we say a hundred times, 'How like a picture!' for once that we say, 'How like the truth!' The forms in which we learn to think of landscape are forms that we have got from painted canvas.

How different from Wilde's is his comment: 'Any man can see and understand a picture; it is reserved for the few to separate anything out of the confusion of nature, and see that distinctly and with intelligence.'[6]

---

[1] *Essays of Travel*, chapter 2.

[2] Ibid.

[3] Hazlitt's energetic genius was widely recognized, but, as Coleridge said, 'he delivers himself of almost all his conceptions with a forceps'.

[4] Laurence Sterne, *A Sentimental Journey* (1768). A 'calèche' or in English usually 'calash' was a light two-wheeled horse-drawn vehicle with a folding hood.

[5] Ransome seems to have written these pages soon after finishing his book on Oscar Wilde (1912). Wilde gives the propositions 'that she [nature] imitates art, I don't think even her worst enemy would deny', and 'Life imitates Art far more than Art imitates Life', in 'The Decay of Lying', in *Intentions, The Critic as Artist* (1891).

[6] *Essays of Travel*, chapter 3, 'An Autumn Effect'.

And in reading that, and comparing it with Wilde, it is worthwhile also to remember that they had both read Musset's *Fantasio*, with his 'Comme ce soleil couchant est manqué ce soir!'[1]

We may illustrate his romantic attitude to art from his opinion of *The Silverado Squatters*,[2] as he wrote to Low: 'I have never at command that press of spirits that are necessary to strike out a thing red-hot. Silverado is an example of stuff worried and pawed about, God knows how often, in poor health, and you can see for yourself the result: good pages, an imperfect fusion, a certain languor of the whole. Not, in short, art;'[3] and again, by comparing the familiarity and charm of his carefully crafted book *An Inland Voyage*, with the straightforward utterance of a letter written on the voyage itself, to Balfour:

> We have had deplorable weather quite steady ever since the start; not one day without heavy showers; and generally much wind and cold wind forby … I must say it has sometimes required a stout heart; and sometimes one could not help sympathising inwardly with the French folk who hold up their hands in astonishment over our pleasure journey. Indeed I do not know how I would have stuck to it as I have done, if it had not been for professional purposes.[4]

A friend of mine who had read little of Stevenson[5] and had not liked what he read, explained his dislike by saying that 'Stevenson was a great deal too familiar.' He went on to remark that he did not like an author to pat him on the shoulder or to be too sure of his sympathy. This qualification of his made me enquire whether he was sure that Stevenson's familiarity was with his reader or with his subject.[6] He replied, 'I felt he presumed a great deal on my slight acquaintance; I have only read one or two of his books, but in both he seemed to trust me as if I had not only read them all, but admired them very much.' There: it seemed to me that he was in error, translating to his own person a familiarity that Stevenson certainly

---

[1] 'What a failure the setting sun is this evening!' Alfred de Musset (1810–57), poet and playwright; *Fantasio* (1834).

[2] *The Silverado Squatters* (1883) is a memoir of his honeymoon trip in the Napa Valley, California. The paragraph is editorially pieced together.

[3] "*Letters*, II, 151."

[4] "Illustrate romantic attitude by comparison of book *Inland Voyage* with letter p. 103 Balfour." The quotation from Balfour is inserted editorially; it continues: 'for an easy book might be written and sold, with mighty little brains about it, where the journey is of a certain seriousness and can be named. I mean, a book about a journey from York to London must be clever; a book about the Caucasus may be what you will.'

[5] We do not know who this friend was. The section is headed "Early Criticism", followed by a check-list.

[6] Ransome is ahead of his time in being so much aware of intertextuality.

shows in his dealings with his imaginary characters. It is true, we are sometimes, if critically minded, led to ask whether Stevenson is not a little too
sure of his knowledge of his men; if he does not a little presume on being
'an observer of human nature,'[1] and if the effect of smallness sometimes
produced by his characterization is not due to a certainty in the author's
mind that he sees all round his characters. There is an air of patronage, of
smiling toleration which, with an unconscious compliment to Stevenson,
we resent on behalf of David Balfour, even on behalf of Mr Utterson.[2] The
impression on the mere reader is that of being beckoned up into a church
tower to look down on the amusing revolutions of men as small as ants. He
is tempted to reply rather rudely that the observer is an ant himself, or to
be annoyed at the condescension with which he has been picked out from
among the antlike multitude to look at the movements of his kind. Nor is it
as if Stevenson worked on a big canvas, chronicling crowds: he concentrates
himself on the adventures of a single ant, with whom he might just as well
be standing face to face. I think my friend, a man of sober dignity, resented
in his own person the indignity offered by Stevenson to his characters.
However that may be, he set his finger on the most noticeable quality in
Stevenson's critical essays, a quality indicated quite unconsciously, or with
a misplaced pride, in their title; *Familiar Studies of Men and Books*.[3] It is
nothing to the point that he had not read them.

Familiarity, of the kind that I have tried to describe, is the key-note of
all these essays, written between his twenty fourth and thirtieth year. Less
noticeable in 'Victor Hugo', which was Stevenson's first adventure in the
kind written before Leslie Stephen's congratulations and publication in the
Cornhill[4] had given him too much confidence,[5] it is clear in the 'Burns' in
spite of occasional phrases like 'a burly figure in literature';[6] clearer in the
'Pepys':[7] Stevenson's finished style would be unbearable on such a book, as

---

[1] cf. 'Woe is me that I may not give some specimens – some of their foresights
of life, or deep inquiries into the rudiments of man and nature, these were
so fiery and so innocent, they were so richly silly, so romantically young.'
(*Across the Plains*, chapter 7).

[2] David Balfour is the hero of *Kidnapped* (1886); Mr Utterson the investigating
lawyer in *The Strange Case of Dr Jekyll and Mr Hyde* (1885).

[3] (1882).

[4] *Cornhill Magazine*, a literary periodical, 1860–1975.

[5] Sir Leslie Stephen (1832–1904), historian of the history of ideas and first
editor of the *Dictionary of National Biography*; father of Virginia Woolf.

[6] From 'Aspects of Robert Burns', included in *Familiar Studies of Men and
Books*.

[7] 'Samuel Pepys', a chapter in *Familiar Studies*. Elsewhere Ransome quotes
Stevenson on Pepys: "Though the manner of his utterance may be childishly
awkward, the matter has been transformed and assimilated by his unfeigned
interest and delight. *Familiar Studies*, 218."

Pepys's. We should want to tear it aside; it would suggest a too serious, and a less pleasurable, intensity of contemplation: it would not be written 'to his own address'. His style is annoying now and then in the admirable 'Villon,'[1] in the too much simplified 'Thoreau'; frightened out of sight almost by the big shouting 'Whitman'; and it spoils the 'Charles d'Orléans' which came so near to being charming.[2] This familiarity is not shown by any patronage of[3] his subjects on the score of literature, but by an assumption of too sure an understanding of their moral difficulties. Perhaps it seemed to Stevenson that his own severe trials of conscience, his own debates over this or that ethical question, his own naïf preoccupation with any action of his own that he considered good (see several of his letters to Mrs Sitwell), had made him something of a doctor in the art of righteousness. Perhaps it was that recognising in each man some phase through which he had himself passed, he was a little too ready to adopt with regard to the whole character, the attitude of personal experience which he could not unjustly assume with regard to the part.

After having said so much, we must turn to the 'Preface by way of Criticism', which he wrote when these short essays in criticism were united in a book.[4] 'One and all,' he says, 'were written with genuine interest in the subject: many, however, have been conceived and finished with imperfect knowledge; and all have lain, from beginning to end, under the disadvantages inherent in their style of writing.' Some of the disadvantages he enumerates explain, if not the familiarity, at least its consistent reappearance in one study after another. He points out that the writer of short studies must 'view his subject throughout in a peculiar illumination', presenting it from one side only, and that as he points out in the essay on Burns, must be chosen by reason of some personal relationship.

Stevenson presents in his critical essays the same phenomenon that is noticeable in his novels. He is a romantic in temperament with respect for a closer technique than the earlier romantics employed, and a willingness to use the details in calm, even prose instead of carrying them on a wave of rhetoric. He is very seldom grandiloquent: on the other hand he is very seldom a mere communicator, and he does not, like

---

[1] He crosses out 'almost revolting' here.

[2] Of this essay, Ransome elsewhere notes "his bringing in the rondel, and ballade writing of Fontainebleau, admiration for Banville [Théodore de Banville (1823–91), French Parnassian poet], again as in Burns knack of portraiture, a little thin, a little too sure of its own comprehensiveness, 'my good copy in pen and ink of an illumination in a fine copy of the Poems given by Henry VII to Elizabeth of York', his word for 'some of our quaintly vicious contemporaries'."

[3] i.e. 'condescension towards'

[4] i.e. in *Familiar Studies*.

Sainte-Beuve,[1] get out of the way of his sitters. His attitude is creative: he wishes his critical essay to be a work of art, and his tendency is to make it the character sketch of the hero of an unwritten novel. He is only tempted away from this main purpose by his interest in technique. There are remarks in the 'Hugo', in the 'Burns', indeed in most of those papers which I shall hope to use later in this book, when I come to consider Stevenson's not unimportant contribution to the knowledge of literary technique.[2] The main purpose is almost certainly romantic portraiture, and these remarks are not an end in themselves but are worked into the background of the picture, if indeed they are not more justly to be considered as part of the preparation of the canvas.

Stevenson's manner is altogether unlike the gay paradox of Wilde. It is earnest, sober, almost professional. When Wilde, impatient of lumbering explanation, says with a smile that 'Nature imitates art', Stevenson, more serious, younger, solemnly shows that 'those predilections of the artist he knows not why, those irrational acceptations and recognitions, reclaim, out of the world that we have not yet realised, ever another and another corner.' It is only by putting two and two together, that we can learn not indeed what was Stevenson's view of art, but in what direction his opinions on that subject tended. Beside that sentence, for example, we have to set this from a later passage in the same essay:

> Art, thus conceived (as by Victor Hugo), realises for men a larger portion of life, and that portion one that it is more difficult for them to realise unaided; and, besides helping them to feel more intensely those restricted personal interests which are patent to all, it awakes in them some consciousness of those more general relations that are so strangely invisible to the average man in ordinary moods.[3]

And before we have time to guess that he is approaching in his own mind a statement of the aim of art being an intensified consciousness of life, he goes hurriedly on to obscure his point with stuff about man realising 'the responsibilities of his place in society.'

He says of his essay on Hugo that he was perhaps dazzled by that 'master of wordmanship', but 'it is best to dwell on merits, for it is these that are

---

[1] Charles Sainte-Beuve (1804–69), influential literary critic, associated with Victor Hugo.

[2] A subject which Ransome had been passionately debating with Lascelles Abercrombie. He was currently planning a book to be called 'The Nature of Technique'. These passages are perhaps intended as a preamble to it.

[3] *Familiar Studies,* chapter 1, 'Victor Hugo's Romances': 'And it is in this way that art is the pioneer of knowledge; those predilections of the artist he knows not why, those irrational acceptations and recognitions, reclaim, out of the world that we have not yet realised, ever another and another corner.'

most often overlooked'. Yet, summing up the book, Hugo and Pepys apart, he says:

> I have found myself ever too grudging of praise, ever too disrespectful in manner ... these were all men whom, for one reason or another, I loved; or when I did not love the men, my love was the greater to their books. I had read them and lived with them; for months they were continually in my thoughts; I seemed to rejoice in their joys and to sorrow with them in their griefs; and behold, when I came to write of them, my tone was sometimes hardly courteous and seldom wholly just.[1]

He wonders why. Are there, perhaps, two reasons. The first, that tendency to familiarity first noticed, noticeable even in the terms of his apology; and the second stranger, more humiliating, known however to everyone who has essayed with zealous care the difficult business of criticism; did he read his books so well that he saw them with their blemishes? Did his lively interest in technique show him the way to dissatisfaction with what he could not himself have equalled? It requires a mind with great momentum, greater perhaps than he possessed, to pass, as Swinburne[2] used to pass, beyond the doubtings of intimate knowledge, to the recovery of his first enthusiasm.

'The readings of a literary vagrant'[3] acquire a serious, critical, biographical significance when the vagrant is himself so versatile a writer as Stevenson. If we add to the familiar studies, one or two later essays, the 'Gossip on Romance', the cheerful dissertation on *The Vicomte de Bragelonne*, we get a fairly sound idea of the cosmopolitan literary background[4] that Stevenson found for his own work. The Covenanters, of course, are absent, but he read them early, and only on re-reading late in life did he discover that he owed them anything. But Knox[5] is there, and Burns and Scott, Victor Hugo who began the movement from Scott that, for the moment at any rate may be said to have ended in Stevenson. Lothian Road, and the hot gazes and tepid sentiment of youth give him a lead through Burns' love affairs. His delight in his own life as a pictorial, dramatic affair gives him an insight into Pepys, and Fontainebleau and the making of valueless but exciting little imitations of old French rondeaux and ballades

---

[1] Ibid., Preface.

[2] Algernon Charles Swinburne (1837–1909), Victorian romantic poet and critic with a reputation for decadence.

[3] Ibid, Preface.

[4] A background which Ransome too had by this time made thoroughly his own.

[5] John Knox (1510–72), theologian, leader of the Protestant reformation in Scotland.

give him at least a reflection of one side of the experience of Charles d'Orléans.

And there is much in the essays themselves that must have suggested to contemporary observers that here was a man not wholly absorbed in criticism. As he goes on, his criticism concerns itself more and more with literature *qua*[1] literature; a good example of this is his summing up of *Cashel Byron's Profession*, Shaw's fourth novel (1882); some of his words were used positively to help sell the book, but on the whole he is disparaging, calling one part 'blooming gaseous folly'. It was a very long time before Shaw found his true métier as a dramatist. Stevenson too was long in finding his true vein as a novelist.

On a very large scale Merezhkovsky[2] has shown how it is possible to write magnificent critical romances[3] in which a period of thought, the Renaissance, the times of Julian the Apostate in Italy, of Peter the Great in Russia, is flowing into vivid drama. On a very much smaller scale Stevenson attempted the same thing, when he took his own suggestion from his essay on Villon and wrote 'A Lodging for the Night',[4] which is, I think, the better criticism of the two. The essay on Charles d'Orléans is very much less concerned with an inadequate criticism of his powers than with just such picturesque anecdote of the time, as a novelist would choose to furnish an historical romance. Nothing could be better for such a purpose than the paragraph on tapestry; nothing could better betray the storyteller than the paragraph on the widow of Louis of Orléans. 'Yoshida Torajiro' is a miniature biography, and no one has been able to read 'Burns', unless perhaps

---

[1] *'qua'* (L) = 'as'. The paragraph is editorially reconstructed.

[2] Dmitri Sergeyevich Merezhkovsky (1865–1941), influential and wide-ranging Russian critic, symbolist poet and novelist exiled from St Petersburg to Paris (1905–7) and again after 1918, author of critical works on Dante, Tolstoy, Dostoevsky, Chekhov, Gogol, and Lermontov and of a trilogy of historical novels that were European best-sellers in their day. In exile he wrote an attack on Bolshevism, *The Kingdom of Antichrist* (1922). Ransome might have met him in Paris; they once discussed a possible Russian translation of *Oscar Wilde*. His thought, promoted through the 'Religious-Philosophical Society' he founded in 1903, has affinities with Yeats and Stevenson's work, and perhaps influenced Ransome's *The Elixir of Life* (1915).

[3] "Let me take this opportunity of directing attention to an English writer with somewhat similar aims, who has written one excellent fantasy of ideas and another on a less strenuous level but also extremely interesting: J. A. Revermort, author of *Cuthbert Learmont* and ..." 'J. A. Revermort' was the pseudonym of John Adam Cramb (1862–1913). *Cuthbert Learmont* was published in 1910. The second book in Ransome's mind (the title of which he could not remember) may have been Revermort's *Lucius Scarfield: A Philosophical Romance of the Twentieth Century* (1908).

[4] 'A Lodging For The Night: A Story of François Villon', in *New Arabian Nights*.

an indignant moralist, and remember that he was not reading a story.[1] Of another writer he wrote when he was thirty-three: 'Let him beware of vanity, and he will go higher; let him be still discontented, and let him (if it might be) see the merits and not the faults of his rivals, and he may swarm at last to the top-gallant. There is no other way. Admiration is the only road to excellence; and the critical spirit kills, but envy and injustice are putrefaction on its feet.'[2]

Stevenson began his novel-writing late and with difficulty. He notices, for instance, how few novels are written with an intention that he can recognise as artistic: 'the purely critical spirit is, in most novels, paramount.'[3] He turns gratefully to Hawthorne.[4] In Victor Hugo, he distinguishes well between the romantic novel and the novel of Fielding,[5] in which there is nothing but a stage background, and the novelist thinks like the dramatist and does not perceive how much he can do with his more flexible medium.

> As for landscape, he (Fielding) was content to underline stage directions, as it might be done in a play-book: Tom and Molly retire into a practicable wood. As for nationality and public sentiment, it is curious enough to think that *Tom Jones* is laid in the year forty-five, and that the only use he makes of the rebellion is to throw a troop of soldiers into his hero's way.[6]

In Scott the personality of a man 'is no longer thrown out in unnatural isolation, but is resumed into its place in the constitution of things.' Stevenson notices that Hugo's advance on Scott is an advance in self-consciousness, that is to say, in the direction of himself.

On Scott, Stevenson is more than most authors obliging to his critics, in giving them examples out of his own mouth for his own conviction or better definition. When we notice a quality in his stories we have but to look in his essays to find that quality the subject of special illustration. We have noticed that with more than a mere memory of the Romantic attitude he had nothing of the free carelessness of technique with which the

---

[1] Ransome additionally notes of this essay: "a portrait of a man in *actions;* a study of the professional Don Juan, showing a considerable knowledge of wayside love, and a keen understanding of its psychology as exemplified by Burns, due partly to impatience with the inadequate, blind sketch by Principal Shairp ..." (i.e. John Campbell Shairp's 1879 biography of Burns).

[2] "Stevenson. Critic. To W. E. Henley. *Letters*, II, 123." Stevenson was referring to Henley's brother Edward's efforts as an actor, rather than writer.

[3] *Familiar Studies*, 'Victor Hugo's Romances'.

[4] Nathaniel Hawthorne (1804–64), American novelist and short-story writer.

[5] Henry Fielding (1707–54), English novelist and dramatist, author of *The History of Tom Jones, a Foundling* (1749).

[6] *Familiar Studies*, chapter 1.

Romantics set that attitude on paper. We have but to look at his 'Gossip on Romance'[1] to find a delightful example of his admiration of the one, his craftsman's pain in contemplating the other. He is writing of *Guy Mannering*.[2] 'The scene,' he says, 'when Harry Bertram lands at Ellangowan is a model instance of romantic method':

> 'I remember the tune well,' he says, 'though I cannot guess what should at present so strongly recall it to my memory.' He took his flageolet from his pocket and played a simple melody. Apparently the tune awoke the corresponding associations of a damsel. ... She imme-diately took up the song –
>
> > Are these the links of Forth, she said;
> > Or are they the crooks of Dee,
> > Or the bonny woods of Warroch Head
> > That I so fain would see?
>
> 'By heaven!' said Bertram, 'it is the very ballad.'

For Stevenson, 'this famous touch of the flageolet and the old song' strikes one of the four strong notes that sound in the mind when the book is laid aside. But, even while exulting in it, he has had to cut away a little of the matter: 'Well,' he says, here is how it runs in the original: 'A damsel, who, close behind a fine spring about half-way down the descent, and which had once supplied the castle with water, was engaged in bleaching linen.' A man who gave in such copy would be discharged from the staff of a daily paper. Scott has forgotten to prepare the reader for the presence of the 'damsel'; he has forgotten to mention the spring and its relation to the ruin; and now, face to face with his omission, instead of trying back and starting fair, crams all this matter, tail foremost, into a single shambling sentence. It is not merely bad English, or bad style; it is abominably bad narrative besides.

And his final summing up of Scott still further emphasises his own position. Scott he says, 'conjured up the romantic with delight, but he had hardly patience to describe it. He was a great day-dreamer, a seer of fit and beautiful and humorous visions, but hardly a great artist; hardly, in the manful sense, an artist at all. He pleased himself, and so he pleases us. Of the pleasures of his art he tasted fully; but of its toils and vigils and distresses never man knew less. A great romantic – an idle child.'[3] This, precisely, is the difference between Stevenson and the generation of Dumas and Scott. For them there was not yet much question of being artists 'in the

---

[1] (1882), in *Memories and Portraits* (1887), chapter 15, 'A gossip On Romance'.

[2] *Guy Mannering, or The Astrologer* (1815), an historical novel by Sir Walter Scott; chapter 41.

[3] *Memories and Portraits*.

manful sense.' Narrative for them was a flexible, compressible, expansible medium, like soft indiarubber. Gautier, while chiseling his cameos, saw and sang that

> L'art sort plus belle
> D'une forme rebelle ...[1]

And the artists of the latter half of the nineteenth century, with a highly developed critical faculty, made prose a difficult medium, and set themselves to a sturdier labour than ever Scott had imagined, a smaller output, but bought by just these toils and vigils of which he knew nothing whatever.

He gets at Pepys by remembering his own habit of making notes of the circumstances of his reading, garden, cockcrow or other detail, to be recalled in later years. He remembers the planned pleasure of building memories, and constructs a credible Pepys out of the reminiscence. 'The whole book' (the diary) 'if you will but look at it in that way, is seen to be a work of art to Pepys's own address.' And he proceeds to show how much that is puzzling is explicable on this hypothesis. 'Now when the artist has found something, word or deed, exactly proper to a favourite character in play or novel, he will neither suppress nor diminish it, though the remark be silly or the act mean.'[2]

We may applaud his attitude towards realism.[3] He complains of Hugo: 'We cannot forgive in him what we might have passed over in a third-rate sensation novelist. Little as he seems to know of the sea and nautical affairs, he must have known very well that vessels do not go down as he makes the *Ourque* go down; he must have known that such a liberty with fact was *against the laws of the game*, and incompatible with all *appearance of sincerity in conception or workmanship*.' In replying to Henley about *Treasure Island* he says again: 'I make these paper people to please Skelt, myself, and God Almighty:' and construct a statement of '*the laws of the game*'.[4]

---

[1] 'Art comes forth more beautifully from a rebellious mould': a slightly inaccurate quotation of Théophile Gautier, *Émaux et Camées* (Enamels and Cameos), 'L'Art'.

[2] *Familiar Studies*, chapter 8.

[3] The sentence is expanded from "Attitude to realism".

[4] "*F[amiliar] S[tudies]*, 19," and "cf. his reply to Henley on *T[reasure] I[sland]*," i.e. 'I make these paper people to please myself, and Skelt, ...' *Letters*, II, 152. The italics here are Ransome's, intensified by a double wavy underlining. He is already on a journey of artistic self-discovery, his own realism perhaps only completely secure by the time of *Winter Holiday* (1933). He habitually called his own fatherly mentor, W. G. Collingwood, 'the Skald' ('poet' in Norse); here he had wrongly placed 'Skelt' before 'myself' in his transcription. Stevenson tells us in *Memories and Portraits* (chapter 13) that he was

It requires little courage to say that Stevenson is a very much greater storyteller[1] than novelist, and even less to say that his short stories are better than his longer tales. He confessed again and again to shortness of breath, and, in an amusing passage, expressed his wonder at the man who could both begin and finish a novel: a thing he was himself incapable of doing. *The Master of Ballantrae*[2] changes key at the end; *Catriona*,[3] *Kidnapped*,[4] are spread too thin. He died too soon to finish *St Ives*[5] or *Weir of Hermiston*.[6] And the wonderful *Ebb Tide*[7] is a long short story, and in no sense a novel. *Treasure Island*[8] alone is without blemish or error in construction. And it is not a novel,[9] though Stevenson called it a novel in his essay on 'My First Book,'[10] when he says: 'although I had attempted the thing with vigour not less than ten or twelve times, I had not yet written a novel. All – all my pretty ones – had gone for a little, and then stopped inexorably like a schoolboy's watch.' And:

> It is the length that kills. ... For so long a time, the slant is to continue unchanged, the vein to keep running, for so long a time you must keep at command the same quality of style: for so long a time your puppets are to be always vital, always consistent, always vigorous! I remember I used to look, in those days, upon every three-volume novel with a sort of veneration, as a feat – not possibly of literature – but at least of physical and moral endurance and the courage of Ajax.[11]

And indeed length, with him, was always a willed thing, like the conquest of a dragon. The pity is that it was the unnecessary conquest of a dragon who for other people is merely a comfortable ambling palfrey.[12]

'a true child of Skelt' in having been absorbed as a boy in Martin Skelt's toy theatres and their world of drama and romance.

[1] The paragraph is headed "Short Stories".

[2] (1889); a story set in the year of the Jacobite Rising, 1745.

[3] (1893).

[4] (1886).

[5] Completed by 'Q' (Sir Arthur Quiller-Couch) and published posthumously (1897).

[6] (1896); published unfinished.

[7] *The Ebb Tide* (1894) by Robert Louis Stevenson and Lloyd Osbourne.

[8] (1883).

[9] A perception which we might wish Ransome had supported with argument. 'Not a novel' because no love interest? Not a novel because 'a boy's book'?

[10] *The Art of Writing*, chapter 5, 'My First Book – *Treasure Island*'.

[11] Ibid.

[12] A lighter breed of saddle-horse used for everyday riding or ceremony, as opposed to the work-horse or war-horse. The archaic term is apt, since the

In writing of his novels we cannot but have an uncomfortable disquiet, in spite of their many pleasant qualities. It is a different thing when we consider his short stories. Then, all our trouble is to choose and classify remembered moments of enthusiastic admiration. Indeed these moments are of many colours, some purple and grey with heather and rock, some lead and white with the anger of the sea, some neat, rich moments of black and white with colour only in a tie-pin or a ring or a pink slip worn under a Mechlin,[1] and others again tinted with old sunlight through mediaeval windows of stained glass.

These last are the earliest, and with 'The Treasure of Franchard' and 'Providence and the Guitar' complete that small section of Stevenson's work which has a strange air of being translated from the French. I mean 'The Sire de Malétroit's Door' and 'A Lodging for the Night'. They were first published in *Temple Bar*, in 1878 and 1877 respectively, and are now included in the volume called *New Arabian Nights*, with 'Providence and the Guitar' and 'The Pavilion on the Links', which fall into a different category.

'The Sire de Maletroit's Door' ('door' being substituted for the original 'mousetrap') was invented in France, first told over the fire one evening in Paris, and ultimately written at Penzance.' In this story,[2] there is something of the careful aloofness from life that makes the Comedy of Manners[3] so charming with its little dancing serpents of immorality who have all of them lost their fangs. But it excuses not immorality but a sort of sur-iced[4] sugar sentiment which would be sickly if it was not so light, so airy a construction. There is the opening with its night town in the possession of mixed troops of England and Burgundy, setting the time; there is the watch passing like one of the prose poems of *Gaspard de la Nuit*;[5] there is the little playful terror of the door, the delicious wickedness of the old gentleman; the threatened death so airily carried off in the suggestion of 'a very efficacious rope'; and then the pretty cross-purposes of the youth and the damsel, weaving a cat's cradle of tenuous loveable sentiment.

---

image is from the medieval legend of St George and the Dragon, where St George's horse must be a war-horse.

[1] 'Mechlin': a type of Flemish lace, here made into a garment; named after the city of manufacture, Mechelen.

[2] "The Sire de Maletroit's Door. There is ..." etc.

[3] A genre of dramatic comedy, dominant in English Restoration comedy, and Molière; and to some extent in the eighteenth-century comedies of Goldsmith and Sheridan; exemplified too in the plays of Oscar Wilde, about which Ransome had recently been writing.

[4] Over-iced.

[5] Aloysius Bertrand, *Gaspard de la Nuit* (published posthumously 1842): Bertrand was one of the inspirers of the Surrealist movement.

A translation from the French; yet no Frenchman has ever touched quite these notes, so airy, so fantastic, so humane.[1]

'Providence and the Guitar' was one of the spoils of Fontainebleau. Stevenson made friends with a pair of travelling actors, and, in the end, sent them the money he earned by the story they suggested.[2] It is one of the most loveable stories in the world, though I am not sure how much of the love we give it is not given to its characters. Leon Berthelini possessing the grand air, with a Spanish touch and a remembrance of Rembrandt, swimming 'like a kite on a fair wind, high above earthly troubles'; his wife with 'a little air of melancholy, attractive enough in its way, but not good to see like the wholesome, sky-scraping, boyish spirits of her lord': these two, the key note of whose external life is sounded so admirably in their dour reception by the innkeeper, following so close on the affectionate description of their souls, those two are the embodiment of the kind.

No one who has lived in France is not reminded by them of other such; as I am reminded of the conductor of a certain orchestra in a cafe in a small Tourangean[3] town, with his great gestures, and his announcement of a violin solo by himself: composer – a bow – Himself. And the black devil of travelling artists in them is the red Commissary. I remember such another, when I happened to be in company with the keepers of some performing bears. We met him in his shirt-sleeves, and he ordered us out of the town. But in his shirt-sleeves even a Commissary is only a man, and we baited him with taunts and jeers, and refused to believe he was a Commissary at all. He plunged away from us into his house, and soon we had the noble spectacle of a half-naked Commissary at an upper window, pulling on his uniform from behind while he threatened us from in front. And how perfectly has Stevenson caught the spirit of the office which has become the spirit of the man. My digressions are justified by this illustration of the excellence of the portraits. For all good portraits plunge their spectators in digression.[4]

The incidents, inevitable as in grand tragedy, follow in a sedate minuet, realistic, painful, somehow smiling to the precipitate, or was it more than precipitate[5] flight of Leon and his wife after their serenade of the

---

[1] Ransome's use of 'humane' in preference to 'human' on several occasions in this book is highly idiosyncratic. It has the sense of a sophisticated perception of human nature, and with a classical context of humanistic values, a connotation of being fully aware of human potentiality.

[2] "R. L. S. by Francis Watt, p. 183." The book is *R. L. Stephenson* [*sic*] (1913).

[3] i.e. of La Touraine (Loir-et-Cher).

[4] Can Ransome here be guilty of the kind of familiarity with his audience that he had earlier disapproved of in Stevenson's essays?

[5] An echo of Stevenson's words at the end of chapter 3 of 'Providence and the Guitar': 'And taking the guitar in one hand and the case in the other, he led

Commissaire. And then their little game under the lime trees, and the guitar touched to comfort Elvira's spirits, awaking the Cambridge undergraduate who asks with no suspicion of wrong, if they too are camping out? – and, almost immediately is urged, he also, to become an artist. Then the quarrelling painter and his wife, the supper, at which 'to see Leon eating a single cold sausage was to see a triumph; by the time he had done he had got through as much pantomime as would have sufficed for a baron of beef, and he had the relaxed expression of the over-eaten.'[1] Then perhaps most sympathetic of all,[2] the discussion of art by the two incompetents, the reconciliation of the quarrelled, and the perfect summary by the reflective Stubbs: 'They are all mad,' thought he, 'all mad – but wonderfully decent.'[3] There are few short stories which bear so well repeated reading; few so easy to begin, on glancing through a book, few so hard to relinquish partly read.

Stevenson discovered a new romance; silent upon the peak of Hyde Park Corner, he looked eastward with a wild surmise,[4] and the swift sophisticated world disclosed its strange perils, its romantic promises. Lieutenant Brackenbury:

> glanced at the houses and marvelled what was passing behind those warmly lighted windows; he looked into face after face, and saw them each intent upon some unknown interest, criminal or kindly ... "They talk of war," he thought, "but this is the great battlefield of mankind.'[5]

Hansom cabs become the gondolas of London, and that phrase strikes the note of the transformation scene that resulted from Stevenson's discovery. The golden lights, the shining silver of the wet streets, the blue sky deepened by the lights, the distant stars, the glowing windows were suddenly made Eastern, made Southern, Venetian, with a hint of Byron,

the way with something too precipitate to be merely called precipitation from the scene of this absurd adventure.'

[1] Ibid., chapter 6.

[2] Such questions were matters of keen debate to Ransome at this time.

[3] These are the last words of the story.

[4] Ransome is alluding to lines from John Keats' sonnet 'On first looking into Chapman's Homer':

> Or like stout Cortez when with eagle eyes
> He star'd at the Pacific – and all his men
> Look'd at each other with a wild surmise –
> Silent, upon a peak in Darien.

These lines were later to colour the perception of the Walker children who gazed from a peak they had named 'Darien' in chapter 1, 'The Peak in Darien', of Ransome's first great novel *Swallows and Amazons* (1930).

[5] In 'The Adventure of the Hansom Cabs', the third and final part of 'The Suicide Club' (1878), within *New Arabian Nights* (1882).

Constantinople, Cairo, Baghdad, polite death lurking at the street corners, young men distributing cream tarts, and, warm in the air, curling spurts of cigar smoke, an incense at once magic and urbane. He discovered the secret of the metamorphosis, and we owe to him the many miraculous Londons[1] that have been discovered in these latter years.

And with the new London came a new atmosphere of narrative. *The Arabian Nights*[2] did no more than suggest the form, and provide a delightful name. Stevenson took nothing from them than the idea of inter-dependent stories. He could have parodied them, had he wished: but all his opportunities were scorned. Meredith in *Shaving of Shagpat*[3] had beaten the Arabian Nights in Araby itself, and Stevenson had no intention of emulating his master. We look in vain for the delightful philosophic tags of verse. We look in vain for the machinery of the East. We are given the new London, a city of infinite probabilities, and in dealing with new place a manner now serious, now whimsical, 'high and stilted' as Stevenson put it,[4] smooth and courteous as the voice of Brackenbury's cabman, and capable of the sedatest nonsense, the most fantastic seriousness. The prince sets the key when he remarks to the young man of the Cream Tarts whom he is entertaining in a café in Soho: 'I must tell you that my friend and I are persons very well worthy to be entrusted with a secret. We have many of our own, which we are continually revealing to improper ears.' All is impossible, all is sublime, and yet when all is done and the Prince, hurled from his throne on account of 'his edifying neglect of public business', is become the handsomest tobacconist in Fleet Street, he sells cigars under such a halo of gallantry and honour and humanity that we approach even the idea of entering his shop with a fine romantic reverence.[5]

---

[1] No doubt he would include his own work, especially *Bohemia in London* (1907). The paragraph gratefully acknowledges Stevenson as his master.

[2] *The Arabian Nights*, or, *A Thousand and One Nights* is a collection of ancient tales from India, Persia, Yemen, Arabia and Egypt, of which the best known is 'Aladdin's Wonderful Lamp,' a rhyming version by Ransome was published in a limited edition in 1919; later (1928) he dramatised the story as a school play.

[3] *The Shaving of Shagpat: An Oriental Romance* (1856), the first published novel by George Meredith (1828–1909), uses a stories-within-story structure in imitation of *The Arabian Nights*.

[4] See below, p. 121.

[5] 'The Adventure of Prince Florizel and the Detective', in *New Arabian Nights*. Compare Ransome's style here with Stevenson's in the ending of the story:

> I am happy to say that a recent revolution hurled him from the throne of Bohemia, in consequence of his continued absence and edifying neglect of public business; and that his Highness now keeps a cigar store in Rupert Street, much frequented by other foreign refugees.

If it had not been for this discovery of Stevenson's, Wilde could never have written: 'Let us go out into the night. Thought is wonderful, but adventure is more wonderful still. Who knows but we may meet Prince Florizel of Bohemia, and hear the fair Cuban tell us that she is not what she seems?'[1]

The two short stories in the Lowland dialect, 'Thrawn Janet' and 'The Story of Tod Lapraik',[2] are among the best of Stevenson's achievements. The dialect seems to knit the words together so that there are no interstices to allow reality to slip out. These two stories are the best examples of dialect prose that have been written in modern times. Expressive, vigorous, firm, and always with that curious feeling of close construction; almost any sentence in either would suffice to illuminate the quality of their excellent vernacular prose. 'Grandfather's silver tester in the puddock's heart of him', is really better than 'Grandfather's silver sixpence in his toad's heart,'[3] and it would be impossible to repeat in other words the precise effect[4] of 'He cam' a step nearer to the corp; an' then his heart fair whammled in his inside. For, by what cantrip it wad ill-beseem a man to judge, she was

> I go there from time to time to smoke and have a chat, and find him as great a creature as in the days of his prosperity; he has an Olympian air behind the counter; and although a sedentary life is beginning to tell upon his waistcoat, he is probably, take him for all in all, the handsomest tobacconist in London.

Ransome's tone has become almost exactly that of the author he is writing about.

[1] The character Gilbert in Oscar Wilde's *Intentions: The Critic as Artist*, not wanting to discuss anything solemnly, says to Ernest:

> Education is an admirable thing, but it is well to remember from time to time that nothing that is worth knowing can be taught. Through the parted curtains of the window I see the moon like a clipped piece of silver. Like gilded bees the stars cluster round her. The sky is a hard hollow sapphire. Let us go out into the night. Thought is wonderful, but adventure is more wonderful still. Who knows but we may meet Prince Florizel of Bohemia, and hear the fair Cuban tell us that she is not what she seems?

[2] 'Thrawn Janet' in *The Merry Men and other Tales and Fables* (1887); 'The Tale of Tod Lapraik' is chapter XV, 'Black Andie's Tale of Tod Lapraik', within Stevenson's novel *Catriona*; see Stevenson, *Vailima Letters* (1895), April 1893: 'Tod Lapraik is a piece of living Scots; if I had never writ anything but that and Thrawn Janet, still I'd have been a writer.'

[3] Ransome has Englished Stevenson's spelling a little here, which diminishes the Scots effect: Stevenson wrote 'but there was grandfaither's siller tester in the puddock's heart of him.'

[4] Unfortunately Ransome does not specify what the effect is.

hingin' frae a single nail an' by a single wursted thread for darnin' hose.'[1]
It seems curious that these especially local stories should be those that
most clearly illustrate the influence of Hawthorne; yet it is not so really, for
in the spirit of the Covenanters, in the remembrance of the persecution,
he found just such a background of religious feeling, that the New England
of the witch-burnings offered to the author of *The Scarlet Letter*, 'Ethan
Brand' and 'The Minister's Black Veil'.[2]

'The Treasure of Franchard'[3] is a sort of genial *Candide*,[4] with the
philosophy that believes that 'all is for the best in this best of all possible
worlds' illustrated in a quite different manner. Nothing could be more
lovable than that small family party, the garrulous doctor, his wife who
was devoted to him 'for her own sake rather than for his', had an imper-
turbable good nature, no idea of self-sacrifice, and an aptitude for falling
asleep, and the wise little offspring of the mountebank. It also is a character story, unlike most of Stevenson's; the few events are only to illuminate these three delightful persons, and events and persons have a warm,
sunny air about them, and seem, like Fontainebleau, to be offering an easy
hospitality.

Stevenson's first three tales of adventure were *Treasure Island*, *The Black
Arrow*, and *Prince Otto*.[5] Stevenson's attitude towards *Treasure Island*
is partly represented in the cheerful lines he addressed to the hesitating
purchaser:

> If sailor tales to sailor tunes,
>   Storm and adventure, heat and cold,
> If schooners, islands and maroons
>   And Buccaneers and buried Gold,[6]
> And all the old romance, retold
>   Exactly in the ancient way,
> Can please, as me they pleased of old,
>   The wiser youngsters of today:

---

[1] The example is from 'Thrawn Janet'.

[2] Nathaniel Hawthorne. *The Scarlet Letter* (1850) is a short novel; 'Ethan
Brand' (1850) and 'The Minister's Black Veil' (1836) are short stories.

[3] In *The Merry Men*.

[4] *Candide, ou l'optimisme* (1759) is a famous satirical novella by Voltaire.

[5] The order of publication was: *Treasure Island* (1883), *The Black Arrow: A Tale
of the Two Roses* (1883), and *Prince Otto* (1885). The introductory sentence
is here reconstructed from "Stevenson. Prince Otto. Treasure Island. Black
Arrow. *Stevenson*. T. A." (i. e. Tales of Adventure.)

[6] The capital letters of 'Buccaneers' and 'Gold' are Ransome's.

> – So be it, and fall on! If not,
>   If studious youth no longer crave,
>   His ancient appetites forgot,
>   Kingston, or Ballantyne the brave,
> Or Cooper of the wood and wave:
>   So be it also! And may I
> And all my pirates share the grave
>   When these and their creations lie!

He offered it as a pious ritual to gods who had stirred his boyhood.[1] He did, piously, what they had done, following their careless furrow with his steel plough in a sentimental emulation. And readers who remembered *The Last of the Mohicans*,[2] *White Ice*[3] and *Coral Island*[4] recovered some of their lost youth in reading these more accomplished pages. More accomplished, and more civilised; for in spite of what he said, the brave adventures of Silver and the others are not 'retold exactly in the ancient way'. There is the old pleasure in hair's-breadth escape, enriched with something of the actuality of adventure-books older still, the actuality of Defoe in *Captain Singleton*,[5] which book he had not read when he wrote *Treasure Island*, the delight in immediate detail that dictated Crusoe's entrancing catalogue of the things found in the wreck, and somehow intellectualizing all this,

---

[1] As, of course, they had stirred Ransome's; his first story, written at the age of seven, has buccaneers and pirates in it; see Introduction, and appendix B.1.

[2] By James Fenimore Cooper (1789–1851), American novelist of adventure and romance (1826).

[3] 'White Ice' cannot be identified for certain. It is most likely to be Ballantyne's *The World of Ice: or, Adventures in the Polar Regions* (1860); or possibly his *Fast In The Ice* (1863) or even *Rivers of Ice* (1875). Ransome does not usually get titles wrong. 'White Ice' may also suggest also Jules Verne's *Hivernage dans les glaces* (A Winter amid the Ice) (1874); or perhaps his *Le désert de glace* (Ice Desert), part two of *Les voyages et aventures du capitaine Hatteras* (1866; the first part is *Les anglais au pôle nord.*) Verne's novels, like Ballantyne's, were made by Ransome part of the Swallows' and Amazons' mental landscapes. Such fantastical adventures in frozen landscapes were to be triumphantly outshone by the much later realism of Ransome's frozen Lakeland landscape in his *Winter Holiday* (1933).

[4] In this, the most famous novel (1858) of R. M. Ballantyne, Jack, Ralph Rover and Peterkin are shipwrecked on a desert island. This was to be a formative tale for Ransome's novels; the scene of Titty and Roger's diving for pearls in *Swallows and Amazons* is inspired by it.

[5] *The Life, Adventures and Piracies of the Famous Captain Singleton* (1720) by Daniel Defoe, an inspiration also for Ransome's *Swallows and Amazons*. Stevenson had asked his friend Sidney Colvin to send him a copy of *Singleton* after *Treasure Island* was published (*Letters*, July 1884).

a sophisticated delight in the goriness of the performance. I remember a later poet's lines:

> And when we'd washed the blood away
>   We'd little else to do
> Than to dance a quiet hornpipe
> As the old salts taught us to.[1]

Something of that quite modern attitude, something of the delight in Grand Guignol,[2] mix with the vigorous love of action and tropical, lurid colour which the great romantics had bequeathed to the boys' storytellers of the preceding generation.

Never were circumstances more apt for such a tale's production. Stevenson, himself a boy, with his young stepson aged thirteen and his father, children both in the simplicity of their imaginative tastes;[3] the drawing of a map in playful imitation of the ancient way, in which maps were not cold-blooded plans but lively pictures, with ships sailing, full-rigged upon the sea, and mountains visible, not merely marked, upon the land;[4] and then with this map a tangible, credible testimony 'to witness if he lied',[5] the construction, for the storyteller's own pleasure and for that of the other two children,[6] of a tale to give the touch of human memory to its hills and creeks. All this too, with no thought of literature or larger

---

[1] 'A Ballad of John Silver' by John Masefield (1878–1967), poet-laureate, and dedicatee of Ransome's *Portraits and Speculations* (1913).

[2] 'Grand Guignol': a style of naturalistic horror drama named after the theatre in Paris where it originated in the 1890s.

[3] Ransome too, like Stevenson and Stevenson's father, never lost his boyish imagination – his, tempered by an idiosyncratic gentle irony.

[4] Just such a map as Steven Spurrier was later to draw for Ransome's *Swallows and Amazons.*

[5] Presented as a quotation but adapted from Lord Macaulay, 'Horatius':

> They made a molten image,
> And set it up on high,
> And there it stands unto this day
> To witness if I lie.

At the bottom of the famous *Treasure Island* map is the testimony: 'Facsimile of Chart latitude and longitude struck out by J. Hawkins'. Jim Hawkins is a fairly trustworthy narrator as witness to the main events of the story. In chapter 28, facing Long John Silver, he offers to bear witness: 'Kill me, if you please, or spare me. But one thing I'll say, and no more; if you spare me, bygones are bygones, and when you fellows are in court for piracy, I'll save you all I can. It is for you to choose. Kill another and do yourselves no good, or spare me and keep a witness to save you from the gallows.'

[6] i.e. his father and his step-son. *Swallows and Amazons* was dedicated 'to the six for whom it was written, in exchange for a pair of slippers'; they were

publication than to the company about the fire in the small Scotch cottage in the northern summer evenings. Its publication was an accident, due to the presence of a critical guest at some of the tellings, and as modest as might be, sharing with many another story less happily conceived, less delicately executed, the columns of a cheap, children's paper, and showing none of its success until two years afterwards when it was issued, quite without trumpets, as a children's book.

We are faced with a strange problem; what is it that makes this tale superior, not only to *The Black Arrow* which won greater esteem in its serial form, but to *Catriona* and *Kidnapped* which in Stevenson's opinion touched his highest level, indeed to *The Master of Ballantrae*, and so indeed to his longer narratives except the stern clean drawing of *Weir of Hermiston*? Nineteen chapters of it were written straight off, a chapter a day, 'no writing, just drive along as the words come and the pen will scratch.'[1] Hawkins in the apple barrel was suggested by his father on *The Regent* sailing in the northern seas, who as a lad crept into an apple barrel, and happened to hear the language of a 'vulgar and truculent ruffian' proceeding from the lips of the deferential captain who was wont to make polite appearances in the cabin, to dine courteously with the new engineer of the lights.[2]

Dr Alexander Japp visited Braemar, and, delighted with the story, immediately arranged its publication in *Young Folks*,[3] at £2.10s a page of 4500 words as Stevenson calculated, with the comment 'not noble is it? But I have my copyright safe ... I'll make this boys' book business pay; but I have to make a beginning.'[4] At once he foresaw other such cheerful books: there was to be *Jerry Abershaw: a Tale of Putney Heath*, and books of the Wild West and so on. This effervescent enthusiasm for a new kind of work lit up

members of the Altounyan family with whom he had sailed dinghies on the lake that he disguised for the purposes of his fiction.

[1] To W. E. Henley, August 24, Braemar, 1881.

[2] "Fam. 41." *Records of a Family of Engineers* (1912): 'He used to come down daily after dinner for a glass of port or whisky, often in his full rig of sou'-wester, oilskins, and long boots; and I have often heard it described how insinuatingly he carried himself on these appearances, artfully combining the extreme of deference with a blunt and seamanlike demeanour. My father and uncles, with the devilish penetration of the boy, were far from being deceived; and my father, indeed, was favoured with an object-lesson not to be mistaken. He had crept one rainy night into an apple-barrel on deck, and from this place of ambush overheard Soutar and a comrade conversing in their oilskins. The smooth sycophant of the cabin had wholly disappeared, and the boy listened with wonder to a vulgar and truculent ruffian.'

[3] *Young Folks; A Boys' and Girls' Paper of Instructive and Entertaining Literature* (1871–1900); the first episode of 'Treasure Island; or, The Mutiny of the Hispaniola' was in vol. 19, no. 565, 1 October, 1881.

[4] Ibid., September 1881.

the actual writing of what was then called 'The Sea Cook'. But the stream suddenly dried, and the serial publication of the book began before the last fourteen chapters were written. Stevenson however, where he caught the note again, wrote them as easily as the earlier batch. No book of his ever cost him so little labour.

But it is worth observing, lest indolent youth should believe that easy writing is a test of merit, that their speed in composition was only made possible by the years of slow, meticulous labour that had preceded it. Stevenson had already written essays, his little travel-books, his *New Arabian Nights*, most of the best of his short stories, all these with an almost passionate taking of pains: he had already wrestled with the planning of *Prince Otto*, which though finished after *Treasure Island* was really his first long story. He had been continually disciplining himself; and when he started 'The Sea Cook' as an amusement only, of the most light hearted kind, he could not but write with skill and certainty, in the same way as the accomplished billiard player will frame with style even on a bagatelle board.

And it is the most seductive of books, hard to discuss because it will be read. I open it to remind myself of some detail of technique, and, from that page, I read willy-nilly to the end. And this happens not once but many times. My edition is dated 1894, and is one of the fifty-second thousand. In the last twenty years I must have read it at least twenty times; and now I cannot write of it as of a literary achievement. No: I speculate upon the fortunes of Long John when he foregathered with his old negress in the port he would not name for fear of causing jealousy. I wonder what became of the three maroons who were left on the island as a punishment for their wicked mutiny. I hear Long John cursing at the flies on his large, red face, or see him smoking silently with Captain Smollett, as in the picture at the log-house door. And then there are delicious, perilous moments, up the mast, with Hands climbing from below, and jerking his dagger murderously through the air to pin me – or was it Jim Hawkins? – to the mast.[1] And then the characters, Livesey and the Squire, and Gunn in the end of the book keeping a gate[2] – oak and walnut characters like those of the eighteenth century novels.

---

[1] 'And there I was, pinned by the shoulder to the mast', at the end of chapter 26, 'Israel Hands'.

[2] Not the heroic Horatius, 'Captain of the Gate' in Macaulay's 'Lays of Ancient Rome', but Jim's meeting with Ben Gunn and the bathos of Ben's final years:

> 'As for Ben Gunn, he got a thousand pounds, which he spent or lost in three weeks, or to be more exact, in nineteen days, for he was back begging on the twentieth. Then he was given a lodge to keep, exactly as he had feared upon the island ...' (Chapter 34, 'And Last').

As for origins, Stevenson, in a letter to Sir Sidney Colvin, was most explicit. 'T. I. came out of Kingsley's *At Last*, where I got the Dead Man's Chest – and that was the seed – and out of the great Captain Johnson's *History of Notorious Pirates*. The scenery is Californian in part, and in part *chic*.'[1] There is one other borrowing, at least so it seems to me, and one particularly interesting as an illustration of the dependence of such events on the personalities that perceive them. And that is the burial of Flint's treasure, and the deaths of the men who helped him. At the end of 'The Gold-Bug'[2] Poe chooses to touch a tragic note:

> 'What are we to make of the skeletons found in the hole?'
> 'That is a question I am no more able to answer than yourself. There seems, however, only one plausible way of accounting for them – and yet it is dreadful to believe in such atrocity as my sugges-tion would imply. It is clear that Kidd – if Kidd indeed secreted this treasure, which I doubt not – it is clear that he must have had assist-ance in the labour. But, this labour concluded, he may have thought it expedient to remove all participants in his secret. Perhaps a couple of blows with a mattock were sufficient, while his coadjutors were busy in the pit; perhaps it required a dozen – who shall tell?'

No other of Stevenson's books cost him such trouble in the execution as *Prince Otto*. In 1880 it was already vivid in his mind: it was then called 'The Forest State – a Romance', and he wrote of it to Henley, who was always urging him towards the theatre:

> A brave story, I swear; and a brave play too, if we can find the trick to make the end. The play, I fear, will have to end darkly, and that spoils the quality as I now see it of a kind of crockery, eighteenth century, high-life-below-stairs life, breaking up like ice in spring before the nature and the certain modicum of manhood of my poor, clever, feather-headed Prince, whom I love already.[3]

In March 1884, it was still unfinished. 'Two chapters of *Otto* do remain: one to rewrite, one to create; and I am not yet able to tackle them.'[4] He took it extremely seriously:

> There is a good deal of stuff in it, both dramatic and, I think, poetic; and the story is not like these purposeless fables of today, but is, at

---

[1] *Letters*, II, 191, July 1884.

[2] The French title of this story, 'Le scarabée d'or', will have resonance for readers of Ransome's *The Picts and the Martyrs* (1942). Ransome had read the whole of Poe for his critical study (1910); the last part of that book is 'The French view of Poe'.

[3] "To Henley, S[an] Francisco, Feb[ruary] 1880. *Letters*, I, 281."

[4] "To Colvin, [*Letters*,] II. 159."

least, intended to stand firm upon a base of philosophy – or morals – as you please ...[1]

and not only was its matter[2] thus earnestly conceived. His first attempt at a novel, intended as the precursor of others, it involved a new and exciting combination of technical processes he had mastered in essays and short stories:

> For me it is my chief o' works; hence probably not so for others, since it only means that I have here attacked the greatest difficulties. But some chapters towards the end: three in particular – I do think come off. I find them stirring, dramatic, and not unpoetical. We shall see, however; as like as not, the effort will be more obvious than the success. For, of course, I strung myself hard to carry it out. The next will come easier, and possibly be more popular. I believe in the covering of much paper, each time with a definite and not too difficult artistic purpose; and then, from time to time, drawing oneself up and trying, in a superior effort, to combine the facilities thus acquired or improved. Thus one progresses. But, mind, it is very likely that the big effort, instead of being the masterpiece, may be the blotted copy, the gymnastic exercise. This no man can tell; only the brutal and licentious public, snouting in Mudie's wash-trough, can return a dubious answer.[3]

He set himself to maintain through a book, and in a continuous story,[4] a definite, artificial note: 'It is all pitched pretty high and stilted; almost like the Arabs, at that; but of course there is love-making in Otto' (which he had hitherto pretty carefully avoided), 'and indeed a good deal of it. I sometimes feel very weary; but the thing travels – and I like it when I am at it.'[5] It is not perfectly successful, but it is an excellent summary of Stevenson's first period. The attempt in the beginning to set the key of fantasy with the tracing of *Otto's* pedigree to the royal race of the sea-bound Bohemia of Shakespeare's discovery,[6] the placing of Perdita at least by suggestion

---

[1] "To Low, Dec[ember] 13, 1883. *Letters*, II, 161."

[2] Classical (and English) rhetoric traditionally makes a contrast between the 'matter' (i.e. content) and 'manner' (i.e. style) of a composition.

[3] "To Colvin, 1884, March 9. *Letters*, II, 169 & 170." Mudie's Lending Library was established in 1842 by Charles Mudie, bookseller.

[4] Ransome probably draws on a quotation he notes: "Prince Otto. In April 1883, to Mrs Sitwell: Hyères: 'I have been, and am, so busy, drafting 'a long story' (for me I mean) about a hundred *Cornhill* pages, or say about as long as the Donkey book.' *Letters*, II, 109."

[5] "To Henley same date *Letters*, II, 108." (He had quoted this phrase twice before; the repetition may be an aspect of the first-draft composition.)

[6] Shakespeare's *The Winter's Tale* (1623) (in which Perdita is the heroine) sets scenes on 'the sea-coast of Bohemia', a land-locked country.

among his maternal ancestry, and the hinted continuation of that airy sweet character of romance with the practical rigour of realistic Saxon Grunewalds,[1] promises something that is not, and but by a miracle could not be, consistently fulfilled. Some of the characters become too real, too vigorous of pulse for the Dresden china masquerade in which they were to appear; and, curiously, it is for those that we remember that Otto disappears beside the Countess von Rosen, with whom all but the most rigid have fallen in love. The princess is called upon to execute too sudden a volte-face, so that the lyrical scenes at the end of the book are acted by a princess of fairy tale who has scarcely a cousinly relationship to the painted minx of the beginning; and the minor characters, Sir John Cotterill, Greisengesang the Councillor, Colonel Gordon, and Gotthold the librarian are more consistent, and lead us to suspect that they owe their consistency to the little use their inventor was compelled to make of them. Gondremark is a pleasant invention: but the most delightful touch in his pretentions is an essayist's, not a novelist's, when in the epilogue it is mentioned that Swinburne has dedicated 'a rousing lyric and some vigorous sonnets' to his memory.

I seem to be carping unnecessarily: it is not so: I am but noticing in *Prince Otto* the signs of a transition, and in so doing perhaps forgetting the wayward grace of the book, and that quality in it which makes it like the Countess von Rosen, curtseying to the Prince in the Castle of Felsenburg, '"You are as adroit, dear Prince, as I am – charming." And as she said the word with a great curtsey, she justified it.' But I can not help feeling that the charm of the book deserves also the description that the Countess fitted to herself: 'Blank cartridge, O mon Prince!'

Stevenson complained that much as he enjoyed his own works, he never read *The Black Arrow*, and the Critic-on-the-Hearth to whom he dedicated it was also unable to get to the end of it. It was, as he put it, 'tushery',[2] a sort of masquerade of old times, with the easy unreality of a pantomime, marred a little by the too great precision of some of the characters for their parts in such stage play. It was, he confessed, written in direct imitation of a school of writers of boys' books. It was the second product of the factory of juvenile literature of which Stevenson had such cheerful hopes, and, strange as it may seem, it was designed, and successfully designed, to catch the favour of those who had gone so far in their disapproval of *Treasure Island*, when it appeared in *Young Folks*, as to write querulous letters to the editor of that

---

[1] Stevenson set the story in the Court of Grunewald.

[2] "*Letters*, II, 116. To W. E. Henley, May 1883: 'I turned me to – what thinkest 'ou? ... to Tushery, by the mass! Ay, friend, a whole tale of tushery. And every tusher tushes me so free, that may I be tushed if the whole thing is worth a tush. *The Black Arrow: a Tale of Tunstall Forest* is his name: tush! a poor thing!'"

magazine. For all that, I liked it as a boy, and like it still, and can turn back without distaste to the picture of Dick and Joanna in the passage with the lamp before them, or to hear the merry Alicia's comforting 'Keep your heart up, lion-driver', or her unfortunate reply to Richard Crookback 'My lord duke, so as the man is straight –'. There are sturdy enough descriptions of fighting, a portrait of Crookback which pleased Stevenson, and some lesser things on a much higher level, like the scene where Dick asks pardon from the old seaman. The old seaman was worthy of a better book, and perhaps it was just the feeling that there were two books, superimposed, destroying each other, written in different keys,[1] that made *The Black Arrow* a disquieting memory for its author. Still it is a pleasant work, and one of those two books that it contains, is full of Stevenson.

Those who are interested in the study of technique will not find many better illustrations of the genesis of a narrative than *Dr Jekyll and Mr Hyde*.[2] Stevenson conceived in a dream a man who by chemical powders was enabled to loose the baser part of his nature in another form than his own, for the unpunished satisfaction of his vicious desires. The character of the man was bad throughout, and he took pleasure in the deeds thus committed in a physical disguise. In this form Stevenson wrote it down before the sharp impression of his dream had evaporated. At that time he was not allowed by his doctor to read aloud, and his wife read the draft, and submitted her criticism in writing. She pointed out (I am leaning here on Mr Graham Balfour's account of the matter)[3] that whereas the tale was really an allegory Stevenson had treated it simply as a narrative. 'After a while his bell rang; on her return she found him sitting up in bed (the clinical thermometer in his mouth), pointing with a long denouncing finger to a pile of ashes. He had burned the entire draft ... not out of pique, but from a fear that he might be tempted to make too much use of it, and not rewrite the whole from a new standpoint.' Now the interest of this anecdote lies not so much in Stevenson's readiness to accept criticism, or in his

---

[1] Ransome seems to draw on a letter he noted from Stevenson to C. W. Stoddard about *Otto*:

> "It is a strange example of the difficulty of being ideal in an age of realism; that the unpleasant giddy-mindedness, which spoils the book and often gives it a wanton air of unreality and juggling with air-bells, comes from unsteadiness of key; from the too great realism of some chapters and passages – some of which I have now spotted, others I dare say I shall never spot – which disprepares the imagination for the cast of the remainder.
> *Letters*, II, 273."

[2] For Ransome's notes on this section see appendix A.2.v.

[3] For Ransome's notes from Balfour, see appendix A.1.

whole-hearted earnestness as a craftsman, as in the reason given by the critic, and the subsequent action of the criticised.[1]

Mrs Stevenson's dissatisfaction was not based on anything outside the draft itself. It was not that she preferred allegory to plain narrative; but that she perceived a discrepancy between matter and manner, the matter demanding a different manner, the manner suggesting a different matter. Her criticism was a suggestion that Stevenson had not gone far enough in knowledge of what he was trying to write, that as it then stood *Dr Jekyll and Mr Hyde* was imperfectly *known*; and Stevenson burned the draft least that imperfect knowledge, stereotyped as it was at a particular degree of imperfection, should be an opaque barrier to further investigation. The original suggestion, from dream or accident, is thus the starting point of a piece of research; the rest is not invention but gradually deepening and spreading perception, and the part played by Mrs Stevenson with regard to the writing of this short story is precisely that of the watchful critical faculty at every stage in the evolution of a work of art.

Some of Stevenson's fantastic tales have been compared to Poe's: but there is always more in them of Hawthorne than of Poe.[2] 'The Body-Snatcher',[3] perhaps, depends like too many of Poe's stories on merely physical horror: the details of blood in, for example, 'Markheim'[4] seem to me to have a wholly different origin. The stricken dealer 'struggling like a hen', the account of the body, 'like a suit half-stuffed with bran', the jolting about of the unstiffened limbs, these things belong to the same category as the visual horror of the murdered man in 'A Lodging for the Night'[5] with his 'bald head and garland of red curls'; or, in another story not in the least horrible in intention, the fight between Hands and Jim Hawkins in the *Hispaniola*,

[1] An extraordinary parallel can be drawn between this observation and what we know to have been the effect of Ransome's second wife's criticism upon his later narratives. In the case of *The Picts and the Martyrs* (1942), her strictures delayed its publication by a year. Amusingly, Ransome notes (but does not incorporate) the following: "*Jekyll and Hyde*, wrote Miss Jeanette L. Gilder (a literary lady who contributed to *The Critic*) 'of course, interested me immensely, but it is hardly a book to enjoy.'"

[2] Hawthorne, romantic writer of historical 'tales' and 'romances' with allegorical content, set in colonial New England; Poe, writer of macabre tales of mystery, inventor of detective fiction, contemptuous of allegory and didacticism, translated into French by Beaudelaire, himself appreciated Hawthorne's 'pure' style and 'wild, plaintive, thoughtful' tone.

[3] Written in 1881 as a 'crawler' but 'laid aside in a justifiable disgust, the tale being horrid' (as Stevenson wrote to Colvin that July) it was published in December 1884 as a *Pall Mall* 'Christmas Extra'.

[4] First published in *Unwin's Christmas Annual* 1885, and included in *The Merry Men*.

[5] 'A Lodging for the Night: A Story of Francis Villon', in *New Arabian Nights*.

when as the boat heeling over, pursuer and pursued tumbled together into the scuppers, 'the dead red-cap, with his arms still spread out, tumbling stiffly after us.'[1] Stevenson is not experimenting in physical thrills, but exulting in the vividness and realism of his vision; his ugly corpses offering him the pleasures of a patch of sunlight and shadow miraculously got into words, and at the same time a delight which in a man of his tenderness, is comparable to the delight in action shown by a man so sedentary by habit and compulsion. He described blood, from his sick-bed, in much the same spirit as the Sidney who died at Zutphen described his shepherdesses.[2]

But though *The Strange Case of Dr Jekyll and Mr Hyde* resembles in some things Poe's 'William Wilson',[3] its scent, its mainspring, was one known to Hawthorne but scarcely realised by Poe except in the crudest manner. To those who have read the book as a simple fantasy, a couple of sentences in a letter from Stevenson to his friend Low must bring with them a shock of surprise and of wonder. 'The gnome,' says Stevenson of this story, 'is interesting, I think, and he came out of a deep mine, where he guards the fountain of tears. It is not always the time to rejoice.'[4] Why, this is as serious as the preachers who made its popularity by advertising the tale from their pulpits! How is it to be reconciled with the fact that the idea of the tale came to him in a vivid dream, and that when he first wrote it down he wrote it as if it were a plain story, not an allegory? Hawthorne is perhaps the only other writer who if in possession of all the facts would have been in no way surprised, unless at the surprise of other people. Hawthorne was himself no fanatic, but he saw that a story may be given coherence and frame by a moral as well as by a physical background, and set his figures at their work, black tortured shadows before the white glow of the morality of his New England forefathers. That is precisely what Stevenson did when in the second revision of *Dr Jekyll and Mr Hyde*, he strengthened the allegorical presentation; he took, as narrator, the moral attitude of his stern, Scottish ancestry, and in doing so, found that one of his own personalities for which that attitude was most real, recovered from the past a Stevenson tortured between good and evil, and in sustaining the mental pose of this unhappy Stevenson found again something of his unhappiness, and translated an artistic device into a vivid, momentary but not for that the less painful reality.

---

[1] *Treasure Island,* chapter XXVI, 'Israel Hands'.

[2] A wonderful reverse-analogy. Sir Philip Sidney (1554–86), English pastoral poet, courtier, and soldier, famous for his *Astrophil and Stella* sonnets, died from a wound received in battle against the Spaniards at Zutphen.

[3] The story tells of a boy and his *Doppelgänger* who acts as voice of conscience to the debauched hero.

[4] "Jan[uary] 2, 1885. *Letters*, II, 253."

In 1896, a collection of short fables and apologues was added to a new edition of *Dr Jekyll and Mr Hyde*.[1] Most of them had been written before 1888, and Stevenson had talked of making a book of them; he added a few during his stay in the South Seas, but they were unpublished at his death. This little collection is a sort of nursery garden, in which we can see less elaborate specimens of the half-romantic, half-moral tales, of which *Markheim*, and *Dr Jekyll and Mr Hyde* are the better known examples. But they are not all on this pattern. Some, not the best, are on an austere Aesopic model; others, like the conversation between Smollett and Silver, in an open place not far from the story of *Treasure Island* are a gentle, balanced, playing with the facts of life; others again like the sentences exchanged between the eager tadpole and the elderly frog,[2] are mainly whimsical illustrations of human attitudes. The best are very short fairy stories, different in handling, and effect, but identical in intention with Wilde's 'Poems in Prose'. Of such are *The House of Eld*, *The Touchstone*, *The Poor Thing* and *The Song of the Morrow*. They are such tales as Blake's poem of the boy and the old woman:[3] the last is indeed identical with that. The king's daughter, speaking to the old crone at the beach, and ending as

---

[1] *The Strange Case of Dr Jekyll and Mr Hyde, with other Fables* (1896). 'Apologues': brief moral fables.

[2] 'The Tadpole and the Frog':

> 'Be ashamed of yourself,' said the frog.
> 'When I was a tadpole, I had no tail.'
> 'That's just what I thought!' said the tadpole.
> 'You never were a tadpole.'

[3] 'The Mental Traveller' by the English romantic poet and painter William Blake (1757–1827) has a similar circular structure; it includes these verses:

> And if the babe is born a boy
> He's given to a woman old,
> Who nails him down upon a rock,
> Catches his shrieks in cups of gold.

> She binds iron thorns around his head,
> And pierces both his hands and feet,
> And cuts his heart out of his side
> To make it feel both cold & heat.

> Her fingers number every nerve
> Just as a miser counts his gold;
> She lives upon his shrieks and cries –
> And she grows young as he grows old,

> Till he becomes a bleeding youth
> And she becomes a virgin bright;
> Then he rends up his manacles
> And pins her down for his delight ...

an old crone, to whom speaks a king's daughter. There is something in the prose of the antique manner of Morris:[1] and a suggestion too of the prose that was to be written years afterwards by J. M. Synge,[2] compound of the fine gesture of old romance and the intimate grammar of the peasantry: for example:

> And the King's daughter of Duntrine got her to that part of the beach where strange things had been done in the ancient ages; and there she sat her down. The sea foam ran to her feet, and the dead leaves swarmed about her back, and the veil blew about her face in the blowing of the wind. And when she lifted up her eyes, there was the daughter of a King come walking on the beach. Her hair was like the spun gold, and her eyes like pools in a river, and she had no thought for the morrow and no power upon the hour, after the manner of simple men.[3]

These fables contain some of Stevenson's most notable images; the man listening to his ancestors, who spoke together with bee-like voices, and stooping his hand among their bones, when 'the dead laid hold upon it many and faint like ants';[4] the elder brother whose soul was as small as a pea, and whose heart was 'a bag of little fears like scorpions';[5] the woman who 'smiled as a clock ticks, and knew not wherefore';[6] and the appearance gobbling like a turkey in the story of 'The House of Eld',[7] which is in its way Stevenson's wistful expression of the relations he feared between himself and his parents. And this compound of vivid imagery, of felt rather than of merely seen pictures, with a contemplation of life separated a little from two particular manifestations, is the main part of many of his longer stories. The Aesopic fables do not succeed;[8] they are wilfully imitation antiques, involving an unnecessary sacrifice of power in exchange for a virtue not now to be obtained. They were to be as hard as nuts, without ornaments, and so they are, but whereas in Aesop the fruit is all of a piece,

---

[1] William Morris (1834–96), English socialist writer and artist, a founder of the Arts and Crafts movement, and of the Kelmscott Press.

[2] John Millington Synge (1871–1909), Irish playwright, poet and folklorist, author of *The Playboy of the Western World*, *Riders to the Sea* and other well-received plays.

[3] 'The Song of the Morrow,' *Fables*, 20.

[4] 'The Poor Thing,' *Fables*, 14.

[5] 'The Touchstone,' *Fables*, 18.

[6] Ibid.

[7] *Fables*, 8.

[8] At Coniston in the autumn of 1910, Ransome experimented without great success in writing fables.

green[1] throughout, in these the kernel rattles dry in the husk, and can be separated from it with advantage. The idea: no child believes that his father was ever young: is more immediate and striking than its gratuitous translation into tadpole and frog. Indeed, in *Fables*, the careful reader will find not only the simplest examples of Stevenson's virtues, but also at least a suggestion of the cause of his occasional blindness to failure, the shorter catechist[2] setting the romancer to polish the chapel door-handle, instead of lifting the roof of the chapel off its walls as he rose with the clouds of romance about his shoulders and the romantic vision in his eyes.

As Happy as Kings[3]

About this time thirty years ago, a Mr Stevenson, severely stricken in wind and limb, sorely troubled with the ridiculous details of drains and smells in a house he had taken in the hope of being well in it, was busied in composition of a kind almost entirely new to him. He had written three or four pretty little books of prose, *The New Arabian Nights*, and a story for boys called *Treasure Island* which had earned much disapprobation when published in a boy's magazine.[4] His friends were mostly poets, and it was with an agitated diffidence that he announced to them the work in which he was engaged: *Penny Whistles for Small Whistlers*, afterwards *A Child's Garden of Verses*. Just about the same time it happened that I was born.[5] It further happened that the book had just had time to percolate the provinces, and induce in provincial parents a readiness to read it aloud instead of Bunyan,[6] when I, in the course of nature, was ready to listen to it. There are accordingly when I read it now, two distinct persons looking at the

---

[1] i.e. fresh and wholesome; but perhaps also an allusion to the quality of thought, from a poem by Andrew Marvell (1621–78), 'The Garden': 'Annihilating all that's made / To a green thought in a green shade', which had become a recognised image for philosophical truth.

[2] As a proper Scottish child Stevenson would have been proficient in 'the Shorter Catechism', a set of questions and answers grounding children in the doctrines of the Church of Scotland.

[3] The only section with a title in the manuscript, a quotation from a poem in *A Child's Garden of Verses*: 'Happy Thought'. The first pages of this section (also headed "Stevenson. Poetry.") comprise the only part of the MS to have been published during Ransome's lifetime; they were written on 26 January 1914 (as his diary shows) and appear under the same title with little alteration in *The New Witness*, 5 February 1914 (see appendix A.3).

[4] *Young Folks*.

[5] Ransome was born on 18 January 1884, in Leeds, Yorkshire.

[6] John Bunyan (1628–88), author of *The Pilgrim's Progress* (1678), inspiration for many children's books, especially Louisa M. Alcott's *Little Women*.

print, a baldheaded person[1] who has read too many books, and a small boy who has read *Robinson Crusoe, Little Arthur's History of England*[2] (a noble work) and *As Pretty as Seven*[3] (the best book of German fairy stories with the most charming woodcuts in the world). I differ from that small boy, alas; on most things. Our tastes are widely divergent. But on the 'penny whistles'[4] of that Mr Stevenson we still preserve a very happy unanimity.

A Child's Garden of Verses is one of those smiling accidents that befall serious, laborious men. When Morris, intent on a thousand other things, delighted his fellow undergraduates with the poems that were afterwards printed in his first volume,[5] and remarked that, if this was poetry, then it was very easy, he expressed very much what Stevenson must have felt when, after long years of technical diligence in other directions, he found himself writing these things, and with his unerring criticism of himself saw with surprise that they were very good. 'These are rhymes, jingles; I don't go for eternity and the three unities,'[6] and he gaily answered criticism on occasional imperfect rhymes, which, he said, were good enough for him. He did not find them easy: 'I can usually do whistles only by giving my whole mind to it: to produce even such limping verse demanding the whole forces of my untuneful soul.'[7]

He did not believe them to be poetry of any very high order. 'Poetry,' he said, 'is not the strong point of the text, and I shrink from any title

---

[1] Writing in early 1914, Ransome was not yet the bald-headed person he was to become, but cultivated a sage and elderly persona, at one point growing a beard to help. By the time he drew Captain Flint (in *Swallowdale*, 1932, a self-portrait) he was indeed bald. The idea of the adult reader of children's books being 'two people' is addressed in recent post-modernist critical theory, where notions of intertextuality and of duality of address in both writer and reader have been discussed in relation to children's literature. For Ransome, as for Stevenson, childhood was never something to be left behind.

[2] (1835), a much-republished children's history by Maria, Lady Callcott (1785–1842). Ransome's mother Edith had published as recently as 1903 her own history-book for children, *A First History of England.*

[3] *As Pretty as Seven, and Other Popular German Tales* [by the Brothers Grimm] by Ludwig Bechstein (1801–60), with illustrations by A. L. Richter (1872).

[4] So much in tune was Ransome with Stevenson as a 'penny whistler' that he used that term in a eulogistic paragraph, intended perhaps as a conclusion or envoi to this study (see note to end of Part I, above, and appendix A.1.i).

[5] *The Defence of Guenevere, and other poems* (1858). J. W. Mackail's *Life of William Morris* had seduced Ransome away from the study of chemistry at Yorkshire College and made him determined to become a man of letters.

[6] To Sidney Colvin, early November, 1883.

[7] "To Henley, Hyères, Oct[ober], 1883. [*Letters*,] II, 140."

that might seem to claim that quality.' He thought of calling them 'Penny Whistles', and publishing them with a sketch of 'a party playing on a P. W. to a little ring of dancing children,'[1] as a frontispiece. When the book was out, he announced to Mr Gosse: 'I have now published on 101 small pages 'The Complete Proof of Mr R. L. Stevenson's Incapacity To Write Verse' in a series of graduated examples with table of contents.'[2] Yet with one or two exceptions he never wrote better verse, and, perhaps, he never elsewhere achieved a completer and more personal success. And in spite of his diffidence in writing to his friends, poets, he loved these verses well. 'They look ghastly,' he said, 'in the cold light of print; but there is something nice in the little ragged regiment for all; the blackguards seem to me to smile, to have a kind of childish treble note that sounds in my ears freshly; not song, if you will, but a child's voice.'[3]

A child's voice in literature had never been achieved before, except for a moment and by a child, the wonderful Marjorie Fleming[4] whose immortal lines on a nurse (I think):

> But she was more than usual calm,
> She did not give a single dam –

are treasured by all who have ever heard them. 'Marjorie Fleming I have known, as you surmise, for long', Stevenson wrote to Mr William Archer. 'She was possibly – no, I take back possibly – she was one of the greatest works of God. Your note about the resemblance of her verses to mine gave me great joy, though it only proved me a plagiarist.'[5]

Some of the *Songs of Innocence*[6] are in the mouths of children, but Blake's children are angels and their clear voices are ecstatic with the hope and the memory of paradise. Stevenson's child is concentrated, humanely,

---

[1] To W. E. Henley, early May 1883, *Letters*, II, 103.

[2] To Edmund Gosse, 12 March 1885, Letters, II, 230.

[3] Ibid.

[4] Marjorie Fleming (1803–11), a Scottish child poet who died of measles. A fine example is 'Isa's Bed', is to her beloved sister Isabel.

> I love in Isa's bed to lie
> Oh such a joy and luxury
> The bottom of the bed I sleep,
> And with great care within I creep
> Oft I embrace her feet of lillys,
> But she has goton all the pillies.
> Her neck I never can embrace,
> But I do hug her feet in place.

[5] "To William Archer, March 27, 1894. *Letters*, IV, 249."

[6] The first of Blake's self-illuminated books, published in 1789.

on the present. The sun in the morning, the lamplighter at night, the rustle of an aunt's skirts, play more serious than life, are the simplest and least questionable version of a philosophy ridiculous in the mouth of Dr Pangloss,[1] but respectable, gallant, and holding for older persons who listen to it, something of the pattern of a forlorn hope:

> The world is [so] full of a number of things,
> I'm sure we should all be as happy as kings.[2]

These things are the real furniture of childish psychology, and give us back our babyhood.

I suppose each reader of the book, each reviewer of that little ragged smiling regiment, must himself have been the child who sang these to a plain but cheerful recitative, like the a. b. ab,[3] we hear when, dusty with age and travel, we pass by a village schoolroom. The only piece of false psychology in the book is the last poem, 'To any reader':

> As from the house your mother sees
> You playing round the garden trees,
> So you may see, if you will look
> Through the windows of this book,
> Another child, far, far away,
> And in another garden, play.

That is not so. Stevenson saw himself, but every child who hears the verses, identifies the land of counterpane with his own bed, and every grown person sees not the little Scottish boy in the old Manse at Colinton, but lives again his own infancy.[4]

I count myself fortunate that I was born late enough to be among the children whose mothers have read aloud them *The Child's Garden of Verses*. For me now they have something of the lovable quality that I suppose everybody attributes to his own childhood. They were translated into my life, and episodes in it seem to have been known to Stevenson though not always quite accurately chronicled by him. Now in writing of them I think I may wisely defer to a childish critic of long ago who was more certain of his favourites than ever I can be. When I was on the fringe of babyhood, before I went to school, older then three but without the hoary dignity of nine or ten; these were the verses I liked best: 'Bed in Summer'; 'Foreign Lands',

---

[1] Dr Pangloss: absurdly optimistic moral philosopher in Voltaire's *Candide* who believes that everything is for the best in the best of all possible worlds.

[2] 'Happy Thought', poem 24 of *A Child's Garden of Verses*.

[3] i.e. phonic chanting.

[4] The adult 'any reader' will always be 'far far away' in time; but Ransome is right in finding this poem the odd-man-out in terms of sentimentality of tone.

principally for the open feeling of the fourth line 'And looked abroad on foreign lands'; the insistent question of 'Windy Nights', 'Late in the night when the fires are out, Why does he gallop and gallop about?' best of all, perhaps. 'The Land of Counterpane' with its real transfiguration of dip and hill in counterpane geography; with contempt of superior science and at the same time a delight in the fantasy, the address to 'My Shadow'; doubtfully with a distaste for the realism of the comb and the mention of girl's names as warriors, the 'Marching Song'. Then I liked the first stanza of 'The Cow', the first and last stanzas of 'Good and Bad Children' partly for the rhyme's sake:

> Children, you are very little,
> And your bones are very brittle;
> If you would grow great and stately,
> You must try to walk sedately ...

and

> Cruel children, crying babies,
> All grow up as geese and gabies,
> Hated, as their age increases,
> By their nephews and their nieces –

this last with a backhand deduction as to the childhood of my aunts,[1] which Stevenson certainly never intended. 'The Lamplighter' was another favourite, though the trees whose leaves were suddenly silenced by the lamp in the autumn evenings made it impossible for Leerie to nod to any little child, listening for his footsteps and watching from the house for the illumination. This Stevenson should have foreseen.[2] 'From a Railway Carriage' was always lovingly associated with journeys to the north country hills, although he[3] wished to edit it, and still thinks that Stevenson would not have disapproved the emendation. In a moving railway carriage one thing always impresses itself on the childish mind, and that is the dip and rise of the telegraph lines as they cut the square of the window. And that Stevenson has omitted. Now it was by that that I knew I was in a train.

---

[1] Ransome had no hated aunt; the 'Great Aunt' who interrupted the holiday lives of her nieces in *Swallowdale* and *The Picts and the Martyrs* is probably a purely literary construct. Of Ransome's aunts, Katy was an excellent croquet-player, and in old age had great fun careering down-hill in her bathchair; his Great-Aunt Susan with her bows and arrows was a weekly refuge from his prep-school at Windermere; his very remarkable missionary aunts, Jessie and Edith, he later visited in China.

[2] Each child reader affirms the experience presented in these poems, to be brought up short here and there by recognition of impossibility; thus literature enlarges a child's world.

[3] That is, the child Ransome.

I liked the sentiment but resented the doll in 'My Ship and I', and always waited in the readings for the thrill of the last line: 'And fire the penny cannon in the bow.' And full of knowledge that the very room in which my parents read possessed a similar occult geography, I had a proprietary pleasure in 'The Land of Story-Books'. Not one of the poems in the section called 'Garden Days' earned my suffrage, except for a few single lines and pictures, and I am now in cordial agreement with my youth. The Envoys were for grown-up people only, and I was no friend to little Louis Sanchez.[1]

I think the childish critic had found the pick of the collection, and I have little to add to his choice by way of commentary. Stevenson was not altogether right when he refused his verses the name of poetry. Much of it is charming prose matter that has gained the lasting, memorable quality of good nonsense-rhymes. He preserves with extraordinary skill the delightful freedom from ulterior motive, which is the chief glory of the childish imagination. He is generous of quite inimitable touches of childish diction:

> The friendly cow all red and white,
> I love with all my heart:
> She gives me cream *with all her might*
> To eat with apple-tart.[2]

There is self-consciousness here and there of a kind bad for children and detested by them, as: 'Who should climb but little me?' But as a rule the psychology is just, and sometimes brilliant in its accuracy, as in the pirate-story, when the geography is made up as the play goes, and only in the last line, when they are sorely needed when the cattle 'are charging with a roar', decides, breathlessly, that 'the wicket is the harbour and the garden is the shore.' Then too there are epithets with the rightness, and the surprisingness of true poetry.

> And in a corner find the toys
> Of the old Egyptian boys.

It would be hard to overpraise the perception and the courage that supplied and left the word 'Egyptian', so true, and so inexplicable.[3] And we have only to write in prose the matter of a story: 'In the winter I get up at night and dress by the yellow light of a candle, whereas in summer, on the contrary, I have to go to bed by day' – and compare it with the verse:

---

[1] 'To My Name-Child' ('little Louis Sanchez', who played 'on the beach of Monterey') is the second last poem in the book.

[2] 'The Cow'. The emphasis is Ransome's.

[3] This is where the section published in *The New Witness* (see appendix A.3) ends.

> In winter I get up at night
> And dress by yellow candle-light.
> In summer, quite the other way,
> I have to go to bed by day –

to perceive that there is more in this than rhymed prose, and that the matter is indeed stamped with the personal and untranslatable form of poetry.[1]

Stevenson was not deceived by the fact of writing verse into thinking– like so many romancers turned poetasters[2] – that in writing prose he had missed his vocation as a poet. He knew that was a difference not only in result but in intuition between his verse and that of those of his contemporaries whom he held to be poets. He asks John Addington Symonds:

> I wonder if you saw my book of verses? It went into a second edition, because of my name, I suppose, and its *prose* merits. I do not set up to be a poet. Only an all-round literary man: a man who talks, not one who sings. But I believe the very fact that it was only speech served the book with the public. Horace is much a speaker, and see how popular! most of Martial is only speech, and I cannot conceive a person who does not love his Martial; most of Burns, also, such as 'The Louse', 'The Toothache', 'The Haggis', and lots more of his best. Excuse this little apology for my house; but I don't like to come before people who have a note of song, and let it be supposed I do not know the difference.[3]

At the same time he had no very low opinion of the muse in her more gossiping moments; he could instance Herrick[4] and Martial[5] and many others whose verses seemed to be mere talk when compared with the solemn music or the intenser song of poets whom he admitted to be greater. But he did not clearly perceive that verse may be talkative and yet poetry, while he cheerfully announced, sometimes mistakenly, that his verse was

---

[1] The scarcely legible handwriting of this preceding section betrays the speed at which Ransome composed his account of this much-loved book.

[2] i.e. incompetent would-be poets.

[3] "To J. A. Symonds. Saranac. Nov[ember] 21, 1887. [*Letters,*] III, 25." John Addington Symonds (1840–93), English poet and essayist, like Stevenson had lived in Davos to recover his health.

[4] Robert Herrick (1591–1674), English lyrical poet.

[5] Martial, Roman epigrammatist whose poems formed part of traditional schoolboy education.

talkative and not poetry at all. He says of his own verse: '... I have begun to learn some of the rudiments of the trade, and have written three or four pretty enough pieces of octosyllabic nonsense, semi-serious, semi-smiling. A kind of prose Herrick, divested of the gift of verse, and you behold the Bard.'[1] To William Sharp, he writes:

> I have never called my verses poetry: they are verse, the verse of a speaker not a singer; but that is a fair business like another. I am of your mind in preferring much the Scotch verses, and in thinking 'Requiem' the nearest thing to poetry that I have ever 'clerked'.[2]

And again, in sending a sonnet to Sharp who edited an anthology, he wrote: 'The form of my so-called sonnets will cause you as much agony as it causes me little.'[3] He was, I think, very uncertain as to the precise nature of the difference, though he willingly admitted its existence.

For Stevenson story-telling was a beneficial drug for the mind:

> When I suffer in my mind, stories are my refuge; I take them like opium; and I consider one who writes them a sort of doctor of the mind. And frankly, Meiklejohn, it is not Shakespeare we take to, when we are in a hot corner; nor, certainly, George Eliot – no, nor even Balzac. It is Charles Reade, or old Dumas, or the Arabian Nights, or the best of Walter Scott; it is stories we want, not the high poetic function which represents the world; we are then like the Asiatic with his improvisatore or the middle-aged with his trouvère. We want incident, interest, action: to the devil with your philosophy. When we are well again, and have an easy mind, we shall pursue your important work; but what we want now is a drug. So I, when I am ready to go beside myself, stick my head into a storybook, as the ostrich with her bush; but fate and fortune meantime belabour my posteriors at their will.[4]

And when we are tempted to compare the airy emptiness of Stevenson's novels with the rich humanity, the filled views, of, for example, Dostoevsky,[5]

---

[1] "*Letters*, II, 121. To W. E. Henley."

[2] "William Sharp (Fiona McLeod) *A Memoir*, Elizabeth Sharp. Heinemann, p. 139."

[3] Ibid., "p. 117."

[4] John M. D. Meiklejohn (1830–1902), Scottish author of textbooks of history, geography and English language. "San Francisco, Feb[ruary] 1, 1880. *Letters*, I, 278."

[5] Feodor M. Dostoevsky (1821–81), Russian novelist, admired for his psychological realism; author of *Crime and Punishment, The Brothers Karamazov*, among others.

or Turgenev[1] or Korolenko,[2] we must remember that such a comparison was never invited by Stevenson. I have chosen these Russian examples on purpose, instead of the Balzac[3] or the George Eliot[4] that to Stevenson represented the exciting but strange antipodes of his storytelling world, because in them the thing that Stevenson lacked is intensified, while his peculiar gifts are almost absent, whereas Balzac or that stern-faced woman both took considerable pleasure in storytelling for its own sake. Those Russians are concerned with life itself: they want to know, to understand, to make life conscious; they sacrifice all else to that end. Stevenson asked for stories, to make life bearable, to make it pleasant, and when he wrote tales, he wrote such tales as he would have wished to find at hand in such a mood as that in which he wrote the paragraph I have just copied out. His is not the tradition of Richardson,[5] Bronte,[6] Hardy[7] and Meredith, though just as Meredith in the beginning of his life wrote *The Shaving of Shagpat* so Stevenson, at the end of his, wrote *Weir of Hermiston* which, more than any other of his books, belongs to the other side of the gulf between the poet and the troubadours.[8]

[1] Ivan Turgenev (1818–83) Russian novelist and playwright, friend of Flaubert; author of the novel *Fathers and Sons* (an important theme for both Stevenson and Ransome).

[2] Vladimir Korolenko (1853–1921), Ukrainian short-story-writer (*The Blind Musician* is one of his collections), opponent of Tsarist policies, exiled to Siberia, published too late to have been an influence on Stevenson. Ransome so admired him as to substitute his name here for that of Tolstoy (crossed out).

[3] Honoré de Balzac (1799–1850), whose series of novels *La comédie humaine* was a landmark in realism.

[4] George Eliot, pseudonym of Mary Ann Evans (1819–80), English novelist acclaimed for psychological realism.

[5] This plethora of names is due to first-draft speed. Ransome's pen races across the page. Here he gives a chronological 'great tradition' of English novelists. Samuel Richardson (1689–1761), novelist, author of *Pamela: Or Virtue Rewarded*, and *Sir Charles Grandison*, another epistolary novel, which was a favourite of Jane Austen's.

[6] *Wuthering Heights* by Emily Brontë (1818–48) is the archetype for novels of romance where the Yorkshire landscapes and qualities of character are interdependent.

[7] Thomas Hardy (1840–1928), poet and novelist, whose powerful sense of place is tied to the passions of his characters in novels such as *Jude the Obscure* and *Far from the Madding Crowd*.

[8] This 'Arabian entertainment', an allegorical fantasy, was Meredith's earliest published prose narrative (1856). Ransome may have already been planning his version of Aladdin, and it is likely that he did admire *Shagpat*. Noting that just as *Shagpat* is odd-man-out among Meredith's novels, so is *Weir* amongst Stevenson's, he implies that just as *Shagpat* is trivial in comparison

A course of Balzac which, as Wilde said, 'reduces our living friends to shadows, and our acquaintances to the shadows of shades' turns Stevenson's creations into the most transparent veils, and a course of Dostoevsky makes them altogether non-existent. But only the crudest criticism would undervalue them on that account, just as only the dullest critics measure a work by comparison with another, and only he who has no right to be a critic at all measures it by comparison with another work in an altogether different kind.[1]

Adventure was what Stevenson cared for in life; adventure was what brought him to his twentieth reading of *Vicomte de Bragelonne*; adventure is what delighted him in his own books; and it is after a course of Dumas that the Scotch novels[2] of Stevenson appear in their true colours, something new, something different, accomplished, graceful sacrifices on the altar of a tradition that will last as long as men are young enough to have the hearts of boys. *Treasure Island* opened the run; *The Black Arrow* perhaps momentarily destroyed his belief in it; but with *Kidnapped* he opened the series of his Scotch novels, and *Kidnapped* was professedly a boy's book: 'This,' says Stevenson, apologising in the preface for the freedoms he had taken with chronology, 'is no furniture for the scholar's library, but a book for the winter evening school-room when the tasks are over and the hour for bed draws near; and honest Alan, who was a grim old fire-eater in his day has in this new avatar no more desperate purpose than to steal some young gentleman's attention from his *Ovid*, carry him awhile into the Highlands and the last century, and pack him to bed with some engaging images to mingle with his dreams.'[3]

Engaging images indeed: Alan Breck with his 'Eh mon, am I no a bonny fighter?', and his love of fine clothes, and that intolerable David, who excuses himself only by his adventures, and, after all is with the less compunction turned out to make room for ourselves: the old uncle, the pretty girl at the inn, and many more. But David is the problem: as Mr Rankeillor remarked he had shown 'a singular aptitude for getting into false positions; and, yes, upon the whole, for behaving well in them': but it is David who chronicles Mr Rankeillor's remark, like so many others, to his own advantage. Now if Alan Breck had written the book, he would have kept up a fine, flaunting,

with *The Egoist*, so are all of Stevenson's narratives in comparison with *Weir* – most readers would agree.

[1] Ransome's ambition to be taken seriously as a critic is evident here. He disarmingly uses a trope which displays the discarded criticism as part of his criticism, before embarking on a quest to define the *kind* of genius that belonged to Stevenson.

[2] Ransome wrote seven pages on 'Scotch novels' on 6 January 1914.

[3] Prefatory letter of dedication to Charles Baxter, university friend and lawyer who acted for Stevenson in some business matters.

boasting, braggadocio vein, which would have amused rather than repelled. There is something repugnant in the smug David, and yet – Stevenson knew what he was about, and yet again; it is no use, no fervour of casuistry will ever make me like David. I read the book with pleasure, with profit, with continual amusement, and an increasing dislike for its narrator. It is one of Stevenson's triumphs that he should have made him live enough to be disliked. And, David apart, the book contains examples of that thrill, that faint stir of the flesh over the cheek bones, that is given by romance, achieved less obviously, less easily than by gold moidores, doubloons, and reminiscence of Captain Kidd.[1] Things like the Red Fox being a hot man wiping his face at the moment of his death, Alan's appearance with the fishing rod, the race through the heather and his drawing the soldiers after him from the murderer, even the *Udolpho*[2] touch in the lightning about the tower when David climbed, so narrowly to escape his death.[3]

In December 1887, he fell 'head over heels into a new tale', *The Master of Ballantrae*, that was to be 'sound human tragedy', no boy's book now, but serious character study and yet with wild enough adventure thrown in.

> The Master is all I know of the devil. I have known hints of him, in the world, but always cowards; he is as bold as a lion, but with the same deadly, causeless duplicity I have watched with so much surprise in my two cowards. 'Tis true, I saw a hint of the same nature in another man who was not a coward; but he had other things to attend to; the Master has nothing else but his devilry.[4]

This is serious enough, but the commentary on it is in an essay in *The Art of Writing* (an essay which carries off in a gentlemanly way its cousin-ship to Poe's 'Philosophy of Composition')[5] which describes the invention and inception of the tale – the starting point being the final resuscitation of the Master, and the novel itself being at first merely the steps to that high culmination. Thus from the very beginning there was conflict, for the novel became more and more real, lively, humane, and the legerdemain of

---

[1] William Kidd (1645–1701), a Scot hanged on counts of piracy and murder. His reputation for piracy may have been ill deserved.

[2] Of thrilling horror, as in *The Mysteries of Udolpho* (1794), a highly popular Gothic romance by the English novelist Ann Radcliffe.

[3] Ransome elsewhere notes this further observation, from Will Low: "Low noticed the strong impression of the country through which David Balfour and Alan Breck escape in *Kidnapped*. Stevenson made him look through the books, to see that there was actually 'not a live description of landscape in it.' Low, p. 426."

[4] "Letter to Colvin. III. 36."

[5] An essay by Poe in which he describes the composition of his poem 'The Raven'.

the finish, which however he would not throw over, retained its need of a conspiring showman and quivering green limelight. And by the time the book was two thirds written, Stevenson was well aware of the danger he was in. In a letter to Henry James written in March 1888, he describes the plot, and his difficulty, and wrote what must be the last verdict upon the book:

> Five parts of it are sound, human tragedy; the last one or two, I regret to say, not so soundly designed; I almost hesitate to write them; they are very picturesque, but they are fantastic; they shame, perhaps degrade, the beginning. I wish I knew; that was how the tale came to me however. I got the situation; it was an old taste of mine: The older brother goes out in the '45, the younger stays; the younger, of course, gets title and estate and marries the bride designate of the elder – a family match, but he (the younger) had always loved her, and she had really loved the elder. Do you see the situation? Then the devil and Saranac suggested this dénouement, and I joined the two ends in a day or two of constant feverish thought, and began to write. And now – I wonder if I have not gone too far with the fantastic? The elder brother is an INCUBUS: supposed to be killed at Culloden, he turns up again and bleeds the family of money; on that stopping he comes and lives with them, whence flows the real tragedy, the nocturnal duel of the brothers (very naturally, and indeed, I think, inevitably arising), and second supposed death of the elder. Husband and wife now really make up, and then the cloven hoof appears. For the third supposed death and the manner of the third reappearance is steep; steep, sir. It is even very steep, and I fear it shames the honest stuff so far; but then it is highly pictorial, and it leads up to the death of the elder brother at the hands of the younger in a perfectly cold-blooded murder, of which I wish (and mean) the reader to approve. You see how daring is the design. There are really but six characters, and one of these episodic, and yet it covers eighteen years, and will be, I imagine, the longest of my works.[1]

I have quoted this long passage because I cannot help thinking that Stevenson pointed with great accuracy to the fundamental flaw in the book, and because it illustrates extremely clearly how in a long composition the original inspiration may wake an older inspiration still, and come in the end to be a mere incubus upon its back, as this ancient inspiration stirs in its sleep, and rises, and at last carries all else sturdily before it. It was more than a year after this letter was written, before the book was finished in Honolulu. But in that time the novel had but grown stronger, the Poesque dénouement more bigoted in retaining its fantastic atmosphere,

---

[1] "[*Letters*,] III, 48."

the fundamental contradiction more noticeable and painful. It is strange to reflect on the persistence of ideas, on that fantastic goblin refusing to be unseated from the shoulder of a tale which as it grew to maturity became only less and less fit to carry it.[1]

A number of passages in Stevenson's *Letters*, in which he discusses the personages of his fictions, as well as his noticeable manner towards them, suggest and indeed demand a discussion of the nature of such imaginary characters.[2] The problems they offer are by no means as simple as less conscious artists than Stevenson, and long tradition, make them appear. They are excellent examples of those problems which long familiarity has led us to believe non-existent. We are in the habit of talking about the characters of fiction precisely as if they were men and women, indeed as if they were men and women whom we know a little better than we know most of our acquaintances. Don Quixote, Sancho Panza, Tom Jones, Willoughby:[3] we can even come so far as to regard these imaginary creatures as standards or types to which we refer our friends in default of closer definition. Such a one, we say, is a Don Quixote: there is more than a touch of Tom Jones in such another ... And yet Don Quixote and Tom Jones are not people, but are vividly present in our minds as we remember sentences of Cervantes and Fielding. There should not be any essential difference between a novel and a poem, as far as our definition of art in general will carry us, and, unless that is incorrect, a novel, like any other work of art, is an act of becoming conscious, performed by its author. But an illusion is produced that the author has left his own life aside, and is merely chronicling the lives of others. We are faced with the difficulty of reconciling this apparent contradiction.[4]

The first contribution to this reconciliation we may take from a passage in Stevenson's letters, written without any such intention. Indeed the problem does not seem to have troubled him at all. It is a little story of Meredith and *The Egoist*.

A young friend of Mr Meredith's (as I have the story) came to him in

---

[1] Ransome's judgement is informed by his recently published and well-received critical study of Poe (1910).

[2] "Stevenson. Characters in Novels" is the heading for this section.

[3] The self-styled Don Quixote de la Mancha, hero in his own fantasy of chivalry, and his earthy companion Sancho Panza, are protagonists of the comic romance by the Spanish writer Miguel de Cervantes Saavedra, *Don Quixote* (1605). Tom Jones is the hero of Fielding's novel of that name; is the foolish adventurer in marriage Sir Willoughby Patterne, 'the egoist' after whom Meredith named his novel (1879).

[4] Ransome here foreshadows questions that become important in late twentieth-century critical debate.

an agony. 'This is too bad of you,' he cried. 'Willoughby is me!' 'No, my dear fellow,' said the author; 'he is all of us.'[1]

That is to say that at least there was enough of him in Meredith to allow his author to learn the rest by separating the promise of him that was in himself from those other qualities which fortunately contradicted and smothered his existence.[2] This development of an imaginary character out of oneself by the elimination of the elements in one's nature which suppress its actual growth is at least analogous to the separation of a moment of life from the unconscious crowded flux of living. It is a choice of a mental attitude from among the many that would be possible in ordinary life, and the voluntary retention of that attitude – in a manner exactly analogous to the careful tuning of a work of art to the note sounded by the particular mood that dictates it. So far, we are on safe ground, and a character within a fiction is a work within a work, itself subject to the same limitations, and produced by the same methods as the larger work, in which it shares in a harmony to which it contributes, by which it is ruled. We can thus imagine that it may sometimes happen that the inner work, the character, may be better realised than the larger piece of consciousness in which it is a part. There are novels in which we feel that the part is greater than the whole,[3] pictures in which a portrait seems to have swelled out of proportion, forced its way through the canvas and destroyed the perspective of the whole. And, indeed, one purpose of the foregoing paragraph of analysis is to enable us to state to ourselves how it is that in *Catriona* for example, David Balfour seems to be so very much more actual than the story in which he takes a part. More than once in Stevenson's books a character seems to stand before us like a reveller the morning after a masquerade, an unimpeachable reality, with remnants of the story hanging about him, the rags and tatters of a fancy dress, pale in the morning light.

It will be worth our while to glance for a moment at the gradual development of character in the personages of narrative. In the beginning they had, properly speaking, no individuality at all.[4] They took part in events, and

---

[1] Stevenson, *The Art of Writing*, chapter 3. He continues: 'I have read *The Egoist* five or six times myself, and I mean to read it again; for I am like the young friend of the anecdote – I think Willoughby an unmanly but a very serviceable exposure of myself.' Under the heading 'Trust', Ransome notes "He very early knew Meredith, and would get M[eredith] to tell his best. Gosse, 76, intro by Colvin."

[2] Ransome is outdoing himself with engaging but mischievous convolutions of sentence-structure.

[3] Ransome's soon-to-be-written *The Elixir of Life* (1915) is one such: its best moment is a splendid horse-race with the Devil.

[4] Ransome glances back to his recent work in his *A History of Storytelling, Studies in the Development of Narrative* (1909).

were credited only with the simplest emotions, common to all men. They had a father's love, a lover's ardour and such courage as their author liked to believe was his own. A remarkable innovation was the first picture of a coward, but not so remarkable as the first picture of a coward which did not make him hateful. The events were at first everything, and the heroes and heroines who took part in them were merely what the listeners would like to think of themselves. The consciousness of life given by this primitive art was a projection of oneself into imaginary action and a general realisation of oneself in delightful, in admirable poses.[1] The good knight is wholly virtuous, the bad simply his opposite, scarcely realised at all except as a thing to be cloven to the chine without remorse. The greater the force conquered, the greater the glory; and so the monster of Beowulf grows large, and Jack kills a giant instead of another Jack.[2] Neither the monster nor the giant are realised except as things horrid and very difficult and dangerous to kill.

Then, in the drama, the persons opposed are visible upon the stage; their actions need more explanation; they begin to speak and move like human beings. The mind wakes slowly to the existence of other minds, unlike itself, but no less vividly peculiar and alive, and these separate dramatic realisations are given their subordinate place in a larger, a circumspicuous realisation. Then, I think of Richardson,[3] with whom actions and personnages became invisible, and we are entirely concerned with thoughts and motives. With the romantics the eye comes into its own again, and throughout the nineteenth century, men play with first one mode and then another, and two or three at once, so that we forget that things have not always been so, and lose sight of the fact that to understand what they are doing we must separate these modes of consciousness, and remember that in a modern story the author may be intensifying his consciousness of life by visual realisation of its pictorial appearance, by the excitement of imagined events, and by the impersonation of characters, and that he may be doing all these three at once, and that the mastery of his work is shown by their complete coincidence, by the perfection with which he disguises from us the separateness of the planes on which he is working.[4]

[1] Ransome is not afraid of grappling with the toughest problems of art, life, and human consciousness; in this he is part of the avant-garde in his time. Here he has just crossed out 'art' and 'life' in favour of 'consciousness', and is about to insert the qualifiers 'imaginary' and 'general', intent on getting his thought clear and right.

[2] Beowulf, hero of the Old English epic, kills the monster Grendel; Jack, the young hero of the English folk-tale 'Jack the Giant-Killer'.

[3] Samuel Richardson, the novelist.

[4] When writing this account Ransome had already published collections of short-stories (they caused no stir); during the period he had Stevenson 'on the stocks', while in Russia, he was inspired to write his first novel, a strange

I think it possible[1] that Stevenson's continual self-transplantation had a little to do with the lack of body in the more ambitious works of the middle period of his life. It is not easy to give deep roots in life to work produced at a time when one's attention is continually arrested by the novel details of one's personal circumstances, when the mind is in a subdued excitability and effervescence, conscious always of the impossibility of tranmitting a true impression of its novel surroundings to the friends in collaboration with whom it exists, in so far as it depends upon its past. The mind strikes deeper, and in whatsoever it is buried, when outer things need no transmission, but are common to its present and past life and to those of its intellectual associates.

Hazlitt, I think, said that he would be glad to spend his life in travel if he could have another life to live at home; for that those years that are spent in foreign parts do not coalesce with the rest of a man's life; and abroad it is as if he had never lived at home; and at home his foreign adventures are a sort of mirage even to himself, and do not make a part of that rising mound of experience from which each man surveys his world. I may be misrepresenting Hazlitt, for I am writing in a little Russian town where there are no English books, and so I can not check my memory.[2] But I am certainly not misrepresenting a thought that may have occurred to Stevenson, and must be present in the mind of any close student of his books.

It would be strange if this phenomenon of travel was without its effect on the writings of a man for whom his art was so identified with his life. Translators, and compilers, men of science, may be laborious when they will, and we shall not detect the influences of their travels in the changing texture of their impersonal styles. Collectors of the husks of travel may write in tents on the Andes or in blown out skins of oxen floating down the rivers of the East,[3] and be as dull or as interesting, as if they wrote at

---

    mixture of philosophy and the macabre, in a genre of fantasy inspired by Poe and Stevenson: *The Elixir of Life* (1915). This knotty analysis shows the apprentice wrestling with the novelist's art.

[1] This very personal paragraph is headed "Stevenson. Novels (Weir perhaps)." Alas, no *Weir*.

[2] This passage may have been written in June 1913, when Ransome had settled down to work on Stevenson at 'Datcha Gellibrand, Terijoki, Finland', the address from which he wrote to his mother, and inscribed on the fly-leaf of his 'Stevenson Exercise-book' (see Introduction, and appendix A.1).

[3] A rich genre of travel writing with wonderfully enticing titles was known to Ransome, including Charles Darwin, who had camped in the Andes, and Ransome's friend and former literary agent Stefana Stevens, whose *My Sudan Year* he reviewed anonymously in 1912. He may have known *Across Asia on a Bicycle: The Journey of Two American Students from Constantinople to Peking* (1894) – a work with a Stevensonian spirit of adventure.

home. But if a book is given a personal vitality, if it is the result of an intimate labour, if it depends upon its author as well as on the facts which it
records, it is subject at once to these subtler influences. Borrow did not
write *Lavengro* or *The Romany Rye* upon the road, or from notes, and the
superiority of these books as literature over *The Bible in Spain* (written
from notes and contemporary letters) or *Wild Wales* the direct result of a
journey undertaken on purpose, is due to the fact that he had had time to
re-collect himself, to refresh his personality until it could indeed translate
those old adventures into the general rhythm of his experience.

When Stevenson was twenty three, and 'ordered south', he wrote in a
letter from Avignon, where he stayed on the way:

> I cannot write while I am travelling; *c'est mon défaut*; but so it is. I
> must have a certain feeling of being at home, and my head must have
> time to settle. The new images oppress me, and I have a fever of rest-
> lessness on me.'[1]

It was not until the novelty of the South Seas had worn away into habi-
tude; not until Stevenson's active existence had closely bound itself up with
the place where he lived; not until observation had had time to slacken the
intensity, the continuity of its business, that his work took deeper roots,
and, always graceful, added strength to grace.[2]

Let us first consider *Catriona* and *St Ives*.[3] There is a curious lack of
meat upon these shapely skeletons. David Balfour is always doing, always
in exciting surroundings, but his escapes, his difficulties do not concern
us as humane adventures, but rather as a series of coincidences, of circumstances which, ultimately, do not matter. When I put down *Catriona* I feel
as if I have been listening to a light overture, sketching the motives of the
ensuing drama, and that the curtain has been rung down before the beginning of the play.

St Ives is on the way to being a novel on the ancient plan of Le Sage,[4]
or of the engaging beggar stories of Spain, like *Lazarillo de Tormes*.[5]

---

[1] "To Mrs Sitwell. Nov[ember], 1873. *Letters*, I, 80."

[2] Again Ransome prefigures his own personal situation. Only returned from
exile to the Lake District and comfortably married to Evgenia, could he write
his new kind of narrative, in novels deeply rooted in countryside he had
known and loved from childhood.

[3] "*Stevenson. Catriona*" and "Stevenson. St Ives."

[4] Alain-René Le Sage (1668–1741), author of *Gil Blas de Santillane* and other
picaresque prose romances.

[5] *The Life of Lazarillo de Tormes, and of his Fortunes and Adversities* (1550), an
anonymous Spanish novella first translated into English in 1576, and thought
to be the first picaresque work of prose fiction.

The character of St Ives is charming, but unchanged by his experiences. He is the same at beginning and end of the book; and the *plot*, the ingenious contrivance of the incredible cousin, pursuing, is merely a device for shifting scenery, for permitting an apparent logic to a succession of independent adventures, all of which are described with equal gusto and detail, no expansion in one place or contraction in another to give the book as a whole a notable shape or internal harmony. The book is a ribbon of adventure,[1] like the North Road; most of the adventures are unnecessary: all are delightful. The point is that all are separate. The episode of the duel among the French prisoners, the escape from the castle, the journey with the Scotch drovers, the adventure with the English smuggler of French prisoners, the claret coloured coach, the interrupted elopement to Gretna Green, the adventures of the drunken Swots of the University of Cramond, the balloon escape, the adventure of the *Lady Nepean* with its special story of Captain Colenso:[2] these things are a succession of short stories, like the chapters in *Gil Blas*,[3] told with something of the insistence in personal charm that makes the success of *A Sentimental Journey*.[4] And Rowley[5] is an admirable companion picture to Le Fevre;[6] and St Ives has several sayings that make him no despicable fellow traveller with Sterne. When he remarks that 'some fire, I think, is needful',[7] to learn French, we rub our hands with pleasure. The book is full of perfect asides: nothing could be better than Rowley's shy induction of his flageolet.[8] The book would be

---

[1] An echo of Alfred Noyes (1880–1958), 'The Highwayman', a fine narrative poem of tragic romance: 'The road was a ribbon of moonlight over the purple moor' and 'The road was a gypsy's ribbon, looping the purple moor …'

[2] Only the first thirty chapters of *St Ives* were completed by Stevenson before his death; the balloon episode, and the *Lady Nepean* and Colenso, were part of Sir Arthur Quiller-Couch's completion of the story. Ransome is napping here. He is disparaging about the book, and the palpable speed of his pen skating across the paper betrays his superficial attention to it.

[3] A novel by Le Sage.

[4] A novel by Sterne.

[5] A character in *St Ives*.

[6] The story of Le Fevre is one of the minor masterpieces within *A Sentimental Journey*.

[7] *St Ives*, chapter III, 'Major Chevenix comes into the story, and Goguelat Goes Out'.

[8] The flageolet is introduced in chapter XXII, 'Character and Aquirements of Mr Rowley':

> He consoled himself by playing for awhile on a cheap flageolet, which was one of his diversions, and to which I owed many intervals of peace. When he first produced it, in the joints, from his pocket, he had the duplicity to ask me if I played upon it. I answered, no; and he put the

entirely satisfactory, if only we could feel that Stevenson had not thought of it as a more serious affair. He seems to be hitting the bull's eye at five hundred yards, but we have an uncomfortable conviction that he has set his sights for a thousand yards, and believes all the time he is firing on the longer range.[1]

And there are wasted touches: of St Ives' French Revolution childhood, due probably to dictation, love of music, etc. Stevenson would probably have seen what he was missing, and would not have let such things go by in the taking of breath.[2] *St Ives* 'is merely a story of adventure, rambling along; ... but there, all novels are a heavy burthen while they are doing, and a sensible disappointment when they are done.'[3]

And then, after *The Master of Ballantrae*, seven years after *Kidnapped*, to which it was a sequel, came *Catriona* taking up David Balfour where he had been left, in the offices of the British Linen Company, and bringing him out with a bag of money, to prosecute a series of adventures, further to illustrate his character (which I cannot abide) and to fall in love with then marry the mother of the children for whom, as we learn with surprise in the last chapter, he is writing the story. Of this book, Stevenson wrote: 'I shall never do a better book than *Catriona*, that is my high-water mark, and the trouble of production increases on me at a great rate – and mighty

instrument away with a sigh and the remark that he had thought I might. For some while he resisted the unspeakable temptation, his fingers visibly itching and twittering about his pocket, even his interest in the landscape and in sporadic anecdote entirely lost. Presently the pipe was in his hands again; he fitted, unfitted, refitted, and played upon it in dumb show for some time.

'I play it myself a little,' says he.

'Do you?' said I, and yawned.

And then he broke down.

'Mr Ramornie, if you please, would it disturb you, sir, if I was to play a chune?' he pleaded.

And from that hour, the tootling of the flageolet cheered our way.

[1] His nonchalance in composition is suggested in another quotation noted by Ransome (see appendix A.2.iv.)

[2] (This sentence is written in an almost illegible scrawl.) *St Ives* was dictated by Stevenson at intervals during the year before his death, while distracted by illness, by his passion for music, and by work on other books, notably *Weir of Hermiston*.

[3] "[*Letters*], IV, 147. See also a remark on Ives. Same page." The full context is: 'merely a story of adventure, rambling along; but that is perhaps the guard that 'sets my genius best,' as Alan might have said. I wish I could feel as easy about the other! But there, all novels are a heavy burthen while they are doing, and a sensible disappointment when they are done.' That 'other', he died in the act of writing: *Weir of Hermiston*.

anxious about how I am to leave my family.'[1] It occurs to me as I transcribe that sentence that Mr Pepys had a ghostly finger in the cooking of Stevenson's epistolary style. But that is not our present subject.[2]

Let me try to discover on what Stevenson based the artwork of *Catriona*, and in how far his opinion is just. It is of course, not his high water mark, but then he could not foresee that with the increasing trouble of production, was to come that firm, jasper manner of the *Ebb Tide* and *Weir*, and with that manner a less limited demand from art. *Catriona* satisfied the Stevenson who believed that 'the one excuse and breath of art' was charm. It is full of charm, and the more charming because of the few grim passages, with Simon Fraser, for example, the few sordid pictures, such as James More's, which show up 'gray eyes'[3] and Prestongrange's daughters like flowers on gray velvet.[4] It is subject to the same criticism as *Kidnapped*; things happen for the sake of the story; it is to be assessed like this beside the works of the great novelists; but as *The Master of Ballantrae* does not, it sustains its note; it all holds together, and leaves at the end a lasting memory of charm. And that was what Stevenson had asked from it.[5]

The writing of *Weir of Hermiston* followed hard upon *St Ives*, but is so much greater and so different an achievement as to demand a separate chapter.[6] Between the two came the tale of *St Ives*, left unfinished for *Hermiston*'s sake, but best discussed in this place.

Nearer to life than any of his novels, his *Memoir of Fleeming Jenkin* is among the three or four best books he wrote. Considered only as a work of imagination, how admirable is its careful discontinuity of texture, the general setting of the family, with its set character sketches of Jenkins and Jacksons, then in a larger pattern the account of Jenkin himself, and finally, the small web again, in the account of the last days not only of Jenkin but the picturesque members of the previous generation, survived from the first chapter. Stevenson never wrote anything better than his picture of the Captain after the death of his wife. Yet the thing is not fiction; it is composed of far less malleable material. And I know of no biography which, without flatulent adulation, leaves so heroic an impression of its subject.

[1] To Mrs Sitwell, 24 or 25 April 1894, *Letters*, IV, 258.

[2] Revision may well have discarded this happy speculative aside.

[3] Catriona herself; her 'gray eyes' are much in the mind of the young hero.

[4] Ransome's image, influenced by Stevenson.

[5] Ransome damns with very faint praise indeed. Though dismissive, he still values the 'charm' the book holds for his generation. Taste has subsequently seen an uneasy mixture of authorial self-deception and failure of voice in the novel.

[6] A section not present, perhaps never written; Ransome leaves us only hints and fragments of his admiration for *Weir*, which he saw to have come from an extreme act of imagination new in Stevenson's work.

And for an understanding of Stevenson, a clear realisation of the nature of his loss of this older, uncouth, childish, heroic, enthusiastic, good man is essential. After reading it, passage after passage of Stevenson's moral essays seem to have the shadow of Jenkin behind them, the cheerful, honest, optimist who was with difficulty persuaded that there was one bad man, and searched his experience in vain for an instance of malice. More than Henley, or R. A. M. Stevenson, or Symonds, or Mr Gosse, this Edinburgh professor carved of virgin rock, smiling like a child and just as serious, influenced Stevenson, and it is pleasant to think that this book, so vigorous, so clear, so heartening, remains to transmit that influence to others.

I think few books have been so curiously underestimated in comparison with the other works of their writer than Stevenson's *In the South Seas*.[1] Sir Sidney Colvin in his edition of the *Letters* tells us that 'there is a certain many-voyaged master-mariner as well as master-writer – no less a person than Mr Joseph Conrad – who ... prefers *In the South Seas* to *Treasure Island*', but Mr Conrad[2] must be almost alone.[3] Yet there are few books of travel so vivid, so sympathetic with the people visited, so rich in a sense of the strange, so precise in its expression of that strangeness. I believe that if it had been written by any other writer than Stevenson it would have earned him an honourable remembrance: I believe the reason of its neglect and the disparagement of silence it has suffered is that it bears Stevenson's name on the title-page, and that persons reading that name, conversant with Stevenson's other works, expect a different book. Their palates are offended, as when one drinks tea, expecting coffee; and they do not forgive the offence.[4]

[1] *In The South Seas*, ed. S. Colvin (1896). This section is headed "Travel In the South Seas".

[2] Joseph Conrad (1857–1924) is usually considered one of the earliest modernist English novelists; his first novel, *Almayer's Folly* was published in 1895, the year after Stevenson's death. His greatest novels (*Nostromo, Lord Jim, Heart of Darkness)* were all known before Ransome wrote this.

[3] Sidney Colvin, *Letters*, III, 262, introducing a letter of 29 April 1891 to himself from Stevenson, explains its context: Stevenson had received a letter from Colvin 'expressing the disappointment felt by [his] friends at home at the impersonal and even at times tedious character of some portion of the South Sea Letters that had reached us. As a corrective of that opinion, may I perhaps mention here that there is a certain many-voyaged master-mariner – no less a person than Mr Joseph Conrad – who does not at all share it, and prefers *In the South Seas* to *Treasure Island*.' Ransome shares Conrad's high opinion of the book.

[4] Ransome himself was later persuaded to abandon 'The River Comes First', a fragment since published in *Coots In The North And Other Stories* (1988), on the grounds that it was not what his public had come to want.

The task that Stevenson attempted was sufficiently difficult to make admirable even a partial success. He wished to describe the life and setting of the inhabitants of several groups of small islands in the Pacific Ocean some two thousand miles from the coasts of New Zealand. The editor of a local paper, *The Pacific Commercial Advertiser*, had suggested that the folk-lore of the Pacific Islands lacked 'a link of homogeneous interest to connect them with the mentation and sympathy of the civilised reader.' 'That,' said Stevenson,

> was almost my first discovery after I began to write of the South Seas, and to my chagrin I found my matter would not work up even into readable travels (from the public's point of view). It seems to me that you have put the difficulty of into a line – everything in the Pacific must be first translated into terms of civilization before being written.[1]

Now all descriptive writing is a translation for the reader of what is unknown to him into terms of what is known, and the greater the discrepancy between known and unknown the greater is the writer's difficulty. The great travel books are written by Europeans, and enable other Europeans to follow the adventures of people not unlike themselves in strange surroundings. Stevenson's object was far less easy to attain. He eliminated, or almost eliminated, the common ground of race, and tried to make Europeans follow with interest the fortunes of strange people in strange surroundings. And apart from the fact that the mere realisation was difficult, with so small a leaven of the known in the mass of the unknown, he has also to contend with the fact that man is a self-centred animal and that his interest in the fortunes of others may be mapped in a series of circles concentric with himself. In the outer circles his free interest to be had for the asking is very small, and at last, in the outermost disappears altogether. Most of those who know of *In the South Seas*, ask themselves some such question as 'Am I the keeper of my fifteen cousins twenty times removed,' and buy *Treasure Island* instead.

Moreover, the book was made still more difficult by the very circumstances that made possible its success. Stevenson was so near what he described, it made so powerful an impression upon him, that he was in danger of forgetting how far from it were his readers, and how averse they were likely to be from a repetition of that impression on themselves. While he wrote, the axes of his black boys were clearing the foundations of the house in which he was to live among them. And he had had scarcely time for learning 'to address readers from the uttermost parts of the sea.'[2]

---

[1] *"Recollections of Robert Louis Stevenson in the Pacific*, p 101."

[2] Op. cit., chapter 1, 'An Island Landfall'.

In November 1890, he was busied in clearing ground in the forest about his house, and wrote this to Sir Sidney Colvin:

> My long, silent contests in the forest have had a strange effect on me. The unconcealed vitality of these vegetables, their exuberant number and strength, the attempts – I can use no other word – of lianas to enwrap and capture the intruder, the awful silence, the knowledge that all my efforts are only like the performance of an actor, the thing of a moment, and the wood will silently and swiftly heal them up with fresh effervescence; the cunning sense of the tuitui, suffering itself to be touched with wind-swayed grasses and not minding – but let the grass be moved by a man, and it shuts up; the whole silent battle, murder, and slow death of the contending forest; weigh upon the imagination. My poem 'The Woodman' stands; but I have taken refuge in a new story, which just shot through me like a bullet in one of my moments of awe, alone in that tragic jungle.[1]

In such circumstances, under such emotions, was conceived 'The Beach of Falesá', which afterwards formed the main part of *Island Nights' Entertainments*.[2] Out of the forest itself came that strange violent tale of Uma and the trader, and the conjuror's magic of the sinister Case.[3] He began the story, left it, took it up months later: 'Oh it's so good, 'The High Woods'' (the story was first called 'The High Woods of Ulufanua') 'but the story is craziness, that's the trouble', and again, on reading through the chapter and a bit that had been written, he found it 'so wilful, so steep, so silly – it's a hallucination I have outlived, and yet I never did a better piece of work, horrid, and pleasing, and extraordinarily *true*; it's sixteen pages of the South Seas; their essence.'[4] Three days later 'the yarn is cured.' He had got rid of some supernatural trick which had originally been part of it, and was surprised at not having done so before. So do stories develop. Three weeks after that it had been written and re-written and he felt as if he never wanted to write 'any more again for ever'. He wrote to Sir Sidney Colvin: 'You will know more about the South Seas after you have read my little tale than if you had read a library.'[5]

Speaking of these stories, he said: 'They all have a queer realism, even the most extravagant, even the 'Isle of Voices'; the manners are exact.'[6] The stories were not meant, however, to go into a volume together. 'The Bottle

---

[1] *"Letters,* III, 202, 205."

[2] (1893).

[3] A character in the story.

[4] *Vailima Letters*, chapter 10, to Colvin, Sunday [6] September 1891.

[5] *Vailima Letters*, chapter 10, 28 September 1891.

[6] *Vailima Letters*, chapter 24, 3 December, 1892.

Imp' was to have been 'the centre-piece of a volume of *Märchen* which I was slowly to elaborate.'[1]

Of the *Island Nights' Entertainments*, only two pretend to have been written for an island audience: 'The Brother Imp' and 'The Isle of Voices'. They are a kind of artificial folklore. The Fables we have already discussed, showed Stevenson's power of coloured allegories. These are not allegories, nor even very moral. They are comparable only with folktales, which rest on elementary principles of psychology – what all men wish, in houses and wives and clothes and musical instruments, and the danger of dealing with the supernatural – they are set in the precious key of island lore.

They should be compared with folklore noted in the *South Seas*. The humane element has been, perhaps, a little elaborated; but not offensively, and the touches of the eastern civilisation in the missionary and the mate in 'The Isle of Voices', and the admirable picture of the drunken boatmen who, free from fear and scruples, rolls off on the way to hell with the bottle imp under his arm, and a bottle of rum bubbling at his mouth, are conceived from the Island point of view.[2] 'The Bottle Imp' curiously is one of Stevenson's most popular tales: I have even met it translated into Russian. It was the first tale to be translated into Samoan.

Of the novels written in collaboration with Mr Lloyd Osbourne the first, *The Wrong Box*, is nothing but 'a little judicious levity' as Michael Finsbury said, by authors of whom one was 'old enough to be ashamed of himself and the other young enough to learn better.'[3] The tale was written first on the typewriter of Mr Osbourne, and, to Stevenson's surprise, when he remembered his own serious and moralising youth, was highly entertaining. Stevenson suggested, removed, and burnished. As he noticed in criticism of his stepson, it would not have been written except for the inspiration of the *New Arabian Nights*, and it is indeed an excellent example of the many half fantastic, half romantic, earnest, farcical tales which followed in the wake of that gay-coloured caravan across the sandy desert of contemporary popular fiction.

---

[1] Märchen: fairy-tales. *Vailima Letters*, chapter 25, January 1893: 'What annoyed me about the use of "The Bottle Imp" was that I had always meant it for the centre-piece of a volume of *Märchen* which I was slowly to elaborate.' Colvin had unilaterally published it along with 'The Beach of Falesá', completely different in style and intention.

[2] Ransome had a sharp eye for point of view, and was ahead of his time in his theoretical understanding of its effects.

[3] The brief Preface to *The Wrong Box* (1889), signed by R. L. S. and L. O., is this:

'Nothing like a little judicious levity,' says Michael Finsbury in the text: nor can any better excuse be found for the volume in the reader's hand. The authors can but add that one of them is old enough to be ashamed of himself, and the other young enough to learn better.

The other two, *The Wrecker* and *The Ebb-tide*, more intimately involved Stevenson's interest and attention, as well as his kindness as a toucher up of youthful masterpieces.[1] His interest in each case was technical, in *The Wrecker* a question of plot, in *The Ebb-tide* an experiment in style.

The idea of *The Wrecker* was given to its author by a conversation on ship-board, while cruising in the South Seas in *The Equator*; a conversation about wrecks, and the piling up of unseaworthy ships with a view to making money out of underwriters.

> Before we turned in, the scaffolding of the tale had been put together. But the question of treatment was as usual more obscure. We had long been at once attracted and repelled by that very modern form of the police novel or mystery story, which consists in beginning your yarn anywhere but at the beginning, and finishing it anywhere but at the end; attracted by its peculiar interest when done, and the peculiar difficulties that attend its execution; repelled by that appearance of insincerity and shallowness of tone, which seems its inevitable drawback. For the mind of the reader, always bent to pick up clues, receives no impression of reality or life, rather of an airless, elaborate mechanism; and the book remains enthralling, but insignificant, like a game of chess, not a work of human art. It seemed the cause might lie partly in the abrupt attack; and that if the tale were gradually approached, some of the characters introduced (as it were) beforehand, and the book started in the tone of a novel of manners and experience briefly treated, this defect might be lessened and our mystery seem to inhere in life ... After we had invented at some expense of time this method of approaching and fortifying our police novel, it occurred to us it had been invented previously by someone else, and was in fact – however painfully different the results may seem – the method of Charles Dickens in his later work.[2]

It is this that makes *The Wrecker* seem less like one book, whether novel of manners or plain police tale, than a compendium of the scenarios of several, the adventures of Loudon Dodd in Paris, of Dodd and Pinkerton in New York, of The Currency Lass, as of Norris Carthew, all striking different notes, all promising more than they quite fulfil, all interesting and pleasant, sufficiently so to make the actual mystery almost an annoying encroachment upon our entertainment. It is as if we are asked to solve a

---

[1] *The Wrecker* by Robert Louis Stevenson and Lloyd Osbourne (1892); *The Ebb-Tide: A Trio and a Quartette,* by Robert Louis Stevenson and Lloyd Osbourne, 1894. Ransome's irony is evident in crossing out 'sketches' in favour of 'masterpieces'.

[2] "*Wrecker*, p. 371. 372." From the Epilogue, a letter to Will H. Low.

chess problem in the progress of the various courses of an eccentrically designed but excellent meal.

In *The Ebb Tide*[1] Stevenson deliberately adopted another manner than the easy, continuous narrative of *The Wrecker*, or the first-personal impressions of David Balfour or *Treasure Island*. It is a dry, economical book. Scenes carefully chosen are worked out in full detail, and burnished, and set side by side. The purpose of the book is never lost sight of: it is the portrait of Attwater with his strange combination of cruelty, Cambridge, and religion on an uncharted island in the Southern Seas.[2] And though, for credibility, precisely half the book is spent on preparing the three adventurers for their subsequent actions when brought into contact with that extraordinary figure, when we look back it is as if we were observing the calm, unhurried preparation of three ocean waves for their final inevitable shattering upon an immovable rock. So perfect is the design of the book in its ultimate form that it is hard to believe that at first in Stevenson's mind the two parts of it stood out as separate stories, the one (Attwater) a 'kind of *Monte Cristo*', the other 'The Beachcombers', 'more sentimental'.[3] It is possible to trace the whole history of the tale, from the combination of these two imagined tales into 'a black, ugly, trampling, violent story, full of strange scenes and striking characters,' and then when a quarter written, 'a great and grisly tale'.[4] Then a clearer vision of what was to be is set down in a letter to Charles Baxter, telling him to sell the serial rights of 'The Schooner Farallone', and continuing:

> I should say this is the butt end of what was once 'The Pearl Fisher'. There is a peculiarity about this tale in its new form: it ends with the conversion! We have been tempted rather to call it *The Schooner Farallone*: a tract by RLS and LO. It would make a boss tract; the three main characters – and there are only four – are barats, insurance frauds, thieves and would be murderers, so the company's good.

---

[1] "Lloyd Osbourne helped in the planning and wrote the original draft up to chapter v. After which nothing but taking over. There was thought of deleting his name."

[2] Ransome's later *Peter Duck* (1932) and *Missee Lee* (1941), although having themes in common with Stevenson's tale, are quite uninfluenced by it. The character of Attwater, washed up on a Pacific shore, is no source for Miss Lee or any of her pirate acquaintance.

[3] To Colvin, 30 September 1889, *Letters*, III, 137; 'Attwater' is 'The Pearl Fisher'.

[4] To Marcel Schwob, 19 August 1890, *Letters*, III, 177; 'great and grisly' not found; however see letter to Baxter from Vailima, Feb[ruary] 1893, 'a most grim and gloomy tale', and to Gosse, 10 June 1893 'a dreadful grimy business in the 3rd person.'

Devil a woman is there, by good luck; so it's 'pure'. 'Tis a most – what's the expression? – unconventional work.[1]

Another letter, of about the same date, in which we get another glimpse of the *Ebb Tide*'s evolution: 'During the last week the amanuensis was otherwise engaged, whereupon I took up, pitched into, and about one half demolished another tale, once intended to be called 'The Pearl Fisher', but now razeed and called 'The Schooner Farralone.'[2] It was then (February 1893) promising to be finished in a month, but on the 25th April he wrote to Sidney Colvin:

> We call it *The Ebb Tide: A Trio and Quartette*; but that secondary name you may strike out if it seems dull to you. The book, however, falls in two halves, when the fourth character appears. I am on p. 82 if you want to know, and expect to finish on I suppose 110 or so; but it goes slowly, as you may judge from the fact that this three weeks past, I have only struggled from p. 58 to p. 82: twenty-four pages, *et encore* sure to be rewritten, in twenty-one days ...[3]

and on May 16th he had only covered another six pages.

> ... I can't think what to say about the tale, but it seems to me to go off with a considerable bang; in fact, to be an extraordinary work: but whether popular! Attwater is a no end of a courageous attempt, I think you will admit; how far successful is another affair. If my island ain't a thing of beauty, I'll be damned. Please observe Wiseman and Wishart; for incidental grimness, they strike me as in it. Also, kindly observe the Captain and *Adar*; I think that knocks spots. In short, as you see, I'm a trifle vainglorious. But O, it has been such a grind! The devil himself would allow a man to brag a little after such a crucifixion! And indeed I'm only bragging for a change before I return to the darned thing lying waiting for me on p. 88, where I last broke down. I break down at every paragraph, I may observe; and lie here and sweat, till I can get one sentence wrung out after another. Strange doom; after having worked so easily for so long![4]

Four days later he was at page ninety-three, and wrote:

> I have made 11 pages in nine livelong days. Well! up a high hill he heaved a huge round stone. But this Flaubert business must be resisted in the premises.[5]

[1] *"Letters*, IV, 148."
[2] "[Ibid.,] 150."
[3] "[Ibid.,] 162."
[4] "[Ibid.,] 162 & 163".
[5] "[Ibid.,] 164."

The next day:

> And here I am back again on p. 85! the last chapter demanding an entire revision, which accordingly it is to get. And where my mail is to come in, God knows! This forced, violent, alembicated style is most abhorrent to me; it can't be helped; the note was struck years ago on the *Janet Nicoll*, and has to be maintained somehow; and I can only hope the intrinsic horror and pathos, and a kind of fierce glow of colour there is to it, and the surely remarkable wealth of striking incident, may guide our little shallop into port.[1]

And two days later again:

> I am discontented with *The Ebb Tide*, naturally; there seems such a veil of words over it; and I like more and more naked writing; and yet sometimes one has a longing for full colour and there comes the veil again.[2]

May 29:

> Still grinding at Chap. XI. I began many days ago on p. 93, and am still on p. 93, which is exhilarating, but the thing takes shape all the same and should make a pretty lively chapter for an end of it. For XII is only a footnote *ad explicandum*.[3]

June 1:

> Back on p. 93. I was on 100 yesterday, but read it over and condemned it ... 10am. I have worked up again to 97, but how ... This is Flaubert outdone.[4]

June 2:

> What kills me is the frame of mind of one of the characters; I cannot get it through. Of course that does not interfere with my total inability to write; so that yesterday I was a living half-hour upon a single clause and have a gallery of variants that would surprise you.

June 4, 4.15:

> Well, it's done. Those tragic 16 pp. are at last finished, and I have put away thirty-two pages of chips, and have spent thirteen days about as nearly in Hell as a man could expect to live through. It's done, and of

---

[1] "[Ibid.,] 165."
[2] "[Ibid.,] 166."
[3] "[Ibid.,] 171."
[4] "[Ibid.,] 171."

course it ain't worth while, and who cares? There it is, and about as grim a tale as was ever written, and as grimy, and as hateful.[1]

And even after that, he said: 'I ought to rewrite the end of this bluidy *Ebb Tide*: well, I can't. *C'est plus fort que moi*; it has to go the way it is, and be jowned to it.'[2] He could not forgive it, heaped epithets of abuse on it and called it 'the excruciating *Ebb Tide*', the 'ever-to-be-execrated *Ebb Tide*', or 'Stevenson's Blooming Error.[3]

I wonder how many of Stevenson's readers have detected the source of all this trouble – which Stevenson himself sets his finger upon:

> The difficulty of according the narrative and the dialogue (in a work in the third person) is extreme. That is one reason out of half a dozen why I so often prefer the first. It is much in my mind just now, because of my last work, just off the stocks three days ago, *The Ebb Tide*: a dreadful, grimy business in the third person, where the strain between a vilely realistic dialogue and a narrative style pitched about (in phrase) 'four notes higher' than it should have been, has sown my head with grey hairs; or I believe so – if my head escaped, my heart has them.[4]

Eight months later he read the tale in print, and was repaid for his torments.

> I retired with *The Ebb Tide* and read it all before I slept. I did not dream it was near as good; I am afraid I think it excellent. A little indecision about Attwater, not much. It gives me great hope, as I see I *can* work in that constipated, mosaic manner, which is what I have to do just now with *Weir of Hermiston*.[5]

If we compare Stevenson's attitude with Flaubert's, allowing for the distinctive 'charm' which each writer possessed, we find that the 'constipated mosaic' of *Weir* is an affirmation of Flaubert's method; while *The Ebb Tide*, in the same category of accomplishment, is quite different.[6]

---

[1] "[Ibid.,] 174."

[2] "[Ibid.,] 176."

[3] "[Ibid.,] 177."

[4] "[Ibid.,] 179." These many quotations about the effort required for a longer work reflect Ransome's own struggle with this extraordinarily difficult reconciliation.

[5] "To Sidney Colvin. Feb[ruary] 1894, *Letters*, IV, 247." This quotation, headed "Stevenson. Ebb-Tide & Weir", suggests that Ransome had intended to treat both works together as sharing the same prime position among Stevenson's works; a view held by most contemporary and subsequent critics of Stevenson.

[6] Reconstructed from a scarcely decipherable note: "Compare Stevenson's attitude with Flaubert's. *Charm*. [vertical line] 'Constipated mosaic' of Weir

Weir … [*and Ransome's trailing dots suggest that there is more to come. But this is the only word on the page. Then the manuscript lets the reader down, for there are no passages on* Weir of Hermiston *at all within the parcel of quarto sheets; and it is only from Ransome's hints along the way that we know he considered* Weir *above all to be Stevenson's masterpiece. It is clear that he had planned to write a substantial account of this compelling unfinished novel, and it is ironical that the missing section of draft should be about an incomplete book: Stevenson had died with his pen poised over a sentence about two-thirds of his way through. There is no doubt that Ransome knew what he wanted to say about what might have been Stevenson's masterpiece, and it is likely that he did set his opinion down, perhaps during that journey to Russia and his time there which began the day after this manuscript was dated, or perhaps in the autumn of 1914, while he was in the north, waiting to return to Russia. Perhaps the Great Russian Bear swallowed the pages down; perhaps they were lost in the fire that destroyed many of his personal papers a few years later in Riga. Their fate is an unsolved mystery.*

Ransome's conclusion is also incomplete. It would evidently have contained a summary account of the personality of Stevenson as a writer, as distinct from the man. We could have expected an account of the part played in his development as a writer by Mrs Stevenson as 'the Stormy Petrel',

> Ever perilous
> And precious, like an ember from the fire
> Or gem from a volcano …,[1]

and by her children, and perhaps an assessment of how Stevenson came to achieve his iconic status and world-wide readership: at the time of his death he was perhaps the most popular writer in the English-speaking world.

The surviving fragments of the conclusion nevertheless relate to matters that interested Ransome greatly (he had already pursued them in relation to Wilde): Stevenson's conversation, his writing viewed as 'executant musicianship', his delight in being the 'amateur', his versatility, his meticulous attention to style, his artificiality and his realism, and finally, his morality. On these matters, then, Ransome now gives us his last word.]

affirmation F: but n. b. that "The Ebb Tide" is in the same – & different." Flaubert's intense workmanship and exacting habits of work were much admired by Ransome, so this missing chapter was set fair to place *Weir* on a high pinnacle of achievement.

[1] "*Memories of Vailima*, p. 54." When the poem was quoted by Nellie van de Grift Sanchez in her *Life of Mrs Robert Louis Stevenson* (1924) she added: 'He called her the "stormy petrel" in reference to her birth in the wild month of March, and because she was such a fiery little person.'

Conclusion

Stevenson's conversation had in it more of the argumentative than, for example, Wilde's. Instead of the aesthetic movement as a nursery it had the Edinburgh Speculative Society. With his cousin or Sir Walter Simpson,[1] he talked for three months at Fontainebleau, and the subject on which they conversed was limited to theology and love. The existence or non-existence of a personal God, the continuance of life after death or sudden extinction, the casuistry of right behaviour in love, illustrated no doubt with distant examples and immediate experience; the character of the conversation they suggest is a combination between post-Darwinian argument between Coleridge and Charles Lamb, and speeches in a court of love between such counsel as Rabelais and Abélard.[2] Most of Stevenson's friends were good talkers as well as good listeners, and there was probably a wholesome public feeling against unbridled monologue. There was:[3]

> one whom I shall call Spring-Heel'd Jack. I say so, because I never knew anyone who mingled so largely the possible ingredients of converse. In the Spanish proverb, the fourth man necessary to compound a salad, is a madman to mix it: Jack is that madman. I know not what is more remarkable; the insane lucidity of his conclusions, the humorous eloquence of his language, or his power of method, bringing the whole of life into the focus of the subject treated, mixing the conversational salad like a drunken god. He doubles like the serpent, changes and flashes like the shaken kaleidoscope, transmigrates bodily into the

[1] A friend since Edinburgh University. Together they travelled on the Continent, and were companions in the canoe voyage described in Stevenson's first book *An Inland Voyage*, in which, named after their craft, Simpson becomes 'Cigarette' and Stevenson, 'Arethusa'.

[2] Samuel Taylor Coleridge (1772–1834), Romantic poet and literary critic, and Charles Lamb (1775–1834), essayist and critic, were for seven years (1782–89) schoolmates at Christ's Hospital in London. 'Post-Darwinian' refers not to the debates following Charles Darwin's publication of his *Origin of Species* (1859) but to those following his grandfather Erasmus Darwin's revolutionary ideas of common descent (1796). François Rabelais (1494–1553) is the French Renaissance satirist famous for *Gargantua and Pantagruel* (1532–52); Pierre Abélard (1079–1142) is the French philosopher, theologian, musician and poet, whose autobiographical romance *Abelard and Heloïse*, is a classic of love-literature. These examples define the passionate and brilliant quality of these young men's conversation.

[3] "Continue with miniatures from "Talk & Talkers"" says Ransome here – so we do. These two 'talkers', from Stevenson's brilliant essay, copied out by Ransome for use, are 'Spring-heel'd Jack' – that is, Bob, Stevenson's cousin R. A. M. Stevenson; and 'Burly': his friend W. E. Henley. This sort of conversation Ransome considered best of all.

views of others, and so, in the twinkling of an eye and with a heady
rapture, turns questions inside out and flings them empty before you
on the ground, like a triumphant conjuror. It is my common practice
when a piece of conduct puzzles me, to attack it in the presence of
Jack with such grossness, such partiality and such wearing iteration,
as at length shall spur him up in its defence. In a moment he trans-
migrates, dons the required character, and with moonstruck philosophy justifies the act in question. I can fancy nothing to compare
with the *vim* of these impersonations, the strange scale of language,
flying from Shakespeare to Kant, and from Kant to Major Dyngwell
– 'As fast as a musician scatters sounds / Out of an instrument' –
the sudden, sweeping generalisations, the absurd irrelevant particu-
larities, the wit, wisdom, folly, humour, eloquence and bathos, each
startling in its kind, and yet all luminous in the admired disorder of
their combination.

A talker of a different calibre, though belonging to the same
school, is Burly. Burly is a man of great presence; he commands a
larger atmosphere, gives the impression of a grosser mass of character
than most men. It has been said of him that his presence could be felt
in a room you entered blindfold; and the same, I think, has been said
of other powerful constitutions condemned to much physical inac-
tion. There is something boisterous and piratic in Burly's manner of
talk which suits well enough with this impression. He will roar you
down, he will bury his face in his hands, he will undergo passions of
revolt and agony; and meanwhile his attitude of mind is really both
conciliatory and receptive; and after Pistol has been out-Pistol'd, and
the welkin rung for hours, you begin to perceive a certain subsid-
ence in these spring torrents, points of agreement issue, and you end
arm-in-arm, and in a glow of mutual admiration. The outcry only
serves to make your final union the more unexpected and precious.
Throughout there has been perfect sincerity, perfect intelligence, a
desire to hear although not always to listen, and an unaffected eager-
ness to meet concessions. You have, with Burly, none of the dangers
that attend debate with Spring-Heel'd Jack; who may at any moment
turn his powers of transmigration on yourself, create for you a view
you never held, and then furiously fall on you for holding it. These,
at least, are my two favourites, both are loud, copious intolerant
talkers. This argues that I myself am in the same category; for if we
love talking at all, we love a bright, fierce adversary, who will hold
his ground, foot by foot, in much our own manner, sell his attention
dearly, and give us our full measure of the dust and exertion of battle.
Both these men can be beat from a position, but it takes six hours
to do it; a high and hard adventure, worth attempting. With both
you can pass days in an enchanted country of the mind, with people,

scenery and manners of its own; live a life apart, more arduous, active and glowing than any real existence; and come forth again when the talk is over, as out of a theatre or a dream, to find the east wind still blowing and the chimney-pots of the old battered city still around you. Jack has the far finer mind, Burly the far more honest; Jack gives us the animated poetry, Burly the romantic prose, of similar themes; the one glances high like a meteor and makes a light in darkness; the other, with many changing hues of fire, burns at the sea-level, like a conflagration; but both have the same humour and artistic interests, the same unquenched ardour in pursuit, the same gusts of talk and thunderclaps of contradiction.

Mr Gosse after insisting on the gravity of Stevenson particularly remarks: 'I cannot, for the life of me, recall any of his jokes; and written down in cold blood, they might not be funny if I did.'[1] This kind of humour is more a laughable manner of expression than any series of separate jests.

Stevenson[2] was not a constructive thinker: he perceived, he felt, but was better at illustration than at argument. And so, instead of a treatise on technique, he left only the record of a few imperfectly understood observations beside a mass of brilliant technical feats. Except in a very few of his works, Stevenson is nearer being an executant musician than a composer. He does not so much invent as re-create and endow with his own charming and marked personality the harmonies and discords created by others. He has left us Stevenson's rendering of Sterne, Stevenson's Ballantyne, a Stevenson Hazlitt, a Stevenson Hawthorne, and even a Stevenson Scott; but as we listen to him in all these moods we think less of Sterne, Ballantyne, Hazlitt, Hawthorne or Scott, than of 'the flashing eye, the floating hair',[3] the delicate fingers, the persuasive, graceful gesture of the performer immediately before us.

Stevenson was one of the most versatile of miscellaneous writers but he never suffered from that melancholy humour of the versatile, in which they wonder what they should be doing, and, frightened at their own inconsistencies, look feverishly for a particular vocation. Plans for a life of Wellington in no way interrupted the joyous progress of the storyteller, and the author of the *Child's Garden of Verses* dreamed, with no infidelity to any of his softer loves, of the eventual publication of a 'small arid book on the Art of Literature'.[4] Oh happy man who could live for days in a story 'and

---

[1] "'Personal Memories of Robert Louis Stevenson', Edmund Gosse, in *The Century Magazine*, July 1895."

[2] This page is headed "Stevenson as *executant musician*".

[3] A phrase from Coleridge's 'Kubla Khan'.

[4] To W. H. Low, 13 March, 1885: 'I shall see if I can afford to send you the April *Contemporary* – but I dare say you see it anyway – as it will contain a paper

only come out of it to play patience' and could play the sober critic without wishing to throw the storyteller's cloak into the lumber room and to forget he ever wore other clothes than the pedagogic drab. He never complained that a man cannot do two things at once. He had seldom fewer than half a dozen on the stocks at once.[1]

There was just this much of the amateur in Stevenson: in spite of his industry, his craftsmanship, he was often preoccupied with the little distinction, the small glamour that is attributed to authorship by those who do not write. He was pleased to be called Tusitala,[2] pleased to put his friends into his books (which an author's acquaintances almost invariably imagine and perhaps hope is the object of his intercourse with them), hugged himself over confessions of his early work, and discussions of method not between himself and other artists, but between himself and men and women who admired him and his books. This is not in the least like the philosophy of literature to be found in Flaubert's correspondence. Charmingly, gracefully written, it has now and again a memory of the egotistic parson describing in a parish magazine the genesis of his final sermon. His method of work may be remembered here: 'Some days,' writes Mrs Strong,

> we have worked from eight o'clock till four, and that is not counting the hours Louis writes and makes notes in the early morning by lamplight. He dictates with great correctness, and when particularly interested unconsciously acts the part of his characters. When he came to the description of the supper Anne has with Flora and Ronald, he bowed as he dictated the hero's speeches and twirled his moustache. When he describes the interview between the old lady and the driver, he spoke in a high voice for the one, and a deep growl for the other, and all in broad Scotch even to 'cuma' (comma).[3]

Mrs Strong also tells how Stevenson once looked in a looking glass to describe a particular expression of 'The Master's' and was astonished to find only his own reflection instead of that of his hero. 'Stevenson,' Wilde

---

of mine on style, a sort of continuation of old arguments on art in which you have wagged a most effective tongue. It is a sort of start upon my Treatise on the Art of Literature: a small, arid book that shall some day appear.'

[1] Ransome crosses out his original phrase, 'quadruplicity of personality', in favour of a metaphor favoured by Stevenson, 'on the stocks'. On 8 October 1883 Stevenson wrote to Colvin that he had 'a great variety of small ships launched or still upon the stocks', *Letters*, II, 155. Ransome himself could never easily move between genres, and was currently frustrated at being stuck in the mode of criticism and essays.

[2] 'The Story-teller', a name given by his Samoan friends.

[3] "Memories of Vailima, p. 8."

wrote in a letter, 'merely extended the sphere of the artificial by taking to digging.'[1]

Yet Stevenson considered himself a realist.[2] He wrote to Low after receiving his drawings for Keats:

> The sight of your pictures has once more awakened me to my right mind; something may come of it; yet one more bold push to get free of this prisonyard of the abominably ugly, where I take my daily exercise with my contemporaries. I do not know, I have a feeling in my bones, a sentiment which may take on the forms of imagination, or may not. If it does, I shall owe it to you; and the thing will thus descend from Keats even if on the wrong side of the blanket. If it can be done in prose – that is the puzzle.[3]

Long afterwards Low reminded him of this. He replied: 'Well, as you see, nothing came of it. The Master of Ballantrae is not precisely inspired by Keats … No, it is not in me, I can do the grim, I can do the Jekyll and Hyde sort of thing, but the trouble with me is that I am at bottom a realist,' and replying to a very sound of objection of Mr Low's, he settled it: 'All that is true enough, but it is the local conditions, the things of the moment and hour that strike the hardest. If it was not for Zola and his gang, who have spoiled the game, I should be a rank realist.'[4] In a letter, 1892, to Sir Sidney Colvin not included in the four red volumes,[5] he says 'I have in nearly all my works been trying one racket: to get out the facts of life as clean and naked and sharp as I could manage it,' and in the same letter he says that in a love story 'you can't tell any of the facts, and the only chance is to paint an atmosphere.'[6]

Stevenson asks: what is realism? He has spoken of the monk who listened to the song of a bird, and found that fifty years had passed in a bar or two of music. 'All life that is not merely mechanical,' says Stevenson, 'is spun out of two strands: seeking for that bird and hearing him.' Wherefore he realises it is to him a puzzling, a seemingly irrelevant business. In the pages of the realist, 'to be sure, we find a picture of life in so far as it consists of mud and of old iron, cheap desires and cheap fears, that which we are ashamed

---

[1] (Robert Ross had allowed Ransome to read Wilde's letters to him – they were not yet in the public domain.) Faint praise; and artificiality was, in the end, what Ransome abjured.

[2] The sentence is expanded from the header "Realism".

[3] To W. H. Low, 2 January, 1886.

[4] "W. H. Low, pp. 422, 423, 424."

[5] The four red volumes of Stevenson's *Letters* (1911) were constantly on Ransome's desk during the months that he was working on this book at Manor Farm, Hatch, Wiltshire in 1913 and 1914.

[6] "'Stevensoniana,' By Sir Sidney Colvin. Article in Scribner's Mag., Nov[ember], 1912." The sentence has been editorially reconstructed.

to remember and that which we are careless whether we forget; but of the note of that time-devouring nightingale we hear no news.'[1] And later he says: 'The true realism, always and everywhere, is that of the poets: to find out where joy resides, and give it a voice far beyond singing.'[2]

Stevenson's own standard of style[3] was of so exacting a nature, so much more in consonance with Gallic requirements, than with those ordinarily enforced in our own tongue, that he never seriously contemplated writing in French. Often enough, however, he would use French terms, or note their exactness of definition approvingly, especially in the rich vocabulary pertaining to art or literature, and in like manner, more than once, when discussing some of his many projects for stories or essays – of which he had an inexhaustible fund – he would break off with 'quite impossible in English. I wish that I could write it in French.'[4]

Marcel Schwob, the subtle author of *Mimes*, and *Le Croisade des Enfants*, the biographer of Villon, who died with his great work unwritten,[5] exchanged a few letters with Stevenson. He surprised Stevenson very much by wishing to translate *The Black Arrow* and by admiring Stevenson's women. The astonished author replied 'Vous ne détestez pas alors mes bonnes femmes? Moi, je les déteste,'[6] and perhaps this reply is the source from which so many have drawn their statement that Stevenson could do nothing with female characters. But that is not the question here. We are here concerned with Schwob's short, luminous essay, reprinted in *Spicilège*,[7] and his by no means negligible contribution to an understanding of Stevenson's method. He was perhaps the first to point out how much Stevenson accomplished by wise silences. 'Nous ne savons pas exactement ...'[8] 'We do not know exactly what Billy Bones had done.

---

[1] "*Across the Plains*, 147 [*sic*]": chapter 7, 'The Lantern-bearers.

[2] "151 [*sic*], Across the P[lains]." Chapter 6, 'Random Memories Continued'.

[3] "Stevenson on French" is the heading of this paragraph.

[4] "W. H. Low, p. 335."

[5] M. A. Marcel Schwob (1867–1905), dedicatee of Alfred Jarry's absurdist *Ubu Roi* (1896) and of Oscar Wilde's *The Sphinx* (1894) 'in friendship', corresponded with Stevenson, translated some of his works, and attempted a voyage to meet him.

[6] 19 August 1890 (an opinion shared by his wife 'who hates and loathes and slates my women': *Letters*, II, 120).

[7] *Spicilège* (1896) brought together Schwob's articles on François Villon, R. L. Stevenson, and George Meredith, along with his prefaces on Théophile Gautier, Gustave Flaubert, and Jules Renard.

[8] 'Nous ne savons exactement ce qu'avait fait BB. Deux ou trois touches de Silver suffisent pour nous inspirer le regret ardent d'ignorer à jamais la vie de Captain Flint et de ses compagnons de fortune.' Ransome interleaves the French with his translation.

Two or three of Silver's touches[1] suffice to inspire us with the burning regret that we are for ever ignorant of the life of Captain Flint and his companions of fortune ...' 'Ce qu'il ne nous dit pas de la vie d'Allan Breck, de Secundra Dass, d'Ollala, d'Attwater, nous attire plus que ce qu'il nous en dit.'[2]

He compared Stevenson's method of realising the unreal with that of Defoe. He points out that Stevenson's realism is quite unreal, and gives many examples to show that 'Stevenson n'a jamais regardé les choses qu'avec les yeux de son imagination',[3] and finds in these examples not errors, but images stronger than real images, indeed 'la quintessence de la réalité.'[4] Finally he insists that Stevenson's stories began, for Stevenson, with pictures, a door, a closed house, a young man with cream tarts, which, by the way, are never explained. He points out that in some of Stevenson's stories the tale is not as good as the picture, but remains a kind of commentary, though, 'dans les romans, *Kidnapped*, *Treasure Island*, *Master of Ballantrae*, etc., le récit est incontestablement très supérieur à l'image, qui cependant a été son point de départ.'[5]

Stevenson won his general recognition in his lifetime in two ways, as the writer of a boy's book, and as the author of a moral allegory which reverberated in a thousand pulpits.[6] His stories all, except a very few, have a showman interested keenly in morality, and his moralisings are the more acceptable from the mouth of such a professed adventurer and romantic as himself. It would have been tedious to comment in every chapter on the morality behind the books discussed, because it did not noticeably vary as he grew older. But to neglect it altogether would be to neglect one of the more or less constant and important factors in his personality. Stevenson in everything, everywhere, was concerned to an unusual extent, for a writer not vowed to a church or to reform, with morals. He was never better pleased than to give advice, and he never felt better employed than when he was giving advice to himself.

---

[1] 'Touches of Silver' may be intended.

[2] 'What he doesn't tell us about the life of Alan Breck, of Secundra Das, of Ollala, of Attwater, fascinates us more than what he does tell us about them.'

[3] 'Stevenson never looked at things but through the eyes of his imagination'.

[4] 'the quintessence of reality'.

[5] 'In the novels *Kidnapped*, *Treasure Island*, *Master of Ballantrae*, etc., the story is incontestably very superior to the picture, which however has been his starting-point.'

[6] This section is headed "Moralist", and was largely written (as his diary shows) on 17, 18 and 19 February 1914. The 'moral allegory' is, of course, *Dr Jekyll and Mr Hyde*.

Even morals took on for him a flavour of the picturesque. He saw them, for example, in brown leather, with emblems, if I may put it so. There was something of an altogether non-moral gusto in his moralising.[1] At twenty-four, he planned a book of 'Essays on the Enjoyment of the World', 'with a motto in italics on the title page – you know the class of old book I have in my head. I smack my lips; would it not be nice?'[2] It is perhaps just this mundane pleasure that prevents us from finding intolerable the spectacle of the lively, dissolute young advocate, whose exploits in the Lothian Road, and Portobello[3] way, were fresh in the minds of his associates, setting up shop as a lay preacher. That, and an honest attitude towards the young advocate, which lay preachers do not commonly emulate. 'One person I have to make good: myself. But my duty to my neighbour is much more nearly expressed by saying that I have to make him happy – if I may.'[4] This quotation is taken from 'A Christmas Sermon' written later in life; but may better show that its sentiment was Stevenson's from the beginning.

And, now, let us consider not piecemeal but in a lump, the essentials of his preaching. It is a preaching, in the first place, of acceptance, and in the second of revolt. Stevenson in the pulpit points with a scornful finger at the man who is bored, and with a finger fiercely denunciatory at the moralist of convention. He wishes to share his pleasant exultation in the world, to silence those who make that exultation difficult. On the plainer levels he only says 'Let all be happy together', and points out a few of the pitfalls that may prevent us. On the higher slopes he outlines a very practicable view of the whole duty of man, which is in notable discord with the teachings, workday and Sunday put together, of the ordinary format.

Lay Morals perhaps contains the most striking examples of his 'Anti-Grundyism'. An unfinished treatise on ethics, its main purpose was a comparison between the ideals[5] [*of Mrs Grundy, a voice of public opinion,*

---

[1] In a different formulation of this Ransome says: 'In his maturer years, with all his seriousness, he preserved something of this altogether non-moral gusto in moralising.'

[2] To Sidney Colvin, summer of 1874. The book was never written. In 1874 Stevenson published *Essays of Travel*, of which chapter 24 is 'On the Enjoyment of Unpleasant Places'.

[3] Edinburgh haunts of the young Stevenson.

[4] "Christmas Sermon, *Across the P[lains]*, 208."

[5] Here, with a dash and multiple dots, Ransome tails off. His notes: 'Morals. Anti-Grundyism. Moral hereditary background combined with sense, instance grandmother and grandfather and the baker. Religion. Prayers. Sect: cf Damien letter. The artist's morality applied to life.' Completion of this paragraph would have been a matter of routine for him. In his essay 'Lay Morals', Stevenson evokes Mrs Grundy:

> Where did you hear that it was easy to be honest? Do you find that in your Bible? Easy! It is easy to be an ass and follow the multitude like a

who like many people has 'an easy view of following at each other's tails' to church, and of one's own conscience, a tough task-master.]

What Stevenson actually does is to transform the technical morality of the scrupulous artist into terms of life's affairs. 'What is right,' he says, 'is that for which a man's central self is ever ready to sacrifice immediate or distant interests; what is wrong is what the central self discards or rejects as incompatible with the fixed design of righteousness.'[1] The best comment on this will be a passage from Poe's essay on Hawthorne's short stories:

> A skilful literary artist has constructed a tale. If wise, he has not fashioned his thoughts to accommodate his incidents; but, having conceived, with deliberate care, a certain unique or single effect to be worked out, he then invents such incidents – he then contrives such events as may best aid him in establishing this preconceived effect. If his very initial sentence tend not to the outbringing of the effect, he has failed in his first step. In the whole composition there should be no word written, of which the tendency, direct or indirect, is not to the one pre-established design. And by such means, with such care and skill, a picture is at length painted which leaves in the mind of him who contemplates it with a kindred art a sense of the fullest satisfaction. The idea of the tale has been presented unblemished, because undisturbed.[2]

'The idea of the tale, unblemished because undisturbed.' Every detail that offers itself, is retained or rejected, regardless of its private beauty, with a single eye to its compatibility or incompatibility with the whole.[3] It is precisely this that Stevenson applies to life. Wilde spoke of a man's life as of

> blind, besotted bull in a stampede; and that, I am well aware, is what you and Mrs Grundy mean by being honest. But it will not bear the stress of time nor the scrutiny of conscience.

And again:

> Christ was in general a great enemy to such a way of teaching ... For morals are a personal affair; in the war of righteousness every man fights for his own hand ... you find Christ giving various counsels to varying people, and often jealously careful to avoid definite precept.

[1] *"Lay Morals"*. Other quotations written out by Ransome for use in this section, but never incorporated, are: 'What a man spends upon himself he shall have earned by services to the race.'; 'To be, not to possess,' for Wilde's 'Oh, not to do'; 'I do not want to be decent at all, but to be good.'

[2] "cf. H[istory] of Storytelling, p. 245." Ransome's own recent book *A History of Story-Telling: Studies in the Development of Narrative* (1909), 'Poe and the New Technique'. He reminds himself to insert here the quotation from Poe used there; it is editorially inserted.

[3] This axiom is one that Ransome himself had rigorously adopted by the time he wrote *Pigeon Post* (1936).

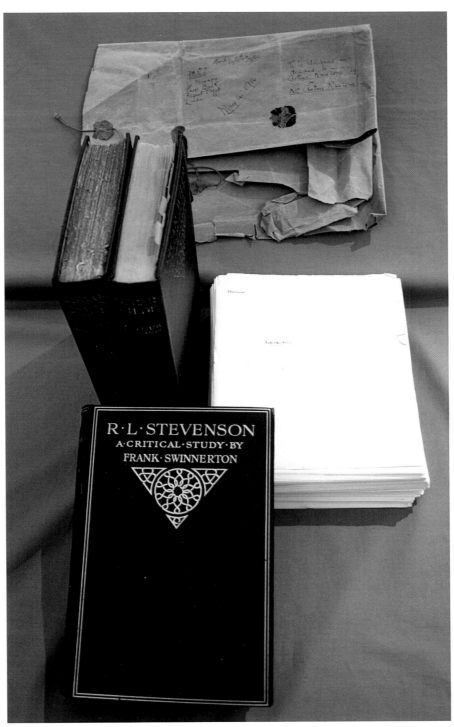

1 Ransome's two preceding 'critical studies' of Poe and Wilde, his Stevenson manuscript, its wrapping paper, and the book that took its place in Martin Secker's series

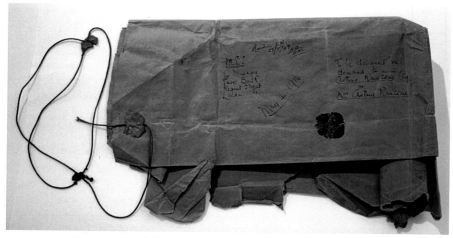

2 The outside of the wrapping paper with string and sealing-wax

3 *(left)* Front cover of Ransome's earliest manuscript, 'The Desert Island', 1892

4 *(below)* First page-opening of 'The Desert Island'

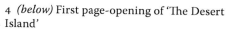

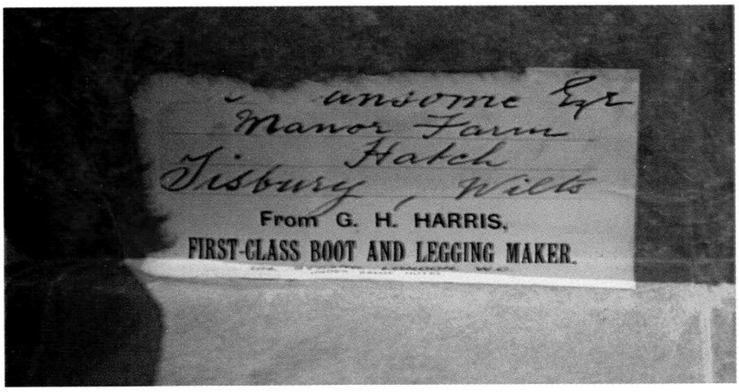

5 The inside of the wrapping paper showing the bootmaker's label

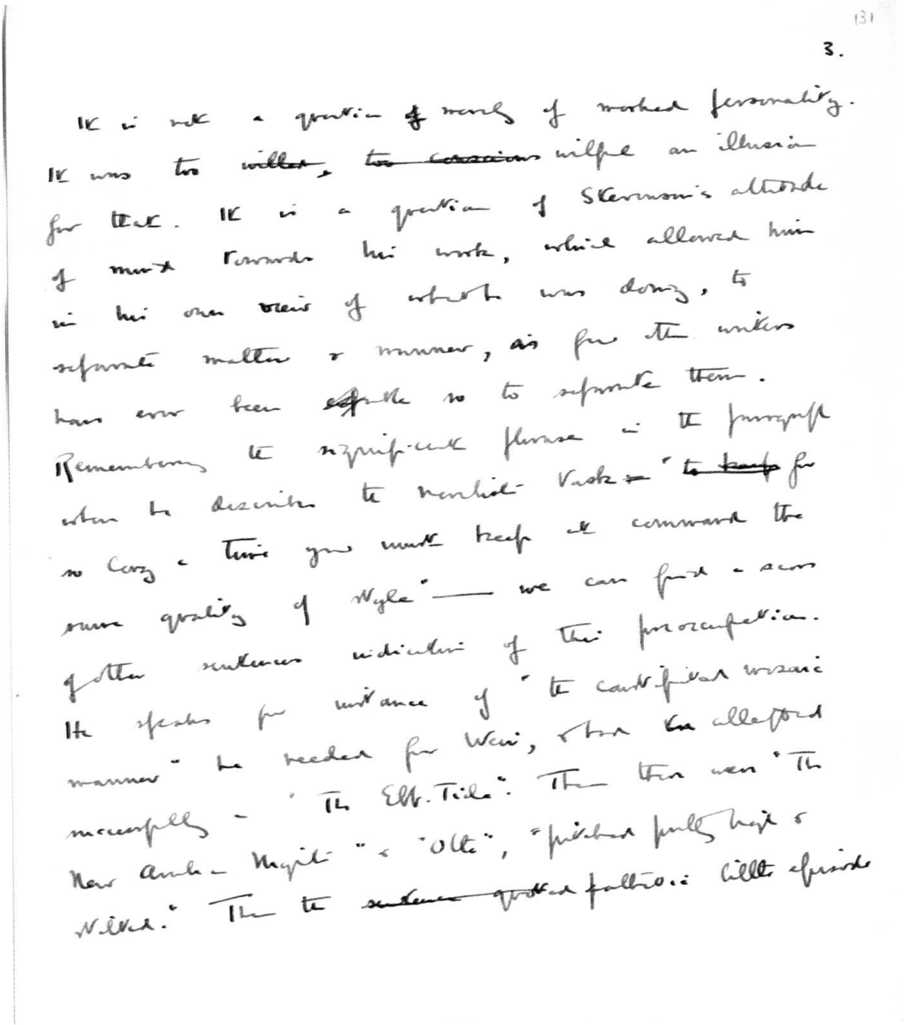

6 A page of the *Stevenson* manuscript showing Ransome's hand at its most legible (fol. 131)

7 Front cover of *The Tramp*, April 1910

8 The young Bohemian Ransome sketched on a piece of grocer's paper in Paris, 1908; artist unidentified

9 'Studio Ideal' portrait of Ransome taken in Moscow between 1915 and 1917

10 Ransome at work in Russian pine forest, 1913

11 The daughter Ransome adored: Tabitha

12 Arthur and Ivy Ransome with Daniel Macmillan outside the law-courts in London, a Press photograph from April 1913

13 Arthur and Evgenia Ransome with Titty, Roger, Taqui and Brigit Altounyan in Syria

14 Robert Louis Stevenson and his family photographed on the verandah steps of Vailima early in 1892 by John Davis of Apia (identified on p. 27)

15 Robert Louis Stevenson in sleeping-bag, illustration by Walter Crane used as frontispiece to vol. I of the Pentland edition of Stevenson's *Works*, ed. Edmund Gosse (1906)

16 R. L. Stevenson writing in bed, by Harry Furniss (pen and ink sketch)

a work of art, with perhaps too much thought of its significant, spectacular effects. Stevenson has the same idea, only, for him the 'idea of the tale' is a 'fixed design of righteousness', or, perhaps, and if so, how much more true, 'the central impulse and direction of a man's nature.'[1]

Lay Morals, that unfinished treatise on ethics is, so far as Stevenson took it, a comparison between the ideals of Christ and those of public opinion. Its motive is an impatience with the people who believe that they can serve God and Mammon, and yet profess themselves Christians. In an ingenious passage he points out that these people are not of Christ's mind, but of a mind with Benjamin Franklin.[2] The essay proceeds with a very noble definition of the Bohemian. 'The man I mean lives wholly to himself, does what he wishes, and not what is thought proper, buys what he wants for himself, and not what is thought proper, works at what he believes he can do well and not what will bring him in money or favour. You may be the most respectable of men, and yet a true Bohemian. And the test is this: a Bohemian, for as poor as he may be, is always open-handed to his friends; he knows what he can do with money and how he can do without it, a far rarer and more useful knowledge; he has had less, and continued to live in some contentment; and hence he cares not to keep more, and shares his sovereign or his shilling with a friend ...' and then the opposing indictment: 'But a young man who elects to save on dress or on lodging, or who in any way falls out of the level of expenditure which is common to his level in society, falls out of society altogether.'[3] Here is the force of Stevenson's

---

[1] Ransome follows this with a large question-mark. The passage from chapter III of *Lay Morals* is: 'All that we know to guide us in this changing labyrinth is our soul with its fixed design of righteousness, and a few old precepts which commend themselves to that.'

[2] (1706–90), Founding Father of the United States, author, scientist, philosopher, politician.

[3] *Lay Morals and Other Essays*, chapter IV. Ransome, author of *Bohemia in London* (1907) which he had recently revised (1912) is bound to think this definition noble, and indeed seems to have emulated Stevenson in his own Bohemian life. He scrawled a large question-mark after this paragraph. He notes: "Bohemianism. The true Bohemian the upright man – L[ay] M[orals] near to end. Criticism of accepted ideas. Christianity and respectability", and elsewhere "Moral hereditary background combined with sense, instance grandmother and grandfather and the baker. Religion – Prayers. Sect: cf. Damien letter. The artist's morality applied to life." Reading Stevenson's letters in Colvin's 'four red volumes' (1911) Ransome would not have had the benefit of a letter omitted from that collection. Writing to Miss Adelaide Boodle in January 1890 about the validity of religious life outside the Church of England, Stevenson had said: 'Who are those whom we respect, who do a fair day's work in life, and keep their blood pure by exercise? The most that I have known do not sit in our friend's church; many of the best Christians sit in none. ... I am pained that a friend of mine should conceive life so smally as

argument. We are not Christian; we substitute for the inner personal virtue
an outward and public conformity. We have dethroned Christ, though we
continue to praise in his name the deity we have set in his place, and that
deity is no other than Mrs Grundy.

It is almost unnecessary to remark on the part played by his Scottish
blood and environment in determining Stevenson's attitude as a moralist.
To say that moralising was hereditary in his family is to say no more than
that his family was Scottish. I do however think it worth while to take a
story from his memoirs to illustrate the family fashion in this regard.
The woman was pre-eminently pious, he has said, the man in comparison worldly and active. His grandmother gathered the godly about her;
his grandfather followed her from an admiring distance, as one walking
beneath an angel. Yet there is one sally of his recorded which is certainly
indicative of Stevenson's personal attitude. 'One of her (the grandmother's)
confidants had once a narrow escape;'

> an unwieldy old woman, she had fallen from an outside stair in a
> street of the Old Town; and my grandmother rejoiced to commu-
> nicate the providential circumstance that a baker had been passing
> underneath with his bread upon his head. 'I would like to know what
> kind of providence the baker thought it!' cried my grandfather.'[1]

Stevenson never allowed his grandfather's critical and circumspicuous
instinct to sleep during his own sermons. He was always mindful of the
feelings of the baker under the impinging heavy weight of godliness, and
he never allowed his own sense of proportion to be distorted by righteousness over-much. Mrs Strong asked him of *The Merry Men*: 'In these stories,
do you preach a moral?' 'Oh, not mine,' he said. 'What I want to give, what
I try for, is God's moral!'[2] And much of Stevenson's most earnest moralising is that of the indignant baker who had suffered from the fall upon
him of too much godliness as he trod his profane and airy way. He moralises as a Scotchman. He moralises against 'morality' because he has been a
Scottish child.

Mrs Stevenson in her preface to the Prayers which her husband wrote
for family use at Vailima says that with him 'prayer, the direct appeal, was
a necessity. When he was happy he felt impelled to offer thanks for that

---

to think she leaves the hand of her God because she leaves a certain clique of
clergymen and a certain scattered handful of stone buildings, some of them
with pointed windows, most with belfries, and a few with an illumination of
the Ten Commandments on the wall. I have forgotten Milton's exact words
but they are something to the purpose: 'Do not take the living God for a
buzzard.'

[1] "*Records of a Family of Engineers.*"

[2] "*Memories of Vailima*, p. 9."

undiscovered joy; when in sorrow, or pain, to call for strength to bear what must be borne.' Those sentences, so precise in meaning, help as few other comments on Stevenson do help, in mapping his private intellectual position. I find that position extremely interesting.[1] The existence or non-existence of God would not alter it. Stevenson *needed* to pray, needed to praise, for his own sake, not for any imagined pleasure given to the deity.

---

[1] Ransome seems to affirm Stevenson's 'free' position. Here is a new scrap of biographical information about Ransome, and a unique instance of his writing about personal matters of belief.

APPENDICES

A.1 Ransome's 'Stevenson exercise-book' transcribed

[Holograph manuscript, in the Brotherton Library, University of Leeds; blue cloth cover, ruled paper]

[spine] STEVENSON. СТИВЕНСОНЪ
[flyleaf] Arthur Ransome,
Datcha [*sic*] Gellibrand,
Terijoki [*sic*],
Finland

A.1.i Preliminary material

[Three loose sheets of MS, same small quarto paper as the parcelled MS; on the first the following paragraph]

Stevenson. *Conclusion.*

It was about this time that Stevenson became 'a great penny-whistler before the Lord', and the fact deserves a little notice. The instrument is unjustly despised, even laughed at, but it is capable of great things. Stevenson and his stepson played duets: it led him to study the technique of music: he even composed for it. And, somehow, it is symbolical of his career. A grown man playing the instrument of youth, playing it with a skill not often dedicated to it, and, in larger matter, playing a penny whistle in the orchestra of English literature. [*A wavy line through the first few lines, perhaps indicating deletion; 'son' crossed out, 'stepson' inserted.*]

[Two loose folio sheets contain a summary list made by Ransome after 1945 from early diaries, of meetings with Robert Ross at the time of his book on Wilde, not relevant to Stevenson.]

The 'Stevenson exercise book'

[many pages remain blank]

A.1.ii Annotated chronology of Stevenson's life and works.

[fol. 1] Stevenson.
1850 Nov. 13. Born 8 Howard Place, Edinburgh.
School. His father's contempt for school learning. 'Tutor was ever a byword with him; "positively tutorial", he would say of people

or manners he despised; and with rare consistency, he bravely
encouraged me to neglect my lessons, and never so much as
asked me my place in school.' *Life*, 20.
Only child. Father, mother, nurse.

1857   17 Heriot Row. Eng. Lakes.
        Colinton Manse. Early preferences in play, *Life* 34.
        Toy theatre, 39. cudgel 43.
        Henderson's prepara[tory] Day school, for a few weeks. '57 again
        in '59, till '61, when he went to Edinburgh Academy, for 18 months,
        64 then day school, till 67 when he went to the University.

1862   His father took him to London, for the 2ⁿᵈ Int. Exhibition, &
        abroad. Riviera, & his first tour of Lighthouse inspection.

[fol. unnumbered page between fols 1 and 2]

1866   The Parlour Diary.
1867   Edinburgh University & practical engineering. Swinton Cottage.
1868   Descent in diving suit, cf. *Random Memories*.
1869   To Shetland in the *Pharos* steamer with his father.
1870   3 weeks on Erraid, where Balfour was shipwrecked.
        Spec. 1869.
        Atheist Socialist. Social enquirer. [?]full town life in Edinburgh.
        grandson of Art. North?
        Friends. R. A. M. S., Walter Ferrier, Sir William Simpson.
        Prof. Fleeming Jenkin.
1871   'New Form of Intermittent Light for Lighthouses'. Worked for W.
        Rogers.
        Scottish Society of Arts.

[fol. 1v]

1874   Victor Hugo (1st ind. paper)
1876   *Burns* commissioned. Fontainebleau. With R. A. M. S. With
        Simpson
        April July 25 early 15th cent. poetry.
        Jan. *John Knox*. June 'Forest Notes'.
1876–77 *Virginibus Puerisque.* 76 Inland voyaging & the Mast[er of]
        Ballantrae
        when he had his imp. Lodging for the Night. *Temple Bar* Oct 77.
1877   Between Edn-Paris-London-Fontainebleau
1878   [illegible] + [?]Burford Bridge & Meredith. Autumn. Travelling
        with a donkey.
1878.   put, Jan, t[o] b[ed] 'Sire de Maletroit's Door'. 'Will o' the Mill' Jan.
        Cornhill.

[fol. 2]
1878   'Inland Voyage', May.
          'New Arabic [*sic*] Nights', in London.
          'Donkey' 'Providence & Guitar', Edinburgh
1879   Spring. 'Deacon Brodie'.
          Lay Morals
1879   Sept to Dec. '*Thoreau*' [illegible]
          Planned *Prince Otto*. [illegible]
          Notes for *Amateur Emigrant*
1881 summer   'Thrawn Janet'. Began *C[hild's] G[arden] of V[erses]*.
          Merry Men
          Treasure Island
1881 autumn   Life of Hazlitt [illegible] it.
          Treasure Island finished.
          Silverado Squatters.
          'Talk & Talkers'
          'Gossip on Romance'

[fol. 3]
March 83 → Oct. 84   *Silverado Squatters*. mission. *Otto. C[hilds] G[arden]
          of Verses. Black Arrow.*
          (*T[reasure] I[sland]* published autumn.)
          Sept. Dec. 1884   Admiral Guinea & Beau Austin.
1885   Finished *Otto. Child's Garden of Verses.*
          New Arabian Nights.
          Attempted: Great North Road. Life of Wellington.
1885   Olalla. ?autumn
          Dr Jekyll & Mr Hyde
1886   Finished *Kidnapped.*
          Preparation of *Fleeming Jenkyn.*
Sept. 1887–12 essays, for [illegible]. *Dreams.* [?] *Paloris of Umbria.*
          Braggarts. Lanterns. Random Memories etc.
May 1888   *Master of Ballantrae*
          Wrong Box.

[fol. 2v]
1887 Sept.   Voyages in *Ludgate Hill.*
          New York. Beginning of Sept.
          End of Sept. went to Saranac Lake in the Adirondacks.
          Penny Whistling.
1888   Saranac, left in April.
          May, New Jersey Coast, cat-boat sailing.
          June 28, sailed in the yacht *Casco* from San Francisco.
          July 28, landfall in the South Seas. Nuka-hiva.

[fol. 4; *On this last page of chronology, 1889–94, some titles are ticked; for Ransome a tick usually means 'section written'. Here it may mean 'book acquired'; see fols 65v and 66.*]

1889, Dec. Finished ✓ *Master of Ballantrae.*
        ✓*Wrong Box*
        ✓ Bottle Imp
1890   ✓ *The South Seas* Father Damien.
1891   ✓ Beach of Falesa (began)
        Stories of [illegible] French.
        ✓ *Wrecker* (Nov)
        Footnote to History
1892   Correcting proofs ✓ *Wrecker* & ✓ 'Beach of Falesá'
        plans Sophia Scarlet
        ✓ *Catriona* (Feb-May) ✓ *Weir of Hermiston* draft of typing
1893   ✓ *St Ives*
        ✓ *EbbTide*
1894   Annals of his family.
Oct.   <u>& *St Ives*</u>.
Oct–Nov–Dec   ✓ *Weir of Hermiston.*

A.1.iii Headed pages

[*Quotations copied but unused, some with brief notes made*]

[fol. 5]   The Sea.
        Compare Stevenson's attitude towards the sea with his attitude towards the letter of Ori-a-Ori, pp. 106 & 109, *Letters*, III.

[fols 7–9] *The Master of Ballantrae* pub. Aug. 1889.
        L[etters], III, 33. Letter to Colvin, Dec. 24, 1887, with 92pp of draft done.
        With good example of S's attitude towards imagined character. 36. 'The master is all I know of the devil. I have known hints of him, in the world, but always cowards; he is as bold as a lion, but with the same deadly, causeless duplicity I have watched with so much surprise in my two cowards. 'Tis true, I saw a hint of the same nature in another man who was not a coward; but he had other things to attend to; the Master has nothing else but his devilry.'
        Letter to Miss Boodle, Christmas '87.

        L[etters] III, 37, 'I am on the jump with a new story which has bewitched me – I doubt it may bewitch no one else. It is called *The Master of Ballantrae* – pronounce Bállan-tray. If it is not good, well, mine will be the fault; for I believe it is a good tale.'

[fol. 8]   *Master of Ballantrae.*
L[*etters*] III, 48, to Henry James.
An account of the plot, with just criticism. e.g.
'Five parts of it are sound, human tragedy; the last one or two, I
regret to say, not so soundly designed; I about hesitate to write
them; they are very picturesque, but they are fantastic; they
shame, perhaps degrade, the beginning. ...
    For the third suppposed death and the manner of the third
reappearance is steep; steep, sir. It is even very steep, and I fear it
shames the honest stuff so far; but then it is highly pictorial, and
it leads up to the death of the elder brother at the hands of the
younger in a perfectly cold blooded murder, of which I wish (and
mean) the reader to approve. You see how daring is the design.'

[fol. 9]   *Master of Ballantrae*
Finished May '89 at Waikiki, Honolulu.

[fol. 11]   *Characteristics of Style*
'Then was a view on a bit of empty wood, a few dark houses, *a
donkey wandering with its shadow on a slope,* and a blink of sea,
with a tall ship lying anchored in the moonlight.' [*Ransome's
italics*] *Squatters*, 5.
Sound and sense
Somerset as the new employé of Prince Florizel (Mr. Goodall of
the Cigar Divan) provides a good example:–
'"Or opulent rotunda strike the sky," said the shopman to himself,
in the tone of one considering a verse. "I suppose it would be too
much to say 'orotunda', and yet how noble it were! 'Or opulent
orotunda strike the sky'. But that is the bitterness of art; you
see a good effect, and some nonsense about sense continually
intervenes." '
M[ore] N[ew] Arabian [Nights]. Dynamiter, 281.

[fol. 12]   *Style.*
War against the adjective and the optic nerve. cf. *Letters*, IV, 231.
aet. 43
but cf. p. 11 here [*i.e. of this notebook*], donkey & shadow: the
visual
propensities of his youth.
'feeling' action, 'hearing' speech; also IV. 231.
'constipated mosaic manner' of *Weir*, & (so he says) of *The Ebb
Tide*, cf. *Letters*, IV, 247.

[fol. 14]   *Character*
The fog in the valley below the mountain suggests the rising
deluge – and – 'The imagination loves to trifle with what is not.

Had this been indeed the deluge, I should have felt more strongly, but the emotion would have been similar in kind. I played with this idea, as the child flees in delighted terror from the creations of his fancy. The look of the thing helped me. And when at last I began to flee up the mountain, it was indeed partly to escape from the raw air that kept me coughing, but it was also part in play.' *Silverado Squatters*, 115.

Lantern bearers. *Across the Plains*, 138.
cf. Balzac on Paris & M[illegible]. *Wrecker*, 26.

[fol. 15]   *Character.   Lighthouses.*
Lighthouses: *Poems*, 44.
'Say not of me that weakly I declined
The labours of my sires ...'
Poems, 42. 'Skerryvore', &, 'Skerryvore: The Parallel'.
Poems, 38. 'To my Father'.

Action.
Letters, IV, 243.
'I ought to have been able to build lighthouses and write 'David Balfour' too. *Hinc illae lacrymae. ...*'[etc.]
cf. also earlier in same letter.

[fol. 16]   The cloak, [*Letters*,] I 123.
Didacticism defended at 18. [*Letters*], I, 17.
me and the birds. [*Letters*,] I, 33.
Enfants, 120.
aet. 18. Don't say anything about the plot because he had not yet finished *The Moonstone* of Wilkie Collins
Scotch songs [*Letters*,] I, 117.

[fol. 17]   The sedulous ape.
Lamb. 'We wore them (tin bull's-eye lanterns) buckled to the waist upon a cricket belt, and over them, such was the rigour of the game, a buttoned top-coat.'
Across the Plains, (The Lantern Bearers), 143.

[fol. 20]   *Letters.*
Used in actual writing.
'what I liked still less ... [etc.]' *The Wrecker*. P. 173, *Letters* p. [*sic*]
Letters, I. 14 – Unpleasant Places. *Essays of Travel*. 225. 'Breezy, Breezy.'

[fol. 23]   Attitude towards art.
cf. 'I would love to have my hour as a native Maker, and be read by my own countryfolk in our own dying language: an ambition

surely rather of the heart than of the head, so restricted as it is in prospect of endurance, so parochial in bounds of space.' Note to 'Underwoods', *Poems.* 7.

'I could never be induced to take the faintest interest in Brompton *qua* Brompton or a drawing-room *qua* drawing-room. I am an Epick Writer with k to it, but without the necessary genius.' *Letters*, IV, 134.

[fol. 25]   *Treasure Island* & *Black Arrow.* 1883–8̶4̶ appearing in serial, *Young Folks* 2.

Black Arrow. Schwob asked leave to translate it, in 1890.
Tushery.

'I had had to leave 'Fontainebleau', when three hours would finish it & go full-tilt at tushery for a while.' [*Letters*,] II, 117.

Written to Colvin who had criticised serial appearance:– *Letters*, 142.

'I am so pleased you liked Crookback; he is a fellow whose hellish energy has always fixed my attention. I wish Shakespeare had written the play after he had learned more of the rudiments of lit. & art rather than before. Some day I will re-tickle the Sabre Missile, and shoot it, *moyennant finances*, once more into the air; I can lighten it much and devote more attention to Dick o' Gloucester. It's great sport to write tushery.'

T[*reasure*] *I*[*sland*]. 'It was the sight of your maimed strength and watchfulness that kept John Silver in Treasure Island. Of course he is not in any other quality or feature the least like you; but the idea of the maimed man, ruling and dreaded by the sound, was entirely taken from you.' To Henley, *Letters*, II, 116. 1883.

B[*lack*] [*Arrow*].
I find few greater pleasures than reading my own works, but I never, O I never read *The Black Arrow*.

Nov 1883, reads this time ('the Lord begot them') pleased ... referring to *T*[*reasure*] *I*[*sland*], [*Letters*,] II, 155.

[fol. 26]   cf. earn my seamanship in journey ...

T[*reasure*] *I*[*sland*] 'I make these paper people to please myself and Skelt, and God Almighty, and with no other purpose. Yet am I mortal myself; for, as I remind you, I begged for a supervising mariner.'

excellent letter on realism etc. [*Letters*,] II, 152.

[fol. 28]   *Catriona*

'I shall never write a better book than *Catriona*, that is my high water mark ...' [etc] *Letters*, IV, 258.

[fol. 30]   Opinions on Contemporaries. etc.
Aestheticism. He congratulates James Payn on *not* having been
an aesthete. *L*[*etters,*] IV, 95.

[fol. 31]   Opinions
'Chateaubriand is more antipathetic than anyone else in the
world.' [*Letters,*] I, 81.

[fol. 32]   Technique of Narration.
Talkative squire in *T*[*reasure*] *I*[*sland*] Continuation.
Knowledge of weakness in heart of *Ballantrae.*

[fol. 34]   The South Seas
Sailed from San Francisco in *Casco.* June 88. Visited eastern
islands early in 89. Honolulu. Thence in trading schooner.
Equator 70 tons, 4 months among the Gilberts. Samoa end of
1889. 3rd cruise – in *Janet Nicoll.*
The sketch of native history in the Gilberts.
The execution by assassination of the unfit [illegible] chief.
character sketches of kings.
Tembinok of Apemana & his Ladies School of a palace.
chronicles, port, etc.
The cannibal high place.
The building of a town for Stevenson's party. p. 289 etc.
Forth Cove. p. 189, to decayed, fast changing, flying corpse.

[fol. 36]   *Poetry.*
Marjorie Fleming.
'Children are certainly too good to be true.'
Letters, I, 105.
Nelitschka. etc. at Menton.

A.1.iv Lists and plans

[fol. 61v]   *Virginibus Puerisque.*
Donkey. Inland Voyage
Silverado Squatters. Amateur Emigrant etc. *Essays of Travel?*
Merry Men

[fol. 62]   Plan.
   I Introductory.
  II Biographical Summary.
 III The Early Essayist.
  IV Short Stories.
   V New Arabian Nights, and The Dynamiter.
  VI *Treasure Island* and *Black Arrow.*

  IX *Jekyll and Hyde*. Markheim. etc. to [?highness] of Hawthorne.
   X The Scotch stories. *Kidnapped* & *Catriona*. *The Master of Ballantrae.*
  XI The collaborations. ? *Fleeming Jenkin*. experiments in style.
 XII *Weir of Hermiston*
 VII *Child's Garden of Verses* & poetry generally.
 VII *The South Seas*. Island Nights Entertainments.
XIII Conclusion.

[*Arrows lead VII and VIII to their places; a sum divides 60,000 by 13, giving 5000; another column lists 4.5, 13, 135, 45, 585 – these relate to numbers of pages written, and word-counts.*]

[fol. 62v] Stevenson's Books
     Inland Voyage
     Edinburgh
     Travels with a Donkey

[fol. 66] Books wanted for Stevenson.
     Gosse. *Critical Kit Kats.*
     Voyages of Capt. Woodes Rogers.
     Shakespearian dramas for toy theatres. (Skelt).
     W. H. Low *Chronicle of Friendships.*
     A Cloud of Witnesses.
     Selections from the Covenanting writers.
     Robertson's *Sermons.*
     G. P. R. James.
     Shorter Catechism.
     Herman Melville.
     Henry James. *Partial Portraits.*
     Rocambole (*Squatters* 133)
     ✓ Barbey d'Aurevilly
     H. J. Moors. *Stevenson in Samoa.*
     ✓ Labiche.

[fol. 68] [*listing number of MS pages completed under each heading.*]
     Sea. 5
     Ballantrae 7
     Style 11
     Character 14
     Sedulous ape 7
     Letters 20
     Contemporaries 30
     Treasure Island}
     Black Arrow} 25
     Attitude towards Art. 23

A.2 Additional material from the main manuscript

A.2.i Ransome's own textual corrections, and editorial emendations (sample pages, annotated)

[fols 131–41]

[fol. 131] It is not a question merely of marked personality. It was too wilful[1] an illusion for that. It is a question of Stevenson's attitude of mind towards his work, which allowed him in his own view of what he was doing, to separate matter and manner, as few other writers have ever been able[2] so to separate them. Remembering the significant phrase in the paragraph where he describes the novelist's task: 'for[3] so long a time you must keep at command the same quality of style' – we can find a score of other sentences indicative of this preoccupation. He speaks for instance of 'the constipated mosaic manner' he needed for *Weir of Hermiston*,[4] and had adopted[5] successfully in *The Ebb Tide*. Then there were *The New Arabian Nights* and *Otto*, 'pitched pretty high and stilted'. Then the pathetic[6] little episode [fol. 132] of Mr Somerset, and again flat, direct statements as in the letter *IV* 231.[7]

[fol. 133] We[8] begin to see now what an intricate affair is any perfect passage; how many faculties, whether of taste or pure reason, must be held upon the stretch to make it; and why, when it is made, it should afford us so complete a pleasure. From the arrangement of according letters, which is altogether arabesque and sensual, up to the architecture of the elegant and pregnant sentence, which is a vigorous act of the pure intellect, there is scarce a faculty in man but has been exercised. We need not wonder, then, if perfect sentences are rare, and perfect pages rarer.[9]

[1] 'too willed, too conscious' *crossed out.*

[2] 'esp' crossed out.

[3] 'to keep' *crossed out.*

[4] 'Weir' > *Weir of Hermiston.*

[5] 'tr' *crossed out*; 'allopted' >adopted.

[6] 'sentence quoted' *crossed out.*

[7] [*a letter to be inserted here*] > as in a letter to Henry James in 1893. [*quote letter*].

[8] [*header for this*] 'Technique of Literature. Art of Writing. 43'.

[9] [fol. 134] [*header*] 'Early [?]movement in words. Essays of Travel. 177.' [fol. 135] [*header*] 'Stevenson. Early Essays'.

In[1] 1878[2] Stevenson had finished *An Inland Voyage* and written *Travels with a Donkey*. In the next year he had his first experience of real travel, voyaging done without too firm a consciousness of the Savile Club at home, without an immediate translation of experience into telling and humorous anecdote. The travelling he did in pursuit of his private romance was touched by realism, whereas the little journeys he had undertaken for fun were[3] at least gilded by the sunset of the[4] Romantic movement– a very different thing. In the two little sentimental journeys, Stevenson pervaded his material: in the journey dictated by a real sentiment he was a dragon fly tossed by a wind of irresistible experiences, blown far from his accustomed reeds, and taking notes while in immediate danger of not finding his way back. In some such way I represent the change in character between *An Inland Voyage* and, for example, *The Amateur Emigrant from the Clyde to Sandy Hook*.[5]

Let me review the circumstances.[6]

[fol. 138] 'Every book is, in an intimate sense, a circular letter to the friends of him who writes it.[7] They alone take his meaning; they find private messages, assurances of love, and expressions of gratitude, dropped for them in every corner. The public is but a generous patron who defrays[8] the postage.' The first of these sentences from the dedication of *Travels with a Donkey in the Cévennes* is strictly true; except in a few rare cases, and of the books of great and isolated man. The third is an ingenious, charming corollary to the second. And the second is not by any means generally true, though it is so[9] of much of Stevenson's own work, and partly explains its peculiar intimate quality. He was thinking of *Otto* when he wrote to Mr. Gosse[10] that it was a deadly fault 'to

---

[1] [fol. 135] [*header*] 'The South Seas' *crossed out.* [*header*] 'Essays. II'.

[2] '78 > 1878.

[3] 'still glowed' *crossed out.*

[4] 'Romance' *crossed out.*

[5] '"The Amateur Emigrant", or "New York to Sandy Hook"' > *The Amateur Emigrant from the Clyde to Sandy Hook.*

[6] 'circumstances:' > 'circumstances.'
[*then the following memorandum:*] 'Thoreau. Torojiro. Pavilion. The story of a Lie? In the ship. Plains – Prince Otto.'

[7] [fol. 137] 'Stevenson. Essays. [?'travels' *crossed out*], 'Unpleasant Places. "Breezy. Breezy." cf. *Essays of Travel* 225, with *Letters* I. 14.'

[8] [fol. 138] 'pays' [*mistranscription*] > defrays.

[9] 'privately' *crossed out.*

[10] 'Mr. Gosse (Letters, II, 177)' > 'Mr Gosse'.

forget that art is a diversion and a decoration, that no triumph or effort is of value, nor anything worth reaching except charm'; but[1] the opinion had long been his, and the expression of it is in the manner of writing, dangerously infectious, easily recognisable, that he [fol. 139] early developed for himself.

Style is so far a man's personal rhythm, that it is as difficult to analyse as a personality. Its characteristics, its differences from other styles, are like a man's differences from other men. Yet something we can seize, in his choice of words, is the tone in[2] which he uses them, and a vocabulary does not make so utterly flexible a vehicle of thought that a writer is not to be known by the repetition of particular effects varied only in detail, and as it were midway between perfect expression and a private convention of his own. He thinks in these effects, but they are approximations stamped with a trademark; he moulds a bust with them, but they do not precisely follow the curves and hollows that they represent. Dr. Johnson always spoke in thunder but sometimes his thunder was a loud and roaring imitation of some smaller noise. Bottom will[3] roar you like the lion, or as gently as a sucking-dove, but the roar is always Bottom's and lion or sucking-dove must be [fol. 140] attributed by courtesy to his wild wood-notes. In so far, every artist is another Bottom, another Johnson where little fishes talk like whales, or, commoner case, when whales converse like little fishes. The wise know the gamut of their own voices and are careful not to stretch them to points where courtesy breaks down and the illusion passes.

This is very unsatisfactory, but[4] it is[5] illustrated with particular clarity by Stevenson's early books.

---

[1] 'the' *crossed out.*

[2] 'with' *crossed out.*

[3] 'roars' *crossed out.*

[4] 'by' *crossed out.*

[5] 'becomes' *crossed out,* 'is' *superscript.*

A.2.ii Ransome's (incomplete) Book-list

[*Missing from the list are Colvin's 1911 edition of Stevenson's* Letters, *and the 1911 edition of Graham Balfour's* Life of Robert Louis Stevenson, *sources which Ransome is known to have used.*]

[fols 325–6]

> Books
>
> *A Chronicle of Friendship* [1873–1900], by Will H[icok] Low.
>   Hodder & Stoughton, 1908.
> *Robert Louis Stevenson. A Record, An Estimate, And A Memorial*,
>   by Alexander H. Japp, LLD. etc. T. Werner Laurie, 1905.
> *Memories of Vailima*, by Isobel Strong and Lloyd Osbourne.
>   Constable, 1903.
> *In the Tracks of R. L. Stevenson and Elsewhere in Old France*, by
>   J. A. Hammerton. Arrowsmith, 1907.
> *With Stevenson in Samoa*, by H. J. Moors. Fisher Unwin, 1910.
> *Recollections of Robert Louis Stevenson in the Pacific*, by Arthur
>   Johnstone. Chatto and Windus, 1905.
> *Robert Louis Stevenson, An Essay*, by Leslie Stephen. G. P.
>   Putnam's Sons, no date. [1903]
> *In Stevenson's Samoa*, by Marie Fraser, 2nd edition. Smith Elder,
>   1895.
> *Robert Louis Stevenson*, by L. Cope Cornford. Blackwood, 1899.
> *Robert Louis Stevenson*, by Eve Blantyre Simpson. T. N. Foulis,
>   1905.
> *Robert Louis Stevenson*, by Margaret Moyes Black. Oliphant,
>   Anderson and Ferrier, 1898.
> *Robert Louis Stevenson*. Bookman Booklet (W. Robertson Nicoll,
>   G. K. Chesterton). Hodder & Stoughton, 1902.
> *Robert Louis Stevenson's Edinburgh Days*, by Eve Blantyre
>   Simpson. 2nd ed., Hodder and Stoughton, 1898.
> *An Edinburgh Eleven*, by J. M. Barrie, 3rd edition. Hodder and
>   Stoughton, 1896.
> *Letters from Samoa*, by Mrs. M. I. Stevenson. Methuen, [1906].
> *From Saranac to the Marquesas*, by Mrs M. I. Stevenson.
>   Methuen, 1903.
> *Robert Louis Stevenson, A Life Study in Criticism*, by H. Bellyse
>   Baildon. Chatto and Windus, 1901.
> *The Home and Early Haunts of R. L. Stevenson*, by Margaret
>   Armour. W. H. White, 1895.
> *The Faith of Robert Louis Stevenson*, by John Kelman. Jr. M. A.
>   Oliphant Anderson & Ferrier, 1903.

A.2.iii Variant passages

[fol. 100] [*a draft passage for p. 82*]

Mr. Johnston [*sic*] records the fact that he left among the whites few enemies, but many critics, and on the other hand a host of friends, in spite of his writings on South Sea problems, which are seldom ever polite to the representatives of civilisation. He quotes the opinion of Captain Otis, the sailing master of the *Casco*, who was present at a discussion of Stevenson's attitude on Pacific matters.

> Well, gentlemen, it seems this way to me: Stevenson was first and last a man of convictions – in fact he always acted promptly and vigorously when he reached a conclusion that satisfied his own mind – but his mental make-up was such that he always took the side of the under-dog in any fight that arose, without waiting to inquire whether the under-dog had the right of it, or was in the wrong. That was the man, gentleman; and I know from personal experience that he did not understand what fear was, when he defended what he thought was right. *Recollections of Robert Louis Stevenson in the Pacific*, p. 13.

[fol. 164] [*The quotation appears in a slightly different formulation on p. 103.*]

'Stevenson. *Critic.* √ [*Ransome's tick, here also circled, often means 'used in the text'.*]

'Not the gay paradox of Wilde, impatient of lumbering explanation: when Wilde says gaily "Nature imitates Art", Stevenson, more serious, younger, solemnly shows that 'those predilections of the artist he knows not why, those irrational acceptations and recognitions, reclaim, out of the world that we have not quite realised, ever another and another corner.' (*Familiar S[tudies]*, 7)

[fol. 173] [*a draft sentence for part of p. 62*]

Familiar Studies

'A new form of intermittent light for lighthouses' was followed three years later by Stevenson's first serious public appearance, with "Victor Hugo" in the Cornhill Magazine; and in that essay we may find a number of indications of what its writer was to become.

[fol. 187] [*an opener perhaps for p. 151*]
New Arabian Nights
From these French stories I turn to those which Stevenson
affectionately called "The Arabs" – *The New Arabian Nights*.

[fol. 378] [*an earlier version of paragraph on p. 84*]
Stevenson. *Biog.*
It is to be presumed that the Gods did indeed know best; for
Stevenson was given the best death that a man can ask. He died
in the midst of the best work of his life, in full vigour, without
pain. Nor is it extravagant to find in *Weir of Hermiston*, with its
'constipated mosaic manner', a work in words as nearly as possible
resembling the work of his father in stones against the beating of
the seas. Here at last Stevenson was building on a promontory in
the uncharted, dangerous seas of humanity; larger than himself,
and doing more difficult work than ever before, and in proud
consciousness of this, Stevenson died suddenly on [*sic*]

A.2.iv Quotations copied by Ransome and notes by him that have not been used in the running text

[fol. 360] 'What a man spends upon himself he shall have earned by
services to the race.'

[fol. 369] He once successfully worked out a theory for a detective in the
criminal case.
Recollections of R. L. S. in the Pacific, p. 281.

[fol. 373] 'In my view, one dank, dispirited word is harmful, a crime of *lèse-humanité*, a piece of acquired evil; every gay, every bright word or
picture, like every pleasant air of music, is a piece of pleasure set
afloat; the reader catches it, and, if he be healthy, goes on his way
rejoicing; and it is the business of art so to send him, as often as
possible.' To W. Archer, Oct. 28, 1885, Bournemouth [*Letters*], II,
248."

[fol. 374] April 20, 1893. Mrs Strong writes: 'I was pottering about my room
this morning when Louis came in with the remark that he was
a gibbering idiot. I have seen him in this mood before, when he
pulls out hairpins, tangles up his mother's knitting, and interferes
in whatever his womankind are engaged upon. So I gave him
employment in tidying a drawer all the morning – talking the
wildest nonsense all the time, and he was babbling on when
Sesimo came in to tell us lunch was ready; his very reverential,

respectful manner brought the Idiot Boy to his feet at once, and we all went off laughing to lunch.' *Memories of Vailima*, pp. 31, 32.

[fol. 379] Travel. Oct 22. 'If we didn't travel now and then, we should forget what the feeling of life is. The very cushion of a railway carriage – "the things restorative to the touch".' To Baxter, Dunblane, March 5, 1872. *Letters*, I, 34.

[fol. 380] 'spontaneous lapse of coin'

[fol. 382] Of art says Stevenson, "The direct returns – the wages of the trade are small, but the indirect – the wages of the life – are incalculably great. No other business offers a man his daily bread upon such joyful terms." *Across the Plains*, 185.

[fol. 383] His uncle Alan, when building lighthouses, used to read Quixote, Aristophanes and Dante, each in the language of its birth.

[fol. 384] Trust
He very early knew Meredith, and would get M. to tell his best.
Gosse 76 intro by Colvin

[fol. 387] 'I have that peculiar and delicious sense of being born again in an expurgated edition which belongs to 'convalescence.' Oct. 29, [*Letters*,] I, 259.

A.2.v Significant working notes for sections of text

[fol. 11]   [*Notes for Part I of the book; the ticks indicate sections written.*]
Biographical Summary
    I *General* ✓
   II Birth and Childhood ✓
  III School days
  IV *University & Edinburgh days. To advocate.* ✓
   V *Ordered South & Health* ✓
  VI *Fontainebleau ......* ✓
VI [*sic*] Monastier. & *Inland Voyage*
  VII *Emigration. San Francisco. Monterey & Marriage.* ✓
 VIII *Scotland & Davos. War game. Printing.* ✓
  IX *Bournemouth* ✓   ?
   X 2nd *voyage to America. At Saranac. New Jersey. Cat boat sailing* ✓
  XI *Yacht Casco. Cruising in the South Seas .*✓
  XII *Vailima* ✓
 XIII Death & Summary. ✓

[*This check-list follows*]

>University ✓
>
>Greek abandoned as hopeless. ✓
>
>With a view to his engineering, he took scientific & mathematics classes instead of the humanities. ✓
>
>In the long vacation lighthouse building. description diver's suit. ✓
>
>Swanston. Vicomte de Bragelonne
>
>Spec. 1869. Boating – to birth.
>
>Velvet Coat in public-houses. Atheism.
>
>Friends R. A. M. S. Fleeming Jenkin.

1871, April.   Told his father he did not want to be an engineer. His father stoically agreed and S. was to be an Advocate.

1872.   Passed public exam for Scottish Bar. Spent some time in an office learning conveyancing.

[fol.48]   July 14. Passed as Advocate
25th with Simpson to France.
R. A. M. S also
23 mile walk: Query
smell the wet forest in morning.
Reading early French verse – writing rondeaux.
Historical sense of the forest: and a personal non-morality, and forgetfulness of argument at home, now – 'a faint far off rumour as of Merovingian wars.'

[fol. 174] Early Criticism   aet. 38, Shaw [*Letters,*] III, 40.
                                Barbey d'Aurevilly, [*Letters,*] IV, 244.
   not the gay paradox of Wilde   aet. 36, Dostoevsky, [*Letters,*] II, 275.
                                aet. 34, Shakespeare & Molière, [*Letters,*] II, 186.

Hugo, Scott & himself cf. Artistic intention. Hawthorne. Main obj. is of art. Admiration. Attitude towards realism. Pepys' style. Personal criticism. Pepys. Burns. Charles d'Orléans.

[fol. 179] Stevenson. Critic. Burns. Biographical study: a portrait of a man in *actions.* Study of the professional Don Juan, showing a considerable knowledge of wayside love, and a keen understanding of its psychology as exemplified by Burns: due partly to impatience with an inadequate, fluid sketch by Principal Shairp, an inadequate, a ridiculously uncomprehending book which judges Burns by a very narrow standard and never attempts to define him.

[fol. 175] "Stevenson. Style. Of Pepys:
'The first and the true function of the writer has been thoroughly performed throughout; and though the manner of his utterance may be childishly awkward, the matter has been transformed and assimilated by his unfeigned interest and delight.' *Familiar Studies*, 218.

[fol. 178] Charles d'Orléans. 1876. His bringing in the rondel, and ballade making of Fontainebleau. Admiration for Banville: again as in Burns knack of portraiture, a little thin, a little too sure of its own comprehensiveness. Fine array of authorities. Very good copy in pen and ink of a illumination in a fine copy of the poems given by Henry VII to Elizabeth of York. His word for 'some of our quaintly vicious contemporaries'.

[fol. 185] *Stevenson.* Short Stories. 6, 1, 3, 1½, ½ [*i.e. numbers of pages written.*]

[fol. 186] *Short Stories.*

1878 Providence. ✓
1877 Villon.
1877 Sire de Malétroit's door. ✓

1878 Arabians. *Dr. Jek[yll]*
1885 Dynamiter

1878 Will o' the Mill.
Markheim.

Scotch novels
1881 Thrawn Janet.
1881 Merry Men.
Body Snatcher.

Pavilion on the Links, 1879

R. L. S. 69.
on ship board

1887 John Nicholson.
1879 Story of a Lie.

[fol. 200] *Tod Lapraik. Thrawn Janet*, an excellent Scotch vernacular prose. 'grandfaither's silver tester in the puddock's heart of him.' Ingenious hitching with the story over to [illegible]'s quarrel.

[fol. 234] *Dr Jekyll and Mr Hyde.*
Markheim, nearer Poe. *Thrawn Janet* nearer Hawthorne. *Jekyll*: W. Wilson of Poe's.
Idea running in head. Dream. Insufficiency of first draft. But correction unimproved by the story itself: 'it was really an allegory.' and so retold.
Stevenson's knowledge that he had written the story before he was sufficiently intimate with it – humming the draft lest his pen should betray him by faltering in the note already made.
'The gnome (Jekyll and Hyde) is interesting, I think, and he came out of a deep mine, where he guards the fountain of tears. It is

not always the time to rejoice.' Jan. 2, 1886. Letter [to] W. H. Low, *Letters*, II, 263.

[fol. 231] *Stevenson. Fables.* By 1888 most written, promised Dougram; a few added in the *South Seas*, published at last 1895 as appendix to new edition of *J[ekyll] & Hyde*.
The characters in *T[reasure] I[sland]*. Vivid picture. The hand among the dead. Dry emptiness in the deliberate antique. J. M. Synge.

[fol. 261] Travel and Solidarity of vision. 'I shall never do a better book than *Catriona*, that is my high water mark.' *Letters*, IV, 258. *Kidnapped*, 1885. *Catriona*, 1893. *Master of Ballantrae*, 1889. A comparison with Russian literature: or Hardy.

[fol. 289] Stevenson. *South Seas*, Oct. 25. 'Awfully nice man here to-night. Public servant – New Zealand. Telling us all about the South Sea Islands till I was sick with desire to go there: beautiful places, green for ever; perfect climate; perfect shapes of men and women, with red flowers in their hair; and nothing to do but to study oratory and etiquette, sit in the sun, and pick up the fruits as they fall.' June 1875, [to] Sitwell, *Letters*, I, 188.

[fol. 290] *The South Seas.* The Church Builder.
'Brother Michel spoke always of his labours with a twinkle of humour, underlying which it was possible to spy a serious pride, and the change from one to another was often very human and diverting. 'Et vos gargouilles moyen-âge,' cried I; 'comme elles sont originales!' 'N'est-ce pas? Elles sont bien droles!' he said, smiling broadly; and the next moment, with a sudden gravity: 'Cependant il y en a une qui a une patte de cassé; il faut que je voie cela.' I asked if he had any model – a point we much discussed. 'Non,' said he simply; 'c'est une église ideale.'

[fol. 291] Stevenson. *The South Seas.*
'In the time of the small-pox in Hapaa, an old man was seized with the disease; he had no thought of recovery; had his grave dug by a wayside, and lived in it for near a fortnight, eating, drinking, and smoking with the passers-by, talking mostly of his end, and equally unconcerned for himself and careless of the friends whom he infected.'
S[outh] S[eas], 31. Marquesas.

[fol. 292] *South Seas. The Church Builder.*
'About midway of the beach (of Hatiheu in the Marquesas) no less than three churches stand grouped in a patch of bananas, intermingled with some pine-apples. Two are of wood: the

original church, now in disuse; and a second that, for some
mysterious reason, has never been used. The new church is of
stone, with twin towers, walls flangeing into buttresses, and
sculptured front. The design itself is good, simple, and shapely;
but the character is all in the detail, where the architect has
bloomed into the sculptor. It is impossible to tell in words of the
angels (although they are more like winged archbishops) that
stand guard upon the door, of the cherubs in the corners, of the
scapegoat gargoyles, or the quaint and spirited relief, where St
Michael (the artist's patron) makes short work of a protesting
Lucifer. We were never weary of viewing the imagery, so innocent,
sometimes so funny, and yet in the best sense – in the sense of
inventive gusto and expression – so artistic. I know not whether
it was more strange to find a building of such merit in a corner
of a barbarous isle, or to see a building so antique still bright
with novelty. The architect, a French lay brother, still alive and
well, and meditating fresh foundations, must have surely drawn
his descent from a master-builder in the age [fol. 293] of the
cathedrals; and it was in looking on the church of Hatiheu that
I seemed to perceive the secret charm of mediaeval sculpture;
that combination of the childish courage of the amateur,
attempting all things, like the schoolboy on his slate, with the
manly perseverance of the artist who does not know when he is
conquered.' *S[outh] S[eas]*, 60. Marquesas.

[fol. 330] [*a record of pages written*]
Robert Louis Stevenson
July

15	Biog. Summary	4
16	" "	3
	Scottish Background	2.
	Treasure Island	2.
18	" "	1½ ✓
	Novels	1½
25	Travel	1½
30	"	2
Aug.		
1	Fables.	3
4	Jekyll	3
	Biog.	1
	Character.	1

A.2.vi   Working notes for the section 'As Happy as Kings'

[fol. 250] *Child's Garden.* 1885.
      Underwoods. 1887.
      Ballads. 1890 or 1891.
      Songs of Travel. Posthumous.

[fol. 251] 'The Shadow' 31
      'The cow' – 'with all her might' 41
      Climbing the tree. Touch of self consciousness in 'little me' 13
      The 'pirate story': with the true psychology that makes up the
      geography as the play goes, and only in the last line, when they
      are needed, decides that 'the wicket is the harbour and the garden
      is the door.' 12.
      Example of poetry transform verse *one*
      In the winter I get up in the dark and dress by the yellow light of a
      candle, whereas in summer I have to go to bed in the day time.
      Something of the lasting quality of nonsense rhyme: something
      too of the freedom from ulterior motive that is so delightful in a
      few of the old nursery songs.
         'And in a corner find the toys
         Of the old Egyptian boys.'

[fol. 252] *Child's Garden* begun at Braemar, 1880. Continued at Nice.
      'Poetry is not the strong point of the text, and I shrink from any
      title that may seem to claim that quality.'
      Also 'The Penny Whistle: nursery rhymes' or Penny Whistles

[fols 253–7 *are pages of quotations to support this section*]

[fol. 253] "Stevenson: on his own verse.
      'Really, I have begun to learn some of the rudiments of that
      trade, and have written three or four pretty enough pieces of
      octosyllabic nonsense, semi-serious, semi-smiling. A kind of
      prose Herrick, divested of the gift of verse, and you behold the
      Bard. But I like it.' To Henley, 1883, *Letters*, II, 121. Refer to the
      source of the verses of *Underwoods*.

[fol. 254] Stevenson, of *Underwoods*.
      'I wonder if you saw my book of verses? It went into a second
      edition, because of my name, I suppose, and its *prose* merits. I do
      not set up to be a poet. Only an all-round literary man: a man
      who talks, not one who sings. But I believe the very fact that it
      was only speech served the book with the public. Horace is much
      a speaker, and see how popular! most of Martial is only speech,

and I cannot conceive a person who does not love his Martial; most of Burns, also, such as "The Louse", "The Toothache", "The Haggis", and lots more of his best. Excuse this little apology for my house; but I don't like to come before people who have a note of song, and let it be supposed I do not know the difference.'

[fol. 255] To J. A. Symonds. Saranac, Nov. 21, 1887. [*Letters*,] III, 25.

[fol. 256] Stevenson. Verse.
'The success of *Underwoods* is gratifying. You see, the verses are sane; that is their strong point, and it seems it is strong enough to carry them.' [To] Colvin, N. Y., Sept. 1887. [*Letters*], III, 8. Stevenson. Poetry. In 1880 'Home is the sailor' etc: imaginary tombstone: moral inscription. Last two lines, with this comment: 'the verses are from a beayootiful poem by me.' To Colvin. S. Francisco, Feb. 1880. *Letters*, I, 283.

A.3   Published article, 'As Happy as Kings' by Arthur Ransome, *The New Witness*, 5 February 1913

[A version of fols 236–49 of the MS (pp. 128–33 above). The only previously published section of the main Stevenson MS; Ransome was paid two guineas for it. There is very little alteration from the MS draft; variants are noted here. The punctuation is that of the original article.]

AS HAPPY AS KINGS

About this time thirty years ago, a Mr. Stevenson, sorely stricken in wind and limb, severely[1] troubled with the ridiculous details of drains and smells in a house he had taken in the hope of being well in it, was busied in composition of a kind almost entirely new to him. He had written two or three pretty little books of essayistical autobiography[2], "New Arabian Nights", and a story for boys called "Treasure Island" which had earned much disapprobation when published in a boys' magazine. He had, of course, written verses, and, admiring the French Parnassians had tried his hand in the old elaborate forms. But he had not printed any,[3] his friends were all real published poets, and it was with an agitated diffidence that he announced to them the work on which he was engaged, "Penny Whistles for Small Whistlers," afterwards "A Child's Garden of Verses". Just about the same time it happened that I was born. It further happened that the book had had just time to percolate the provinces, and to induce in provincial parents a readiness to read it aloud instead of Bunyan, when I, in the course of nature, was ready to listen to it. Accordingly, there are, when I read it now, two distinct persons looking at the print, a baldheaded creature who has read far too many books, and a small boy who has read little but "Robinson Crusoe," "Little Arthur's History of England" (a noble work), and "As Pretty As Seven" (the best book of German fairy stories, with the most charming woodcuts in the world). I differ from that small boy, alas! on most things. My taste, perhaps, has been vitiated by years and libraries. But on the 'penny whistles' of that Mr. Stevenson, we still preserve a very happy unanimity.

   "A Child's Garden of Verses" is one of those smiling accidents that befall serious, laborious men. After long years of technical diligence in other directions, Stevenson found himself writing these quite unforeseen things,

---

[1] 'severely stricken ... sorely troubled'.

[2] 'books of prose'.

[3] 'He had ... any' omitted.

writing them with a surprise, comparable perhaps, to that of Morris when, intent on a thousand other matters, he delighted his fellow undergraduates with the poems that were afterwards printed in his first volume, and remarked that if this was poetry, it was very easy. Poetry was not at all easy to Stevenson, but he had a surprise like Morris's in finding he could do it at all.[1] "I can usually do whistles only by giving my whole mind to it," he wrote to Henley, "to produce even such limping verses demanding the whole forces of my untuneful soul." He did not believe them to be poetry of any very high order. "Poetry," he said, "is not the strong point of the text, and I shrink from any title that might seem to claim that quality." For this reason, partly, he wanted to call them[2] "Penny Whistles" and imagined them in a little book with a sketch of "a party playing on a P. W. to a little ring of dancing children" as a frontispiece. And indeed when the book was announced[3] to Mr. Gosse:– "I have now published on 101 small pages, 'The Complete Proof of Mr. R. L. Stevenson's Incapacity to write Verse' in a series of graduated examples with a table of contents." Yet with one or two exceptions he never wrote better verse, and, perhaps, he never elsewhere achieved a completer and more personal success. And, in spite of his shyness in exhibiting them to his friends,[4] poets, he was too good a critic not to like these verses well.[5] "They look ghastly", he said, "in the cold light of print: but there is something nice in the little ragged regiment after all; the blackguards seem to smile, to have a kind of childish treble note that sounds in my ears freshly; not song, if you will, but a child's voice."

A child's voice in literature had never been achieved before, except for a moment, and by a child, the Marjorie Fleming, whose lines -

> "But she was more than usual ca'm
> She did not give a single dam."

are treasured by all who have ever heard them. "Marjorie Fleming," Stevenson wrote to Mr. Archer, "I have known as you surmise, for long. She was possibly – no, I take back possibly – she was one of the greatest works of God. Your note about the resemblance of her verses to mine gave me great joy, though it only proved me to be a plagiarist."

Some of the Songs of Innocence are in the mouths of children, but

---

[1] 'When Morris ... soul.' This whole section is recast here, retaining the same concepts and phrases but achieving more fluent rhythm and point. This suggests the published article was the later, revised version.

[2] 'He thought of calling them ...'

[3] 'When the book was out, he announced ...'

[4] 'diffidence in writing to his friends'.

[5] 'he loved these verses well.'

Blake's children are angels, and their clear voices are ecstatic[1] with the hope and memory of paradise. Stevenson's child is concentrated, humanely, on the present. The sun in the morning, the lamplighter at night, the rustle of an aunt's skirts, play more serious than life, and the simplest and least questionable version of a philosophy ridiculous in the mouth of Dr. Pangloss, but respectably gallant, and holding for those who have left the nursery the pathos of a forlorn hope:

> "The world is so full of a number of things,
> I'm sure we should all be as happy as kings."

This is the real furniture of childish psychology, and gives us back our babyhood.

I suppose each reader of the book, each reviewer of that little smiling[2] regiment, must himself have been the child who sang these verses to a plain but cheerful recitative, like the a. b. ab. we hear when, dusty with age and travel, we pass by a village schoolroom. The only piece of false psychology in the book is the last poem – "To any reader":

> "As from the house your mother sees
> You playing round the garden trees,
> So you may see, if you will look
> Through the windows of this book,
> Another child, far, far away,
> And in another garden, play."

That is not true. That is not so.[3] The verses were translated into my own life and back again, and the episodes of my own childhood seem to have been known to Stevenson, though not always quite accurately chronicled by him. Let me defer to that childish critic who looks over my shoulder whenever I open that book.[4] When I was on the fringe of babyhood, older than

---

[1] 'are ecstatic'.

[2] 'ragged smiling regiment'.

[3] 'That is not so'.

[4] 'Stevenson saw himself, but every child who hears the verses, identifies the land of counterpane with his own bed, and every grown person sees not the little Scottish boy in the old Manse at Colinton, but lives again his own infancy.

I count myself fortunate that I was born late enough to be among the children whose mothers have read aloud them *The Child's Garden of Verses*. For me now they have something of the lovable quality that I suppose everybody attributes to his own childhood. They were translated into my life, and episodes in it seem to have been known to Stevenson though not always quite accurately chronicled by him. Now in writing of them I think I may wisely defer to a childish critic of long ago who was more certain of his favourites than ever I can be.'

four[1], but without the hoary dignity of nine, these were the verses I liked best: "Bed in Summer", "Foreign Lands," principally for the open feeling of the fourth line, "And looked abroad on foreign lands", the insistent question of "Windy Nights":

> "Late in the night when the fires are out,
> Why does he gallop and gallop about?"

best of all, perhaps, "The Land of Counterpane," with it real transfigurations of dip and hill in counterpane geography. With a contempt due to superior science, and at the same time a delight in the fantasy I liked[2] the address to "My Shadow" and doubtfully[3], with distaste for the realism of the comb and the mention of girls' names as warriors, the "Marching song." Then[4] the first stanza of "The Cow", and the first and last stanzas of "Good and Bad Children," partly for the rhyme's sake:

> "Children you are very little,
> And your bones are very brittle;
> If you would grow great and stately,
> You must try to walk sedately."

and

> "Cruel children, crying babies,
> All grow up as geese and gabies,
> Hated, as their age increases,
> By their nephews and their nieces."

this[5] with a backhand deduction as to the childhood of my aunts, which Stevenson certainly never intended. Then the childish critic approved[6] "From a Railway Carriage" which he associated with journeys to the north country hills, although he wished to edit it, and still thinks Stevenson would not have rejected his emendation. In a moving railway carriage one thing always impresses itself on the young mind, and that is the dip

---

[1] 'before I went to school, older than three but without the hoary dignity of nine or ten'.

[2] New sentence beginning 'With' and inserting 'I liked …'

[3] '"My Shadow"; doubtfully …'

[4] 'Then I liked …'

[5] 'this last …'

[6] '"The lamplighter' was another favourite, though the trees whose leaves were suddenly silenced by the lamp in the autumn evenings made it impossible for Leerie to nod to any little child, listening for his footsteps and watching from the house for the illumination. This Stevenson should have foreseen. "From a Railway Carriage" was always lovingly associated with …'

and rise of the telegraph wires as they cut the square of the window. This Stevenson has omitted.[1] It was[2] by that I knew I was in a train. I liked the sentiment but resented the doll in "My Ship and I," and always waited in the readings for the thrill of the last line – "And fire the penny cannon in the bow." And, full of the knowledge that the very room in which my parents read possessed such an occult geography,[3] I had a proprietary pleasure in "The Land of Storybooks".[4] Not one of the poems in the section called "Garden Days" earned my suffrage, except for single images, and I am now in cordial agreement with my youth. The envoys[5] were for grown up people only, and I was no friend to little Louis Sanchez.

I think the small boy[6] had found the pick of the collection and I have but little to add to his choice by way of commentary. Stevenson was not altogether right when he refused his verse the name of poetry. Much of it is charming prose that has gained the lasting, memorable quality of good nonsense-rhymes. But, besides the inimitable touches of childish diction, there are again and again epithets chosen with the rightness, the surprisingness of the best of poets.[7]

> "And in a corner find the toys
> Of the old Egyptian boys."

[1] 'And that Stevenson has omitted.'

[2] 'Now it was ...'

[3] 'And full of knowledge that the very room in which my parents read possessed a similar occult geography, ...'

[4] 'Story-books' [which is correct].

[5] 'Envoys'.

[6] 'the childish critic'.

[7] 'He preserves with extraordinary skill the delightful freedom from ulterior motive, which is the chief glory of the childish imagination. He is generous of quite inimitable touches of childish diction:

> The friendly cow all red and white,
> I love with all my heart:
> She gives me cream *with all her might*
> To eat with apple-tart.

There is self-consciousness here and there of a kind bad for children and detested by them, as: 'Who should climb but little me?' But as a rule the psychology is just, and sometimes brilliant in its accuracy, as in the pirate-story, when the geography is made up as the play goes, and only in the last line, when they are sorely needed when the cattle 'are charging with a roar', decides, breathlessly, that 'the wicket is the harbour and the garden is the shore.' Then too there are epithets with the rightness, and the surprisingness of true poetry.'

It would be hard to overpraise the perception and the courage that found and left the word Egyptian, so true and so inexplicable.[1]

ARTHUR RANSOME.

[1] [the passage continues:] 'And we have only to write in prose the matter of a story: 'In the winter I get up at night and dress by the yellow light of a candle, whereas in summer, on the contrary, I have to go to bed by day' – and compare it with the verse:

> In winter I get up at night
> And dress by yellow candle-light.
> In summer, quite the other way,

I have to go to bed by day. – to perceive that there is more in this than rhymed prose, and that the matter is indeed stamped with the personal and untranslatable form of poetry.'

B BIOGRAPHICAL AND CONTEXTUAL MATERIAL

B.1 Ransome's first story, 'The Desert Island', 1892.

[*Written at the age of eight in a tiny notebook now with the Ransome papers at Abbot Hall Museum and Art Gallery, Kendal, and first published in* Mixed Moss, *The Journal of The Arthur Ransome Society, vol. 1, no. 1, 1990.*]

The Desert Island.
By A. M. Ransome.

There was once a boy called Jack. His father had gone to Liverpool and had never been heard of since, everybody thought that he had been seized by a press-gang, and taken away to the South Seas. So Jack made up his mind to go and find him. When he was fourteen he went to Portsmouth and went on board a ship called the White Bird. This ship was bound for the Friendly Isles. They had very good weather till they got round Australia. Then a terrible storm began to blow and the ship lost its rudder. The next day the main mast fell and crushed two of the men. Four hours after this disaster the ship sprang a leak and they had to take to the boats. Jack and one of his friends called Tom escaped in a very small boat by themselves. The land was about two miles away. They rowed to it but all the other boats sank at least they thought so. They rowed back to the ship the next day and took a lot of planks, guns, pistols and swords back with them.

They built a house and a stockade round it to keep it safe from wild beasts or savages if any should come. Tom shot a wild duck and a sort of pigeon which lasted for breakfast and dinner and they found some bananas and coconuts for tea. There was a little stream running through the stockade so they should never run short of water. Jack nevertheless took two or three barrels and filled them with water in case the stream dried up. They also gathered a good deal of fruit to preserve because if they were attacked by savages they would not be able to get out and get away. They caught a wild goat which they tamed because as they had no cow they could get its milk. When they were walking about one day they found a small hut with provisions in it and a note saying "If anyone is wrecked here he will see a ship some time in December and he must hoist a red flag. John Smith." Jack at once recognised his father's handwriting and John Smith was his father's name. However, they did not think much about it then. It was plain Jack's father had been there and thinking it was a likely place for a ship wreck had left the message so that he could save them. They found a large red flag to hoist as a signal. They made one of the coconut trees that were in the stockade into a lookout place by placing wooden steps all the way up. They also put two spikes at the top to fasten the red flag on. Jack and Tom went out about fifteen days after the finding of the hut to look for food and to explore the island. When they got on the top of the high hill in the middle of the island they saw two other islands a long way out to sea which they thought might be inhabited. Two or three days after this happened they went out in their boats to fish. They saw several sharks which were swimming past them and they caught some bright coloured fish which were not good to eat and at last they caught some fish very like our plaice and one like a sea-trout. They caught a young pig and a parakeet which they taught to talk but it used to copy their voices and call them in when they found it was the parakeet the whole time. The pig grew very well and soon was too big to be allowed in the stockade so they made a little clearing outside and fastened it with a tether to a post. It began to get near December so they fastened the red flag up because of the note they had found in the hut. One day they heard a cry and the pig squealed and when they climbed to the lookout place they saw rows and rows of canoes and hundreds of savages running up the beach. They ran down and got all the guns and ammunition ready to fire through the loopholes of the stockade. With a yell the savages charged against the stockade and some of them succeeded in climbing to the top of it but these Jack and Tom quickly shot down. Then Jack and Tom fired through the loopholes of the stockade and killed about six more. Suddenly there was a flash of lightning and a peal of thunder and the frightened savages fled to their boats for they thought that a thunderstorm is more dangerous on land than at sea. So this battle ended satisfactorily for Jack and Tom. The next day they climbed to the top of the lookout place. But they could see nothing of the savages. So they got some more provisions ready in case they were attacked again. And sure enough that evening which was the twenty fourth of December when they went up the lookout place they saw a huge fleet of brown sailed canoes making straight for the island. So they climbed down as quick as they could and loaded their guns ready to fire upon the enemy. As soon as the enemy were in reach Jack and Tom poured shot and bullets into them but all the same they charged again and again all through the night and Jack and Tom were just going to be defeated, when there was a great boom, and a cannon ball came scattering the enemy on all sides, killing and wounding large numbers. This happened again and again till the savages fled and found that their boats had been seized by a British ship and that there were lots of soldiers and sailors by the shore who shot them. Jack and Tom ran out of the ship and Jack suddenly saw his father who was captain of the ship. Jack's father said that it was he who had written the note and built the hut, and that he had been wrecked on that very island and had been found by an English ship and been taken on board. He had afterwards got to be captain and was on his way back to England. Jack and Tom went with him and arrived safely.

The End.

B.2 'The Plate-Glass Window'

Unsigned review article, *The Eye-Witness*, 3 August 1911, p. 220

[*Biting ironical criticism, full of entertaining faint praise and sledge-hammer blows of damnation, with Ransome's style and preoccupations evident; the very title a wry mockery. Punctuation is that of the original article.*]

The Plate-Glass Window

The technique of those writers, gradually increasing in number, who usually style themselves 'creative artists' is now reasonably familiar to the majority of readers. Mr. Swinnerton is a promising recruit to the band. In his third novel* he proves his ability to write a novel, a stage of artistic development which many more popular writers will never attain. He observes justly and translates the nicety of his observation with accuracy. He knows exactly what he wishes to say and says it. Both his characterisation and his descriptions are always well done, and he avoids the appearance of a studied effect by substituting gentleness for the acerbity so characteristic of the phraseology of some better-known novelists. And he is something of a symbolist in that he prefers suggestion to explanation. Throughout the book there is a spirit of natural grace delicately expressed.

But all that can be said simply amounts to stating Mr. Swinnerton's ability as a novelist. The fact remains that he has wasted that ability in writing "The Casement." The book was not worth writing. It is a mass of platitudes decked in the guise of subtleties. It is an attempt to make a Kemp [*sic*] window out of plate-glass. Mr. Swinnerton is selling soiled goods in gilded wrappers, and the name of Swinnerton is on every packet. There is not a character in the book we have not met before. Paul Trevell with his philosophic maundering is as Michael Reay with his undigested anarchy. That the writer should apparently fail to see this infuses into the book a discordant sentimentalism that rises to a shriek in the last few pages where Michael's future regeneration is suggested. Robert Burton, as an antithesis to Paul Trevell, is a mere lay figure, and Olivia, as a foil to Loraine, is even less interesting. Loraine, herself, is a delicate study, but she is too indeterminate, too vague, too self-conscious to be fascinating to anyone less weak than herself. It explains Paul Trevell's character that he fell in love with her.

Mr. Swinnerton calls his book "A Diversion." To him it may be; to us it is not. It is rather the pitiable spectacle of an artistic ability wasted by lack of courage to attack material worthy the craft. If he will throw aside his timidity and grasp at things he can only as yet apprehend he may become a novelist of distinction.

*The Casement. By Frank Swinnerton. Chatto and Windus. 6s.

B.3 'R. L. S.' by 'K.'

The Eye-Witness, 28 September 1911, pp. 471–2

[*Ransome used the 1911, sixth edition (here reviewed) of Balfour's 1901 biography of his cousin Stevenson while writing his book; this is confirmed by his page-references. The article shows in places clear evidence of Ransome's typical preoccupations and sentence-rhythms; others in the* Eye-Witness *office may however also have had a hand in it. The pseudonyms 'K.' and 'K. Q.' used by Ransome date from 1904 and may have associations with chess. Punctuation is that of the original article.*]

R. L. S.

It is well that a cheap edition of Mr. Graham Balfour's "Life of Robert Louis Stevenson"* should be published just now, when the glories of the wonderful sunset of that life are beginning to fade. There is no danger that men will forget Stevenson's work so long as they can appreciate good English (or rather, good Scottish) and good story-telling. But there may be some danger that the personality which lay behind that work may be too easily forgotten; and that would be regrettable for, apart from its intrinsic fascination, without an understanding of it men will fail to understand Stevenson's relation to his age, and consequently the enthusiasm he evoked and the fame he achieved.

If we want to understand Stevenson we must try to recapture the atmosphere of the time in which he lived. He was born in 1850. He was not quite of age when the grave closed on the most glorious of English story-tellers. The period that followed the death of Charles Dickens was one during which many brilliant talents were displayed, but almost all these talents seemed to be devoted to the task of discouraging mankind. Those who prided themselves especially on being "artists," whether with words or brush, threw themselves into this task with singular enthusiasm. It was in those days that we were told that it was the function of the poet "to count the falling leaves"; it was in those days that a painter set himself to reproduce lovingly the rainbow hues of a dying corpse.

Against all this Neo-Satanism Stevenson set himself with a refreshing manliness and gaiety. He was not, indeed, the man to offer to the world a constructive philosophy to oppose the nightmares of negation. But he could do something that was, perhaps, at the moment more effective. He was himself exquisitely deft in the use of words. No man belonged more to his age in careful perfection of the technique of writing. He was the very man to have moved its admiration by writing about White Nights or the Flowers of Evil. He wrote instead a boy's adventure story; and in writing it, he showed that as much artistic beauty could be got out of a boy's adventure story as all the decadents ever got out of their decaying corpses. "Treasure Island" is an extraordinarily good adventure story, and all boys love it as such, and get more delight out of it than they get out of the poor stuff usually served out to them, simply because it is better done. It is also a very perfect work of art, in which one can find scarcely a flaw, in which scarcely a word could be altered without depreciation. Superficially it reads as if the author were hurried along from adventure to adventure, rejoicing only in the thought of rum and blood and gunpowder like a boy of fourteen. Yet Mallarmé in all his glory was not arrayed like one of these.

The unconquerable elfish gaiety of Stevenson was what was really valuable to him to his age and to ours. I must confess that to me he seems not only most delightful but most inspiring when he takes himself least seriously. That he could take himself and life lightly were his two best qualities not only artistically but morally, for the former touched his vanity with humour and humility, while the latter showed a rare and admirable courage, for it is not easy to take lightly a life of almost continual sickness and suffering. When he begins to take himself seriously he often jars. There is a touch of priggishness in some of his more solemn essays. He talked incredible nonsense about politics; nor is the vague sort of "undenominational" religion which he seems to have taken to so strongly in later life likely to be the final comfort of humanity. In some of his moralisings one does catch a note that goes some way to justify Henley's taunt about "the Shorter Catechist," and reminds one not altogether pleasantly of what he himself called his "Covenanting childhood."

His Calvinistic origins did Stevenson harm as a moralist, but I think he owed no small debt to them as an artist. Their medieval folk-lore was rich in wonders, yet even then touched with something that was eerie and sometimes cruel. The Reformation swept away their saints and banned the fairies. It left them with a cold abstract God utterly aloof from men – and with the Devil. They turned eagerly to the latter, and into their conception of the Devil they poured all the magnificent poetry of their natures. On the wonderful devil-stories of Scott and Stevenson was fed from his childhood, and anyone who has read "Thrawn Janet" or the glorious episode of Tod Lapraik embedded in "Catriona" can see how powerfully they moved him. But it is not only in his direst imitations of the wild tales that Scottish peasants whisper, when they think that their terrible God is sleeping, that the influence of Scottish Diabolism can be felt. It flames in the blind eyes of Pew in "Treasure Island"; it hangs like a black cloud over "The Master of Ballantrae"; it is the energy of "The Ebb Tide," that wonderful product of his mature genius; and it touches here and there, as a pearly cloud is touched with fire, the irresponsible gaiety of "The New Arabian Nights."

There is among the old Scottish ballads one that is, perhaps. The noblest of them all, called "Tamlane". Those who know it will remember the very

Scottish myth that it speaks of – of the "Tiend to Hell." The fairies are represented as happy, irresponsible, unmoral creatures rejoicing in their utter ignorance of good and evil. But once in seven years they must "pay the Tiend (or Tithe) to Hell," that is, send one of their number to Hell as a sort of tribute to an Infernal Suzerain. Stevenson was at his best an elf. His most exquisite stories are the most elfish – "The New Arabian Nights" and "The Dynamiter" and, above all, that incomparable monument of human absurdity, "The Wrong Box." But, elf as he was, he never quite forgot "the tiend to Hell"; and in his most light-hearted fantasies, in his most boyish tales of adventures, one catches now and again a glimpse of that red and thirsty abyss over which his Covenanting ancestors saw the whole human race suspended like flies. K.

* The Life of Robert Louis Stevenson. By Graham Balfour. Methuen, 1s.

B.4 Family trees for Stevenson and Ransome, including their extended families

(a) Robert Louis Stevenson and his family

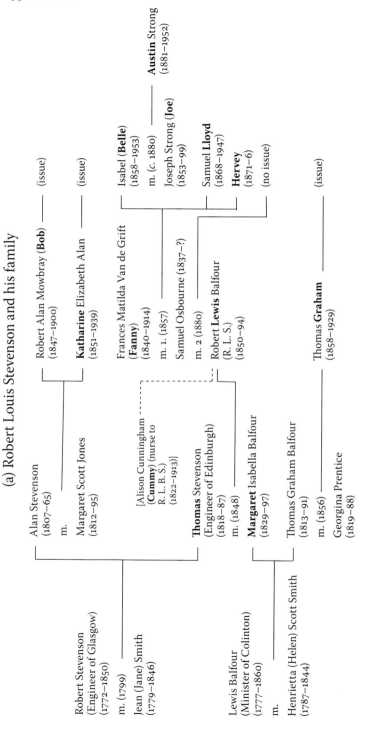

(b) Arthur Ransome and his immediate family

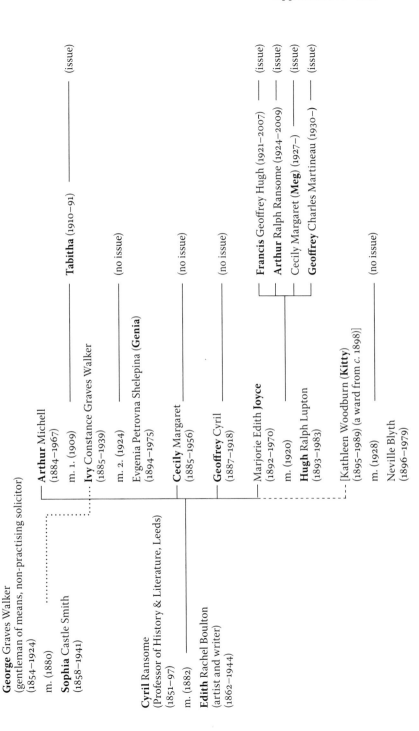

George Graves Walker
(gentleman of means, non-practising solicitor)
(1854–1924)

m. (1880)

Sophia Castle Smith
(1858–1941)

Cyril Ransome
(Professor of History & Literature, Leeds)
(1851–97)

m. (1882)

Edith Rachel Boulton
(artist and writer)
(1862–1944)

Arthur Michell
(1884–1967)

m. 1. (1909)   **Ivy** Constance Graves Walker
(1885–1939)

m. 2. (1924)

Evgenia Petrovna Shelepina (**Genia**)
(1894–1975)

Cecily Margaret
(1885–1956)

Geoffrey Cyril
(1887–1918)

Marjorie Edith **Joyce**
(1892–1970)

m. (1920)   **Hugh** Ralph Lupton
(1893–1983)

[Kathleen Woodburn (**Kitty**)
(1895–1989) (a ward from *c.* 1898)]

m. (1928)

Neville Blyth
(1896–1979)

Tabitha (1910–91) ———— (issue)

(no issue)

(no issue)

(no issue)

Francis Geoffrey Hugh (1921–2007) ——— (issue)

Arthur Ralph Ransome (1924–2009) ——— (issue)

Cecily Margaret (**Meg**) (1927–) ——— (issue)

Geoffrey Charles Martineau (1930–) ——— (issue)

(no issue)

(c) Arthur Ransome's 'adopted' family, the Collingwoods, contemporary with him

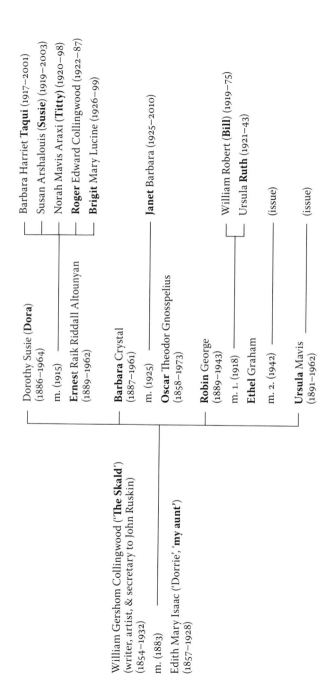

Index

Abbot Hall Museum of Lakeland Life and Industry, Kendal, 20

Abélard, Peter, 158, 158*n*

Abercrombie, Lascelles, 4, 30, 103*n*

Aeneid, 75, 75*n*, 79

Aesop, *see* Stevenson: *Fables*

Altounyan family, 27, 28, 118*n*; Plate 14

Andersen, Hans, 24

The Arabian Nights, 16, 113, 113*n*

Archer, William, 184

Armour, Margaret: *The Home and Early Haunts of Robert Louis Stevenson*, 182

Austin, Stella: *Stumps*, 31

Baildon, Dr H. B.: *Robert Louis Stevenson: A Life Study in Criticism*, 83, 93*n*, 83*n*

Balfour, David (character), *see* Stevenson: *Kidnapped*

Balfour, Graham, 21, 43, 56*n*, 80, 100, 204
   The Life of Robert Louis Stevenson, 64*n*, 84, 201, 203

Balfour, J. and M. C., 1*n*

Ballantyne, R. M., 4, 116*n*, 160
   The Coral Island 22, 23, 116

Balzac, Honoré de, 34, 55*n*, 135, 136, 136*n*, 137

Banville, Théodore de, 102*n*, 187

Barbey d'Aurevilly, Jules Amédée, 178, 186

Barrie, Sir J. M., 48, 51, 51*n*
   An Edinburgh Eleven 182

Barthes, Roland, 30

Baudelaire, Charles, 124*n*

Baxter, Charles, 63, 63*n*, 137*n*, 153, 153*n*

Bechstein, Ludwig, 129, 129*n*

Bell, John, 3, 47

Belloc, Hilaire, 12

Bennett, Arnold, 37

Beowulf, 142

Bertrand, Aloysius, 110, 110*n*

Bible, 74, 74*n*

Binyon, Laurence, 4, 5

Black, M. M.: *Robert Louis Stevenson*, 182

Blackmore, R. D., 24

Blake, William, 29, 126, 126*n*, 130*n*

'Bohemia', 113, 114*n*, 121, 122, 167, 167*n*; Plate 8; *see also* Ransome: *Bohemia in London*

Boodle, Miss Adelaide, 167*n*, 173

The Bookman, 7, 43

Borges, Jorge Luis, 45

Borrow, George, 98, 98*n*, 144

Boswell, James, 94*n*

Bottomley, Gordon, 4

Brash, Peter, 88*n*

Brodie, Deacon William, 61

Brogan, Hugh, 11, 38

Brontë sisters, 24, 136, 136*n*

Brotherton Library, University of Leeds, 20, 169

Brown, Curtis, *see* Curtis Brown

Browne, Alice, 43

Browning, Robert, 71, 71*n*

Bruce, Kathleen (Lady Scott), 5

Bunyan, John, 128, 128*n*

Burne-Jones, Edward, 73, 73*n*

Burns, Robert, 52, 60*n*, 101, 102, 104, 186

Busby, Dr, 75

Byron, Lord (George Gordon), 112

Callcott, Maria, Lady, 129, 129*n*

Camisards, 96, 96*n*

Candide, *see* Voltaire

Cape, Jonathan, *see* Jonathan Cape

Carroll, Lewis, 24

The Century Magazine, 160*n*

Cervantes Saavedra, Miguel de, 140, 140*n*

Chapman & Hall (publishers), 5, 6

Charles d'Orléans, 65, 65*n*, 102, 105, 186

Chateaubriand, Vicomte de, 56, 56*n*, 177

Chatto & Windus (publishers), 38

Chesterton, Cecil, 5

Chesterton, G. K.
   Robert Louis Stevenson, 182
   Twelve Types of Biography, 43, 44, 83*n*

The Chronicle of the London Missionary Society, 80*n*

Clarke, W. E., 80

Cole, Alphaeus P. and Peggotty, 25

Coleridge, S. T., 1*n*, 99*n*, 158, 158*n*, 160

Collingwood, Barbara, 5, 38, 206

Collingwood, Dora (later Altounyan), 5, 27, 206

Collingwood, Robin, 7, 206

Collingwood, Ursula, 7, 206

Collingwood, W. G., 5, 13, 24, 41, 108*n*, 206

Collins, Wilkie: *The Moonstone*, 175

Colvin, Lady, *see* Sitwell, Frances

Colvin, Sir Sidney, 43, 48, 62, 62*n*, 63, 64, 70, 73, 93*n*, 116*n*, 120, 148, 150, 154, 162

Conrad, Joseph, 44, 148, 148*n*

Cooper, James Fenimore, 116, 116*n*

The Coral Island, *see under* Ballantyne, R. M.

Cornford, L. Cope: *Robert Louis Stevenson*, 182

Cornhill Magazine, 101, 101*n*, 121*n*, 183

Cunningham, Alison, 58, 204

Curtis Brown (literary agency), 5, 11, 41

The Daily News, 41

Darwin, Charles, 143*n*

Darwin, Erasmus, 158, 158*n*

Daudet, Alphonse, 95, 95*n*

Defoe, Daniel, 24, 116, 164
   Captain Singleton, 116, 116*n*
   Robinson Crusoe, 23, 33, 56, 56*n*, 129

Dickens, Charles, 201

Don Quixote, *see* Cervantes Saavedra, Miguel de

Dostoevsky, Fyodor, 34, 35, 48, 135, 135*n*, 137, 186

Douglas, Lord Alfred, 11, 16

Drower, Lady, *see* Stevens, Stefana

Drummond, William, of Hawthornden, 52

Dryhurst, Sylvia, 4

Dumas, Alexandre, 35, 53, 53*n*, 137
   The Count of Monte Cristo, 153
   Vicomte de Bragelonne, 35, 60, 60*n*, 104, 137, 186

Edinburgh, *see under* Ransome *and* Stevenson

Edinburgh University Magazine, 25

English Illustrated Magazine, 61*n*

Eliot, George, 136, 136*n*

Ewing, Mrs Juliana, 24

The Eye-Witness, 200

Farr, Ann, 3

Fergusson, Robert, 48, 52, 52*n*, 59*n*, 61

Ferrier, Walter, 53, 53*n*

Field, Isobel, *see* Strong, Isobel

Fielding, Henry, 106, 106*n*, 140, 140*n*

Flaubert, Gustave, 53, 53*n*, 154, 155, 156, 156*n*, 161

Fleming, Marjorie, 130, 130*n*, 177

The Fortnightly Review, 7

Franklin, Benjamin, 167, 167*n*

Fraser, Marie: *In Stevenson's Samoa*, 182

Gaspard de la Nuit, *see* Bertrand, Aloysius

Gavin, Jessie, 4, 38

Gautier, Théophile, 108*n*

Gellibrand family, 17, 170

Gissing, George, 7

Goldsmith, Oliver, 61, 61*n*, 94*n*

Goschen, Max (publisher), 17, 18

Gosse, Edmund, 70, 94, 94*n*, 130, 148, 153*n*, 160, 160*n* 178; Plate 15

Gourmont, Remy de, 12

Granville, Charles, *see* Steven Swift

Gray, Douglas, 39

Gray, Eileen, 5

Greene, Graham, 36

Grimm, Jacob and Wilhelm, 24

Hackston, David, of Rathillet, 53

Hamley, Sir Edward, 73, 73*n*

Hammerton, J. A.: *In the Tracks of R. L. Stevenson*, 182

Hardy, Thomas, 4, 8, 34, 136, 136*n*

Hardyment, Christina, 38, 47

Hart-Davis, Sir Rupert, 3

Hawkins, Jim (character), *see* Stevenson: *Treasure Island*

Hawthorne, Nathaniel, 106, 106*n*, 115, 115*n*, 124, 124*n*, 160, 187

Hazlitt, William, 7, 29, 98, 99, 99*n*, 143, 160, 172

Henley, W. E., 4, 63, 63*n*, 64*n*, 73, 89, 108, 148, 158*n*, 176, 202
   'Robert Louis Stevenson', 64*n*

Henty, G. A., 4

Herrick, Robert, 134, 134*n*, 135

Horace, 57

Huckleberry Finn, *see* Twain, Mark

Hugo, Victor, 26, 48, 53, 103, 104, 106, 171, 186

Iliad, 90, 90*n*
Illustrated London News, 42

Jack, T. C. & E. C. (publishers), 6
James, G. P. R., 178
James, Henry, 33, 43, 53*n*, 55*n*, 56*n*, 57, 57*n*, 75, 139, 178
Japp, Dr Alexander H., 118
  Robert Louis Stevenson, 182
Jarry, Alfred, 162
Jefferies, Richard, 5
Jenkin, Fleeming, 60, 60*n*, 62, 74, 74*n*, 147, 186
Johnson, Dr Samuel, 94, 94*n*
Johnstone, Arthur: *Recollections of Robert Louis Stevenson in the Pacific*, 78*n*, 82, 182, 183, 184
Jonathan Cape (publishers), 14
Jonson, Ben, 52*n*, 64, 64*n*

Kalakaua, King David, 26
Kant, Immanuel, 21, 158
Keats, John, 63, 111*n*, 112
Kelman, John: *The Faith of Robert Louis Stevenson*, 182
Kelmscott Press, 126*n*
Kempe, C. E., 200
Kidd, William, 138, 138*n*
Kingsley, Charles, 24
Kingsmill, Hugh, 35
Kipling, Rudyard, 43
Knox, John, 104, 104*n*
Korolenko, Vladimir, 136, 136*n*

L. J. R., 61, 62
Labiche, E. M., 178
Lamb, Charles, 29, 59, 59*n*, 158, 158*n*, 175
Lang, Andrew, 24
Lazarillo de Tormes, 144, 144*n*
Le Gallienne, Richard, 42
Le Sage, Alain René, 144, 144*n*, 145
Lear, Edward, 9
Leavis, F. R., 44
Leeds, University of, Brotherton Library, 20, 169
Lewis, Sir George, 15
Linklaters (Linklater & Paines, solicitors), 2, 3
Little Arthur's History of England, Callcott, Maria
Lodge, Margaret, 38

London, *see under* Ransome *and* Stevenson
Longman's Magazine, 55*n*
Low, W. H.: *A Chronicle of Friendship*, 65, 67, 75, 76, 88, 125, 138*n*, 162
Lowell, James Russell, 73, 73*n*
Lupton, Joyce, *see* Ransome, Joyce
Lynd, Robert, 4

Macaulay, Lord, 117*n*, 119*n*
Mackail, J. W., 28
Mackay, Aeneas, 70, 70*n*
Macmillan (publishers), 4
Macmillan, Daniel, 11, 12; Plate 12
Mallarmé, Stéphane, 29, 202
Mansfield, Katherine, 12
Marryat, Frederick, 22
Martial, 134
Martin Secker (publisher), *see* Secker, Martin
Marvell, Andrew, 128*n*
Masefield, John, 4, 5, 117*n*
  'A Ballad of John Silver', 43, 117
Masterman Ready, *see* Marryat, Frederick
Maupassant, Guy de, 6
Meiklejohn, J. M. D., 135, 135*n*
Melville, Herman, 178
Meredith, George, 34, 113, 113*n*, 136, 136*n*, 140, 140*n*, 141, 171, 185
Merezhkovsky, D. S., 105, 105*n*
Methuen, Sir Algernon (publisher), 7, 9, 11, 12, 20, 38, 39, 41
Mills & Boon (publishers), 5
Milton, John, 94*n*, 168*n*
Molière (J. B. Poquelin), 186
Montaigne, Michel de, 57
Moors, H. J.: *With Stevenson In Samoa*, 178, 182
Morris, William, 127, 129, 129*n*
Mudie, Charles, 121, 121*n*
Munro, Neil, 43
Murry, John Middleton, 12
Musset, Alfred de, 100

Nelson, Admiral Lord, 71
New Witness, 12, 52*n*, 128, 128*n* 192
Nicoll, W. Robertson, 182
Nietzsche, Friedrich, 64, 64*n*
North, Capt. George, *see* Stevenson, names and pseudonyms
Noyes, Alfred, 145*n*

Osbourne, Belle (Isobel), *see* Strong, Belle
Osbourne, Fanny, *see* Stevenson, Fanny
Osbourne, Lloyd, 26, 27, 28, 43, 69, 70, 72, 74, 80, 153, 204; Plate 14
Otis, Captain, 77, 78
Ovid, 137
The Oxford and Cambridge Review, 29

The Pacific Commercial Advertiser, 149
Pall Mall Gazette, 64*n*, 124*n*
Pangloss, Dr (character), *see* Voltaire: *Candide*
Paracelsus, 21
Pares, Bernard, 2
Parr's Bank, 1, 2, 3
Payn, James, 177
Peacock, Thomas Love, 8, 21
Pepys, Samuel, 101*n*, 102, 104, 108, 186, 187
Perry, Matthew, 68*n*
Petrarch, Francesco, 52
Poe, Edgar Allan, 26, 120, 120*n*, 124, 124*n*, 125, 125*n*, 138, 138*n*, 166, 166*n*, 187; *see also* Ransome: *Edgar Allan Poe*
Ponson du Terail, Pierre Alexis: *Rocambole*, 178
The Portfolio, 97, 97*n*

Quiller-Couch, Sir Arthur ('Q'), 109*n*, 145*n*

Rabelais, François, 158, 158*n*
Radcliffe, Ann, 138, 138*n*
Radek, Karl, 26
Ransome, Arthur, Plates 8, 9, 10, 12, 13
❦ LIFE
'Bohemia', 113, 114*n*, 121, 122, 167, 167*n*, 130*n*; Plate 8
early reading, 22
family, 22, 204
first marriage, 13ff
First World War, 20, 26, 41
folktales, 142
lawsuit, 11, 12, 14
mouse-breeding, 9, 17
music, flageolet, 25
pseudonyms, 52*n*
projected work on R.L.S., 8, 9, 11, 12, 15, 16, 17, 19, 21, 28ff
Russian folklore, 15, 17

Ransome, Arthur *(continued)*
schooldays, 28
second marriage, 26
❦ PLACES ASSOCIATED WITH
Aleppo, Syria, 28; Plate 13
Coniston and Lanehead, 4, 8, 9, 18, 24, 41, 127*n*
Edinburgh, 97*n*
Finland, 15, 16, 20; Plate 10
Hatch, Tisbury, 1, 6, 9, 18, 40, 162*n*
La Touraine, 111
Lake District and Carlisle, 52, 52*n*, 53*n*
Leeds, 3, 20, 22, 24
London, 113
    Chelsea, 112
    Fulham, 14
    Hyde Park Corner, 112
    John Street, 12
Paris, 2, 14, 17, 20, 25
    Montparnasse, 5
Riga, 26
Russia, 15, 20, 21, 26, 27, 32, 39, 90*n*, 105, 143, 157; Plates 9, 10
St Petersburg (Petrograd), 17, 21, 40, 41
Stockholm, 15
❦ THEMES
literary or critical theory, 8, 178
literary technique, 32, 33, 46, 98, 103*n*
'real life', realism, 162
religious opinions, 34, 168–9
romanticism, 55
style, 31, 46, 91, 94, 95, 163
❦ WORKS
– Articles and essays
    'Art for Life's Sake', 29
    'Friedrich Nietzsche: An Essay in Comprehension', 64*n*
    'Kinetic and Potential Speech', 8, 28, 55*n*
    'The Plate-Glass Window', 200
    'Poe and the new technique', 55*n*
    'R. L. S.', 201–3
– Books
    The A.B.C. of Physical Culture, 5
    Aladdin and his Wonderful Lamp, 113*n*
    Autobiography, 8, 34
    The Blue Treacle, 17
    Bohemia in London, 5, 32, 167*n*
    The Book of Friendship, 2, 6
    The Book of Love, 2, 6

Ransome, Arthur *(continued)*
  Coots in the North, 148*n*
  Edgar Allan Poe, 7, 8, 9, 11, 36, 39
  The Elixir of Life, 38, 41, 105*n*, 141*n*
  A History of Story-Telling, 5, 7, 8, 53*n*,
    141*n*, 166*n*
  The Hoofmarks of the Faun, 7
  Missee Lee, 153*n*
  A Night in the Luxembourg (trans.),
    12
  Oscar Wilde, 8, 9, 11, 12, 20, 29, 36, 39,
    47, 105*n*
  Peter Duck, 28, 153*n*
  The Picts and the Martyrs, 102*n*, 132*n*
  Pigeon Post, 166*n*
  Portraits and Speculations, 12, 29,
    64*n*, 117*n*
  Secret Water, 88*n*
  The Souls of the Streets, 5
  Swallowdale, 53*n*, 129*n*, 132*n*
  Swallows and Amazons, 4, 21, 35, 90*n*,
    112*n*, 116*n*, 117*n*
  We Didn't Mean to Go to Sea, 23
  Winter Holiday, 108*n*, 116*n*
  – Juvenilia
    'The Desert Island', 22, 23, 198–9;
      Plates 3, 4
  – Stories and fragments
    'Ankou', 17
    'The River Comes First', 36, 148*n*
Ransome, Cecily, 5, 23, 204
Ransome, Cyril, 4, 22, 204
Ransome, Edith, 4, 15, 28, 41, 204
Ransome, Evgenia (née Shelepina), 3, 26,
  28, 204; Plate 13
Ransome, Geoffrey, 5, 16, 23, 38, 97*n*, 204
Ransome, Ivy (née Walker), 1, 2, 3, 7, 12,
  13, 14, 15, 18, 21, 26, 41, 97*n*, 204; Plate
  12
Ransome, Joyce (later Lupton), 23, 73*n*,
  204
Ransome, Tabitha, 3, 14, 16, 17, 18, 19, 26,
  41, 97*n*, 204; Plate 11
Renard, Jules, 163
Revermort, J. A. (J. A. Cramb), 105*n*
Rhythm, 12
Richards, Grant (publisher), 4
Richardson, Samuel, 34, 136, 136*n*, 142
Richter, A. L., 29
Robertson, John, 178
Robinson Crusoe, see under Defoe, Daniel
Rocambole, see Ponson du Terail, Pierre
  Alexis

Rogers, Woodes, 178
Le Roman de la rose, 6
Ross, Robert, 10, 47, 162*n*, 170
Rouse, W. H. D., 8, 29
Ruskin, John, 4, 5, 53*n*

'St John, Christopher', 4
Sainte-Beuve, Charles Augustin, 103,
  103*n*
Sanchez, Louis, 133*n*, 195
Sanchez, Nellie, 157*n*
Sargent, John Singer, 27, 29, 73, 73*n*
Schiller, Friedrich, 55*n*
Schwob, Marcel, 47, 153*n*, 163, 163*n*, 176
Scott, Sir Walter, 52, 52*n*, 79, 79*n*, 82, 104,
  106, 107, 108, 160, 186
Scribner's Magazine, 71*n*
Secker, Martin (publisher), 4, 7, 8, 9, 10,
  11, 37, 39; Plate 1
Sewart, David and Elizabeth, 47
Shairp, J. C., 106*n*, 186
Shakespeare, William, 52*n*, 91*n*, 94*n*, 121,
  121*n*
Sharp, Elizabeth, 135*n*
Sharp, William (Fiona McLeod), 135, 135*n*
Shaw, George Bernard, 104, 105
Shelley, Sir Percy Bysshe, 29
Sheridan, Richard Brinsley, 110
Sidney, Sir Philip, 125, 125*n*
Silver, John (character), *see* Masefield,
  John: 'A Ballad of John Silver'; and
  Stevenson: *Treasure Island*
Simpson, Mrs E. B., 9, 171
  Robert Louis Stevenson, 59*n*, 182
  *Robert Louis Stevenson's Edinburgh
    Days*, 182
Simpson, Sir Walter, 158, 158*n*
Sinclair, Catherine, 24
Sitwell, Frances (Fanny, later Lady
  Colvin), 62, 62*n*, 63, 102
Skelt, George, 108, 108*n*, 178
Speculative Society of Edinburgh, 55, 55*n*,
  158
Spenser, Edmund, 29
Spurrier, Steven, 117*n*
Stephen, Leslie, 101, 101*n*
  Robert Louis Stevenson, An Essay, 182
Sterne, Laurence, 93*n*, 96, 99, 99*n*, 145,
  160
Steven Swift (publisher, Charles
  Granville), 12
Stevens, Stefana (Lady Drower), 4, 5, 143*n*

Stevenson, Alan, 185, 204

Stevenson, Fanny (formerly Osbourne), 26, 27, 43, 67, 69, 70, 74, 75, 124, 169, 204; Plate 14

Stevenson, Margaret, 27, 58, 74, 75, 157, 204; Plate 14

Letters from Samoa, 182

From Saranac to the Marquesas, 182

Stevenson, R. A. M., 1, 61*n*, 62, 65, 67, 72, 77*n*, 158, 158*n*, 171, 186, 204

Stevenson, Robert Louis, Plates 14, 15, 16

❀ LIFE

   childhood, 58

   education, 58–61

   marriage, 26

   music, 73, 76, 145

   names and pseudonyms, 58, 69*n*, 161, 204

   Scottish Bar, 65

❀ PLACES ASSOCIATED WITH

   Adirondacks, 75

   Avignon, 144

   Barbizon, 65

   Bournemouth and 'Skerryvore', 72, 74, 81, 83, 118, 175, 185

   Braemar, 70, 118

   Burford Bridge, 83

   Colinton, 131, 171, 193, 204

   Davos, 64, 70, 71, 83

   Edinburgh, 11, 24, 185

      Calton Hill, 51

      Drummond Street, 61

      Lothian Road, 104, 165

      The Old Town, 168

      Portobello, 165

      Princes Street, 51

      University, 60, 171, 186

   Fontainebleau, 24, 65, 66, 71, 102*n*, 104, 111, 115, 158, 170, 185

   Hawaii, Honolulu, 77, 79, 139

   Hyères, 72

   Mentone, 65, 69, 177

   Monastier, 98, 98*n*, 185

   Mont Lozère, 25

   Monterey, 68

   Mull, Erraid, 171

   Nice, 72

   Paris, 25, 65, 70, 110

   Penzance, 110

   Pitlochry, 70

   Samoa (Apia, Mt Vaeia, Vailima), 14, 26, 27, 28, 79, 80, 84*n*, 85, 185

Stevenson, Robert Louis *(continued)*

   San Francisco, 68, 76

   Saranac, 75, 76, 185

   Shetland, 171

   Silverado, 70

   Swanston, 186

   Sydney, 79

   Tahiti, 78, 78*n*

   Wick, 98

❀ SHIPS ASSOCIATED WITH

   Casco, 76, 77, 82, 172, 177, 183, 185

   Devonia, 67

   The Equator, 79, 152, 177

   Janet Nicoll, 79, 155, 177

   The Ludgate Hill, 74, 76, 172

   Pharos, 171

   The Regent, 108

❀ THEMES

   boys' books, 122

   craft of writing, 166

   penny whistle, 73, 74, 76, 86, 107, 128–30, 145, 172

   religious opinions, morality, 164, 165, 166

   style, 46, 101, 174

❀ WORKS

– Articles and Essays

   'An Autumn Effect', 99, 99*n*

   'A Christmas Sermon', 165, 167

   'Father Damien: an open letter …', 79, 79*n*, 167*n*, 173

   'My First Book', 109

   'A Footnote to History', 173

   'A Gossip On Romance', 55*n*, 104, 107, 172

   'A New Form of Intermittent Light …', 25, 62, 171

   'Ordered South', 64

   'Samuel Pepys', 101, 104

   'Some Aspects of Robert Burns', 101, 171

   'Talk and Talkers', see *Familiar Studies*, 158, 172

   'The Thermal Influence of Forests', 62

   'Victor Hugo's Romances', 101, 103, 183

   'Walt Whitman', 102

   'Yoshida Torojiro', 105

Stevenson, Robert Louis *(continued)*
– Books
    Across The Plains, 48, 59, 66*n*, 163,
      165*n*, 175, 185
    The Amateur Emigrant, 42, 68, 68*n*,
      93, 177, 180
    The Art of Writing, 109*n*, 141*n*
    The Black Arrow, 24, 115*n*, 118, 122,
      122*n*, 123, 137, 163, 176, 177, 178
    Catriona, 114*n*, 118, 141, 144, 147, 173,
      176, 178, 187, 188, 202
    A Child's Garden of Verses, 22, 25, 30,
      31, 32, 58, 71, 71*n*, 72, 128, 128*n*, 130,
      131, 131*n*, 160, 172, 178, 190
    'David Balfour', see *Kidnapped*
    Dr Jekyll and Mr Hyde, 39, 40, 45, 72,
      75, 101, 101*n*, 123, 125, 126, 164*n*, 172,
      178, 187, 189
    The Ebb Tide, 39, 109, 109*n*, 147, 152,
      152*n*, 153, 154, 155, 156, 173, 179, 202
    Edinburgh, 97, 178
    Essays of Travel, 98, 98*n*, 177
    Fables, 32, 126, 127, 128, 188, 189
    Familiar Studies of Men and Books,
      33, 68*n*, 101, 101*n*, 102, 102*n*, 105,
      105*n*, 106*n*, 108*n*, 158*n*, 183
    Fleeming Jenkin, 39, 46, 60, 60*n*, 147,
      172
    In the South Seas, 33, 39, 42, 51, 79,
      148, 149, 173, 178, 188
    An Inland Voyage, 25, 93, 96*n*, 97,
      100, 171, 177, 178, 180
    Island Nights' Entertainments, 150,
      151, 178
    Kidnapped, 22, 24, 51*n*, 60, 72, 73,
      101*n*, 109, 118, 137, 138, 138*n*, 147,
      164, 164*n*, 172, 175, 178
    Lay Morals, 39, 67, 67*n*, 165, 167, 167*n*
    Letters, 48, 140, and *passim*
    The Master of Ballantrae, 75, 79, 109,
      118, 138, 147, 164, 171, 172, 173, 174,
      177, 178, 188, 202
    Memories and Portraits, 47, 59, 107,
      107*n*
    The Merry Men and Other Tales and
      Fables, 70, 89*n*, 91, 91*n*, 115*n*, 124*n*,
      168, 172, 177, 178, 188, 202
    More New Arabian Nights: The
      Dynamiter, 72, 173, 177, 179, 187,
      203
    New Arabian Nights, 65, 105*n*, 110,
      112*n*, 113*n*, 119, 124*n*, 128, 151, 172,
      183, 187, 202
    Penny Whistles for Small Whistlers,
      see *A Child's Garden of Verses*

Stevenson, Robert Louis *(continued)*
    Poems, 84, 84*n*, 88, 89, 175
      Ballads, 190, 202
      Songs of Travel, 42, 190
      Underwoods, 176, 190, 191
    Prince Otto, 71, 72, 86, 94, 105*n*, 119,
      120, 121, 122, 123*n*, 172, 179, 180
    Random Memories, 171, 172
    Records of a Family of Engineers,
      118*n*, 168*n*, 173
    St Ives, 42, 60, 60*n*, 144, 145, 173
    'The Sea Cook', see *Treasure Island*
    The Silverado Squatters, 69, 69*n*, 100,
      100*n*, 172, 175, 177
    Travels with a Donkey, 25, 39, 93, 97,
      172, 177, 178, 180; Plate 15
    Treasure Island, 12, 22, 23, 24, 26, 313,
      34, 40, 45, 69, 69*n*, 70, 71, 72, 109,
      109*n*, 115,
      118*n*, 119, 122, 125*n*, 126, 128, 137,
      148, 149, 153, 164, 164*n*, 172, 176, 177,
      178, 188, 189, 202
    Vailima Letters, 42, 48, 150*n*, 151*n*
    Virginibus Puerisque, 171, 177
    Weir of Hermiston, 19, 36, 40, 42, 84,
      109, 118, 143*n*, 147, 147*n*, 156, 156*n*,
      157, 173, 178, 179, 183
    The Wrecker, 32, 39, 57, 78, 152, 152*n*,
      173, 175
    The Wrong Box, 151, 151*n*, 172, 173,
      203
– Juvenilia, 22
– Plays
    Deacon Brodie, 73; *see also* Henley,
      W. E.
– Projected works
    'Art of Literature', 87, 160
    'Essays on the Enjoyment of the
      World', 165
    'Jerry Abershaw', 118
    'Life of Wellington', 160
– Stories
    'The Adventure of the Hansom Cabs',
      112
    'The Adventure of Prince Florizel
      and the Detective', 113*n*
    'The Beach of Falesà', 150, 173
    'The Beachcombers', 153
    'Black Andie's Tale of Tod Lapraik',
      see *Catriona*
    'The Body Snatcher', 124
    'The Bottle Imp', 39, 150, 151, 151*n*, 171
    'The High Woods of Ulufanua', 150

Stevenson, Robert Louis *(continued)*
'The House of Eld', 126, 127
'The Isle of Voices', 150, 151
'A Lodging for the Night', 105, 110, 124, 124*n*, 171
'Markheim', 124, 126, 187
'Pavilion on the Links', 68, 110, 187
'The Pearl Fisher', 153*n*
'The Poor Thing', 126, 126*n*
'Providence and a Guitar', 33, 110, 111, 111*n*, 187
'The Schooner Fallarone', 153
'The Sire de Maletroit's Door', 110, 171, 187
'The Song of the Morrow', 126, 126*n*
'Sophia Scarlet', 173
'Spring-Heel'd Jack', see *Memories and Portraits*
'The Story of a Lie', 67
'The Tadpole and the Frog', see *Fables*
'Thrawn Janet', 39, 70, 114, 187, 202
'The Touchstone', 126, 127, 127*n*
'The Treasure of Franchard', in *Merry Men*, 40, 89, 90, 110, 115
'Will o' the Mill', 171, 187
Stevenson, Thomas, 58, 59, 60, 74, 118, 204
Stoddard, C. W., 123*n*
Strong, Austin, 27, 81, 204; Plate 14
Strong, Isobel (Belle; née Osbourne, later Field), 27, 81, 83, 96*n*, 161, 168, 204, 99/14
    Memories of Vailima, 83*n*, 96*n*, 157*n*, 161*n*, 168*n*, 182, 184
Strong, Joe, 27, 204; Plate 14
The Studio, 71, 71*n*
Swinburne, A. C., 104, 104*n*
Swinnerton, Frank, 37ff, 200
    Robert Louis Stevenson: A Critical Study, 39; Plate 1
Symonds, John Addington, 134
Synge, J. M., 127

T. P.'s Weekly, 7
Temple Bar, 5, 171
Terence, 57
Thackeray, W. M., 24
Thomas, Edward, 4, 5, 6, 98*n*, 136*n*
Thoreau, Henry David, 68, 68*n*, 102
The Times Book Club, 11
The Times Literary Supplement, 5
Tolstoy, Leo, 105, 136*n*
The Tramp, 6, 7, 9; Plate 7
Turner, Walter, 59
Turgenev, Ivan, 34, 136, 136*n*
Twain, Mark, 22, 24

Unwin's Christmas Annual, 124*n*

Verlaine, Paul, 53
Verne, Jules, 26, 88*n* 116*n*
Villon, François, 102, 105, 105*n*, 124, 163, 163*n*
Voltaire: *Candide*, 105, 131*n*

Walker, George, 13, 204
Walker, Sophia, 14, 204
Watt, Francis, 111*n*
Wells, H. G., 37
Whitelaw, Robert, 28
Wilde, Oscar, 34, 42, 52, 52*n*, 99*n*, 103, 110*n*, 114*n*, 126, 158, 163*n*, 166*n*, 170, 183, 186; *see also* Ransome: *Oscar Wilde*
Winterson, Jeanette, 48
Wordsworth, William, 29

Yeats, W. B., 48, 52, 52*n*, 105*n*
Yonge, Charlotte Mary, 24
Yoshida-Torojiro, 68, 68*n*
Young Folks, 69*n*, 72, 118, 118*n*, 122, 128*n*

Zola, Émile, 162